To my late mother, Rachel Gawthrop Coe, keeper of his memory.

Contents

Full Fathom Five

FULL FATHOM FIVE

A Daughter's Search

MARY LEE COE FOWLER

The University of Alabama Press   Tuscaloosa

Copyright © 2008
The University of Alabama Press
Tuscaloosa, Alabama 35487-0380
All rights reserved
Manufactured in the United States of America

The excerpts from the poem by Arthur Howard Taylor, Rear Admiral,
USN (Ret.) are reprinted by permission of Patterson C. Taylor, Captain, USN (Ret.) and Anthony R. Taylor, Captain, USNR (Ret.)

Designer: Michele Myatt Quinn
Typeface: AGaramond

∞

The paper on which this book is printed meets the minimum re-
quirements of American National Standard for Information
Sciences-Permanence of Paper for Printed Library Materials, ANSI
Z39.48-1984.

Library of Congress Cataloging-in-Publication Data

Fowler, Mary Lee Coe, 1946—
    Full fathom five : a daughter's search / Mary Lee Coe Fowler.
        p.   cm.
    Includes bibliographical references and index.
    ISBN 978-0-8173-1611-2 (cloth : alk. paper) — ISBN
978-0-8173-8039-7 (electronic) 1. Fowler, Mary Lee Coe, 1946–
2. Fathers and daughters—United States. 3. Mothers and daughters—
United States. 4. Parent and adult child—United States. 5. Children of
military personnel—United States. 6. World War, 1939–1945—Naval
operations. I. Title.
    HQ755.85.F689 2008
    306.874′2092—dc22
    [B]

                                                2007043864

Acknowledgments

Besides the people named at the end of the book for their generous personal communications, I am grateful to the readers who reviewed my manuscript in various drafts, giving me cogent and helpful feedback to make it better: Elaine Reisenberg; John Bowdren; Tom Corwin; Frank Jeton; the late Jim DeRose; Ron Martini; and Elizabeth Moore. I also received valuable copyright advice from reference librarians Frank Wihbey of the University of Maine at Orono and Ginny Hopcroft of Bowdoin College. I'd like to thank those who helped me with research at the Portsmouth Naval Shipyard: David Davenport, Richard Winslow, and the New Hampshire Chapter of Subvets of WWII. I'm grateful to oldtime radio collector David S. Siegel for giving me the miracle of my father's voice from a 1943 CBS broadcast. And friends who supported me throughout the long years of writing and marketing this book are: Professors Kathy Ashley, Jacque Lynn Foltyn, Sara Shute, and Dave Boyer; authors Robin Lippincott, Sena Jeter Naslund, Peter Sasgen, and David Jones; AWON members Jeanine and Lorie Allen, Patty Wheeler, and Dixie Maurer-Clemons; neighbors Jock and Barbara McDonald, Joe and Delores Raymond, Bo Chesney and Liza Nichols; and my family, Win and Scheherazade Fowler and the late Alexander Fowler, plus my siblings, Jean Coe Cronk, Henry Coe, and Fred Wildebush.

Full Fathom Five

PART I

Ghost Dad

1

I see myself squeezing past old trunks, suitcases, cardboard boxes, and rolled-up maps to a dark mahogany wardrobe that stands at the far end of our attic under a high, lone window. I push one end of a trunk in front of the wardrobe, then pull myself on my belly up onto it. Kneeling, I stretch my hands up to small knobs on the double doors. I wrench the stiff doors open, and they smack against the trunk; puffs of dust waft up from the door jambs, and I sneeze. I climb back down from the trunk and pull it back from the wardrobe. The doors swing open with a creak, and there are his ghost-robes: two white naval uniforms hanging from a rack. On either side of them are long silk dresses Mother wore to dances in Honolulu and Manila. There's a shelf above the clothes, and I climb back up on the trunk, this time teetering on the balls of my feet and stretching my neck to see what's on it. There's a lady's hatbox and a white, flat-topped officer's hat beside it.

Climbing down, I feel among the legs of the uniforms and skirts till my hands hit boots at the back of the wardrobe. I pull them out, one by one, making two pairs of riding boots—one brown, one black. The leather is dry and cracked. The toe-ends curl upward from their soles. The brown pair is bigger, with wide, round toes. The black ones are ladies', with thin, pointy toes.

After dusting the boots off, I put the black ones aside, cradle the brown ones under each arm, and march down to the kitchen. Mother turns from the stove, then her face pales and her lips tighten into a thin line. "Put those back!" she says, turning away, and I know they're more than forbidden: they're my father's.

Irresistibly pulled into the vacuum she's made of her former life, I climb back up to the attic and—despite the heat and the itchy bits of insulation I stirred into the air—sit on a suitcase. Feeling rebellious, I pull the brown boots on over my feet. They extend past my knees, and for the first time I feel my father's size as my feet slide back and forth in the old leather. "My father's bigger than yours!" I want to yell, picturing myself on the playground, joining in as never before. I clump around the cardboard boxes and leather trunks in the sweltering, dusty air, stiff kneed and triumphant. Here in my father's boots, I'm suddenly big and noisy, someone to reckon with. I stump past my mother's boots, forgotten now. I wave an invisible sword while I charge ahead of a battalion of men, kicking my white horse up a smoky rise, cannons roaring all around.

My father sits on the bottom of the ocean against a bone-white mound of coral, the water green around him. He's in his khaki navy uniform, without his officer's plank hat, and his copper-colored hair billows back and forth in the current. He has a half smile on his face, as if to say, "This is what happened. Don't worry."

This stops my breath in midline. I'm forty-five years old now, speed-reading Shakespeare's *The Tempest,* which I've been called in midsemester to teach for a colleague suddenly taken ill. In act 2, scene 2 of the play, Ferdinand, son of the king of Naples, has just dragged himself up onto a deserted beach after the ship he and his father were sailing founders in a vicious storm. Ferdinand finds himself on a lonely island, and he cries over his father, Alonso, whom he last saw struggling in the waves. Ariel, an invisible island sprite, comes upon the grieving Ferdinand and sings him this song:

Full fathom five thy father lies;
Of his bones are coral made;
Those are pearls that were his eyes;
Nothing of him that doth fade
But doth suffer a sea change
Into something rich and strange.
Sea nymphs hourly ring his knell:
Ding-dong.
Hark! Now I hear them—ding-dong bell.

This passage conjured the image of my own father, lost at sea in the fall of 1943. It makes me wonder about him, something I haven't let myself do most of my life.

My mother remarried on the bounce, in the gap between news of my father's submarine declared overdue and presumed lost, November 6, 1943, and his being declared officially dead by the navy, January 8, 1946. Pregnant with me when she got the terrible news, my mother met her future husband, Frank, at the naval hospital in Annapolis where I was born five months later. He was a neurosurgeon on staff there at the time, and later he worked at the Naval War College on logistics of medical support for the planned invasion of Tokyo. "He must have given her plenty of TLC," Lil Nelson, the wife of my father's fellow submariner and close friend Bill Nelson, speculated when I reached her by telephone one summer morning in 1999.

Mother and Frank were married in April 1945, a year after I was born. In those days, with the men off to war, women far outnumbered men, and widows with small children were at a marked disadvantage in the competition for a provider. Mother considered herself lucky that any man would want her and three kids, much less a captain in the navy with a promising future in the new specialty of neurosurgery. "He was the catch of Annapolis," agreed Mary McGregor, wife of Rob Roy McGregor, another submarine friend of my father's. Mary went on to say that Frank was very good-looking in those days, a fact that surprised me. We kids were too busy staying out of his way to admire his looks.

In the late forties, we moved to Swarthmore, a suburb of Philadelphia. Large homes of stone or brick with slate roofs and leaded glass windows sat back from the roads on leafy, half-acre lots. Our house, just built, sat on a hill overlooking a large, leafy front yard with a stream running through it. In fall, I teetered over the water on a high stone wall running down the side of our yard bordering woods, exhilarated by the smell of wet ferns and raked leaves. In spring, I caught crayfish and tadpoles in jars and dammed up the stream to make ponds. Dogwoods laced the woods, and rhododendrons, azaleas, and boxwoods bordered lawns so lush that their greens seemed to rise, tingeing the air with a bottle-green hue that makes a child pretend she's underwater, an adult imagine it's always after dinner in daylight savings time. The neighborhood was full of kids, and our calls as we played capture-the-flag and hide-and-seek ring forever through green air in my memory.

This beautiful world illustrated a sense of arrival, entitlement, even a smugness that permeated the era. We had everything. But I was confused. My family was the only one in town with two last names, and it made people curious. When they asked me about my parents, I'd say, "My mother's a housewife; my stepfather's a doctor." It wasn't long before I put a lilt in my voice to stave off the next question.

"And your real father?" the unwary would press on.

"He died in the war." I used the word "died" because people could understand it; I never told the real truth—that my father "was lost," just disappeared and never came back.

And by nine or ten I'd learned to jump into the breach, to spare them the odd flick of their eyes to the side, the flush pinking their necks, the lowered voice: "Oh! *I'm* sorry."

"Oh no," I'd shrug before they did any of this. "I didn't know him. He died before I was born."

And so I minimized my father to save people—and me—embarrassment and because I should know better—know all about heroes and patriotism and dying for one's country. I should be an expert, like those gold-star mothers who proudly propped their losses in the window for all to see. The flag emblem, whose blue star changed to gold with the death of a son, was small and discreet, so pretty that people didn't mind looking at it. The tone in which people talked about the war, our country, heroes, and sacrifice made me feel that I should be doing something noble or humble, like picking up trash in the school lunchroom or helping my grandmother and her creaky friends up the stairs to Quaker quilting. In school, we were told in short order that men who didn't come back from the war "died for their country" or "gave their lives for their country," signaling that we should feel grateful for their sacrifice. But far from being grateful or proud, I was pissed. Here these people were showing me that any anxiety, curiosity, disappointment, or surely anger about my father's loss was off-limits. These ungrateful feelings did not measure up to his heroic act. I should square my shoulders, get my fingers out of my mouth, paste on a smile, and shut up.

And so my sister and I pretzled ourselves into Villager clothes and circle pins, my brother into Ivy League khakis with a buckle in the back. Our mother wore Peck and Peck suits and got her hair done at Elizabeth Arden. Our new brick house had the epitome of fifties' architecture: an open-floor plan and a picture window, accentuating the feeling that we were on display. To get some privacy, our stepfather retreated to the basement, laying down linoleum and lining the walls in knotty pine. Overlooking this "game room" were shelves of what he'd brought from medical school: his textbooks, with a jar of pickled human brains and a human skull serving as bookends. Frank stashed a bottle of bourbon behind the brains, and balancing the amber liquid in a shot glass, he paced back and forth. When I came down to practice the piano, he talked about the war as he roamed the room, head down as if studying the linoleum squares. He'd been a ship's doctor somewhere, treating the wounded. "You'd bandage 'em up with one hand, and push 'em out to fight with the other, Spook," he said, using the nickname he'd given me when, as a toddler, I believed I disappeared when I covered my eyes.

Upstairs in the open-plan main floor where the living room flowed into the dining room and kitchen, there was a beautiful blue-green glass globe. It sat on an intricately carved teak bureau that Mother called the "Chinese chest"; she and my father had brought these things back from the Orient. Bigger than a basketball, the globe was shiny, ethereal, and riveting. The small bubbles trapped in the glass mesmerized me. Like our father, they were there, permeating the globe, yet not there—out of reach and intangible.

The glass ball sat on a big plate of the same fresh, sea-foam color. Beneath them, the fine-grained, honey-colored teak chest gave a rich, buttery warmth to the dark-green dining room wall. On either side of the glass ball, toward the back of the chest, stood two carved figures of the same golden teak, a man and a woman, both bent under heavy baskets on their backs. The man carried a walking stick, and the woman had a dog at her side.

This tableau was the only remnant of my father in our living space. Everything else—his photos, letters, uniforms, shoes, and medals—were hidden away in the attic. And so I came to associate the glass ball with him. That ethereal, sea-glass color—like the shiny green curl of a rising wave just before it breaks—is his. Despite the fact that I've only seen his image in sepia photographs of the late thirties and early forties, I've always pictured him against a background of this color, his pale skin, red hair, and khaki uniform in vivid contrast.

But the glass ball association took something away from him as well: movement. In my mind's eye, he was always still, frozen in time and memory like those bubbles in glass. This is a shame, because everyone who knew him speaks of his physical grace. He was tall and lithe, with music in his bones, and my mother's friends—all widows in their eighties when I interviewed them—still raved about his dancing.

⸺◦◦◦⸺

It's daylight savings time, and I get to stay out past my bedtime because Mother is away. I stand with some other kids in the neighbors' circular driveway, watching our friend Joan sneaking around her lawn, catching lightening bugs. She claps the cap on the jar and comes over, holding it up like a torch. "Look. A real lamp," she crows.

"Can I see it?" I say.

She hands it over.

"You gotta poke holes in the top, so they can breathe," I say.

But she turns away, gazing at more tiny flashes over the grass, and I know she won't. I unscrew the cap and raise it to give the bugs some air, and suddenly they're all over my hand, crawling and flying out. I shake them off as Joan grabs the jar. "You're mean and cruel and stupid!" she yells, and her big sister Suzanne jumps on my back, crushing me to the ground.

Joan leaps on me, straddling me. Something explodes in my chest, and I corkscrew myself onto my back to free my hands. But she clamps her knees on my upper arms, rising like someone in a saddle and slaps my face back and forth. I scream that I'm sorry, and Suzanne is suddenly pulling on her shoulders. "Let her go!" she says. "I'll get you some more."

Joan stands up, and I curl to my side to hide my face, rubbing my upper arms. My friend Judy kneels and brushes the end of my ponytail out of my mouth. I get to my knees. Joan and Suzanne are back on the lawn, clapping their hands over fireflies.

Judy offers a hand, but I get up myself and run down the hill to our house. I open the back door to Frank sitting at the kitchen table under the round fluorescent light. "A fight," I say, breathing hard. I grab a dish towel and wipe my eyes.

Frank's veined eyes widen. He puts down his whiskey glass and peers at me with new interest. His face is gray and puffy, only a shade lighter than his close pelt of squirrel-gray hair.

I hold my stomach against a stitch in my side. "Joan jumped on me for letting her lightning bugs out of the jar."

He juts out his chin. "She's got no right!"

This is what I came for.

He gets up, catches the door jamb into the living room to steady himself, then motions me after him. "You gotta learn to fight, Spook." He puts his drink down on the living room table, then turns to face me, telling me to put both hands on his throat. He bends his knees so I can reach him.

I freeze, not wanting to be within the radius of his quick hands. But I've started us down this path and can't turn back. I put wobbly hands on his shoulders as he bends lower so that our faces are level. I smell something sour, like vinegar and rotten peaches. I hold my breath.

"No," he says, lifting his arms to grab his own throat with his hands. I flinch at the sudden movement, then lean forward to cover it, not wanting to disappoint him by showing that he scares me. "Like this," he says, as he tightens his hands on his throat. I picture the safest place I know: my friend Deanie's house, as we run up the hill and into the front door that her mother holds open for us. The smell of baking bread fills the front hallway.

But Frank's face bobs in front of me, and I square my shoulders, force myself forward, and put my hands on his neck.

"That's it," he says, dropping his hands to his sides and planting his feet, raising his chin through my hands like a hanged man. Then with a sudden chop upward, he brings his fists against the bottom of my forearms, knocking them off his neck. I jerk back, then resist an urge to rub my stinging arms. Again, I try to be nonchalant, relax, and suddenly I'm back in Deanie's house as her father waits for Deanie to step onto his shoes, then waltzes her around the living room to the "Tennessee Waltz."

Frank dances away from me, ducking his face behind a left fist, his heavy head bobbing. "Always guard yourself," he says, jabbing the air with quick upward thrusts. Like a mule, I plant my feet solid, then hold up my left fist, crossing my eyes at the firm ball it makes between my face and his, still bobbing in the background.

Suddenly, knuckles glance off my cheek, and my braces spring loose against my gums. I fall backward, hot coppery liquid filling my mouth. Putting out a hand to steady myself, I curse the tears flooding my eyes and turn my head away from Frank. An image of Joe Louis springs into my mind, and I push up and dance away from him in small semicircles. But he weaves forward flat-footed, peering at my mouth. "Spook," he says, bunching up his brows and pulling on his chin. "Looks like I caught you there."

"No, it's just my braces."

"Go upstairs, take a look," he says.

2

I'm sitting on my mother's living room rug in 1997, warmed by the California sun streaming in the patio door at my back. I'm surrounded by cardboard boxes. Last week Mother had a sudden heart attack and lived only a day afterward. She was eighty-six.

Although I couldn't catch a flight out in time to be with her, I'm comforted by stepping into her shoes here for a few days, being in her home and trying to sense how she wanted things done. It's late January, and my husband and I had to snow-blow ourselves out of our driveway in Maine to catch my flight from Portland. Now I'm surrounded by sun lighting up the regulation-white walls and off-white carpeting of the small, rectangular living room. The glass ball on the Chinese chest faces me from the far wall, the tableau too big for this tiny apartment. The wooden man and woman are still there, unchanged. A doorway beside them leads into Mother's bedroom, where more cardboard boxes cover the floor and bed.

Mother moved here a few years ago after selling her house on the Goleta side of Santa Barbara. Vista del Monte was said to be the best bargain in town, and my mother loved a bargain. Started by schoolteachers as a place to guarantee them a pleasant retirement on limited funds, it has a cozy library, a spacious dining hall, and a small fitness room. No golf course, swimming pool, café, screening room, or other frills of more-affluent retirement homes, but it does have plenty of oleander, lemon trees, eucalyptus, gardenia, and other fragrant plants to make the morning's walk around the grounds a treat.

I'm packing up my mother's things into boxes that I've labeled with Magic Marker: Good Will; Vista del Monte (for their yearly rummage sale); my siblings, Jean, Henry, and Fred; and four more for various friends and cousins of my mother. My work is helped by a new sense of finality; certain objects bring on memories, but as they're playing out in my mind, I'm working steadily, the decisions quick and intuitive because my mother's story is now done. There's no more possibility between us, no more wondering how I can make things better. She's gone—and in the way she wanted—fast, without lingering.

I tackled the hardest job as soon as I arrived, going to the funeral home to make cremation and burial arrangements and planning a Quaker memorial service. The rest—packing up her things, closing accounts with the retirement home, and meeting with her accountant and banker—is easier, and so I spend most of the time between appointments sorting and boxing things up. Keeping my hands and mind busy feels like I'm resolving something, closing a chapter of my life, packing up the past. "You feel lighter," my cousin's wife, Alanna, told me on the phone the previous evening, trying to cheer me up. I swallowed down a hard place in my throat, grateful as she went on about the death of her last living parent, the father she'd adored, in a wobbly voice. "In even the best relationship in the world, you still want to please them, live up to their expectations, or resist them sometimes."

I felt a shiver of recognition and curled more deeply into the couch, not wanting to think of how much I'd resisted my mother. "And that's a burden," Alanna said. Then her voice rose a notch. "But once they've gone, you're free to become the person *you've* always wanted to be."

I sigh, wondering if I'll ever feel that way. It's too soon; I'm still kicking myself for not getting here in time. Again, I bless my half brother, Fred, who held Mother's hand in the hospital here last night. Fred and his son just left, and I'm the next shift. In a week Henry, my older brother, will take my place while I go back to my teaching job in Maine. He'll go over the last of Mother's items in storage and contact her friends and extended family for the memorial service. Our older sister, Jean, lives in London and can't get over, but calls me often while I'm here. "Let me pay your plane fare," she said this morning, trying to find something she can do. There's a wonderful feeling of us pulling together, which I hope my siblings savor as much as I do, because we've never been close. I'm proud that there's been no disagreement, no squabbling over Mother's effects, no childhood jealousies flaring up. In this sense, we're all putting the past behind us.

I fold the last sweater from Mother's upper bureau drawers into the box for Juanita, Mother's best friend here at Vista del Monte. They took a couple of cruises together in the three years Mother lived here, two tall, elegant women who could wear each other's clothes and loved to travel and dress up. I close up the box for Juanita, then turn to the last drawer of my mother's bureau, the large bottom one full of papers. I start through it, drawing the plastic-bag wastebasket closer. Mother was never organized, and all her drawers and shelves have old bills, bank statements, letters, and photographs mixed in with clothes, gloves, and old pocketbooks. And everywhere, in every drawer and shelf, are unused sewing patterns and fabrics. Mother loved fabric, much more than words or even photographs. And every fabric has folds, so I shake bills and rent receipts out of percales and silks.

The papers demand attention, edging out the reflecting I've been doing since I got here, but the job is simplified by having only one decision: to keep or throw out. I think of putting on the radio, but then remind myself that there are only five days left to finish everything. I don't need distractions. I work fast, making it down to some older, more yellowed papers near the bottom of the drawer: my grandfather's will, my grandmother's deed to the house that was sold in 1954. A corner of a photograph sticks out. I pull it out, and everything stops.

A middle-aged "Daddy Jim," the name my mother used the few times she mentioned our father, sits on a rock, flanked by two small children who each rest an arm across his shoulders. Realizing he can't be middle-aged—he was only thirty-three when he was lost—I peer at the two children at his sides. Yes, they're Jean and Henry, my siblings as young kids. The naval officer in the middle, looking too old to be their dad, is in a dress-white uniform. The suggestion of lines—not there in prewar pictures—slant down from his temples to meet in vertical furrows between his brows. His eyes are dark-circled and bagged, making him look anxious, sad, even a bit fearful. I cover the part of his face that doesn't match—the tentative half-smile—with a horizontal finger. Now he looks like a man in anguish, even mourning. His tall frame slumps backward on the rock as if he's bone weary. My brother's and sister's hands rest lightly, tenderly, on his neck, and I feel a stab of envy.

I peer closer and make out two baby rabbits he holds, one on each thigh,

Jim with Jean and
Henry, rabbits on
his lap, Portsmouth,
New Hampshire,
Easter 1943.

the black one showing up better against his white uniform, the white one
barely distinguishable. They suggest that it's Easter, and bare branches in the
background indicate a cold climate, probably Portsmouth, New Hampshire,
where my mother told me they were stationed for a while. From the age of
my brother and sister, looking about three and six, I'm wondering if it's the
last photo ever taken of him, if this is why Mother kept it. She told me, in
the early nineties when I helped her move out of her house into this retirement home, that she had long ago destroyed most of the photographs of our
father with his kids. "It was just too sad," she said. So I'm holding a precious
link that escaped her wastebasket.

I strain for a clue in my father's troubled eyes, wanting to know what he's thinking, why he's so worried. It's the first photo that's invited me in like this, that shows him as vulnerable, flawed, someone I can identify with, rather than the stern, distant war hero of earlier, more official naval photos taken on ships. At last I can see something of myself—my own worry, doubt, and fear—in this man I never knew. Although this is the first time I've seen this picture, there's a familiarity to it, a feeling of connection.

—◦◦◦—

Over the next day of packing and running errands, I'm haunted by the photo. Why did Jim Coe, whose pictures always looked either relaxed and happy or posed and gazing into the middle distance like a hero, look so worried? Did he know that something terrible was going to happen? That he would never come back to these children who rest their hands on his neck so trustingly? I remember Uncle James—the husband of my father's sister—telling me once that "he *knew*." The last time my uncle and aunt saw my father, it was at some party, and Uncle James said Jim Coe just sat and stared into the middle distance, ignoring the people around him. He had always been gregarious, the life of the party, so this unusual preoccupation stood out in my uncle's mind. "Things were very bad over there [the Southwest Pacific], and he knew he was going down," Uncle James said.

The next day I go to the funeral home to settle up. The funeral director gives me the jewelry from my mother's body, a single ring. He asks me if I want to view the body before today's cremation. "No," I shudder, then wonder what he must think. "I can't," I say, then turn on my heel to stave off any show of consolation. I'm glad that we've got all the paperwork done and I can leave.

Driving back to the retirement home, I look at the ring on the dashboard. It has a small, sea-green stone in it—maybe tourmaline. Yes, it's the ring Mother started wearing in the mid-sixties after she divorced my stepfather, took back Jim's name—becoming Rachel Coe again—and moved to California. The stone is encased in heavy gold, and at a stoplight I pick it up. Its weight seems solemn, a reminder that there's a whole life my mother had with this man that she never talked about. I see that it's engraved with their initials and a date on the inner curve: JWC to RHG, 1935, and I feel like

I'm peeking at an intimacy I haven't the right to know, a crucial, defining relationship that lived and died before I was born.

Driving back to Vista del Monte, I have a growing sense of disorientation. The photo and ring are puzzle pieces turning me in another direction. I'd come here to close a door, lay my mother to rest. But instead, these pieces have opened a new door. Instead of burying my mother, I'm pulled to unearth my father. His face, newly worn and anxious in my mind, says, "Things aren't right. Come closer. *Know* me."

Suddenly I think of Sherry, our only child, now grown up and on her own, and I'm overcome with the enormity of what I've closed out all these years. I pull over to the side of Modoc Road and park on the shoulder. Resting my forehead against the steering wheel and taking a couple of deep breaths, I try not to cry. If I ever disappeared like my father did, I'd want Sherry to come looking for me, find out what happened. I'd want her to remember me, to tell her kids about me, show them pictures. Realizing I've hardly ever *mentioned* my father to Sherry, I find myself startled to think of him as her *grandfather!*

I wait for a break in traffic and make a U-turn back to Hollister Avenue. I drive to a photo shop, where I have Jim's picture blown up and copied. I then mail one copy off to my sister in London and another to my brother Henry in Vermont, asking them both if they want to help me find out about this man, how he lived and died. I buy two copies with cardboard frames to stand up on my desk and library at home.

━━◦◦◦◦◦━━

The next day I wrap the glass ball and its plate in foam padding. I notice how the ball and plate just match the stone from Mother's ring. I picture her walking the beach with Rocky, her black standard poodle, which she did almost every day once she moved out here. I see the glint of my father's ring as her hands swing up and down, its sea-green stone matching the waves in the background. Crumpling up newspaper to line a sturdy cardboard box, I remember Mother telling me the Pacific was more beautiful than the Atlantic, not as gray and rough. As I lower the glass ball deep into the crumpled newspaper, I realize that it's all coming together, the story of her years here. They were built around Jim Coe.

I top off the box with more crumpled paper, then close up the top, tape it, and address it to my brother Henry. He's getting the teak bureau and figures, too. I'm glad the tableau will stay together, and I realize that back in my twenties, I would have resented Henry getting the best things. But here on the wiser side of the intervening years with families of our own, I'm glad they're going to him.

Henry, a rangy, freckled twelve-year-old, is on his knees on the hard-packed clay outside our house, chipping bricks. Surrounding him is an area marked off by stakes and string for a terrace that will wrap around the house. A big pile of concrete edgings and a taller pile of powdery-surfaced bricks behind him show that he's been at it for a while—nearly half the summer, to be exact. But Henry works steadily, eager to get through in time to spend the remaining summer days with friends.

Our stepfather stands over him, a squat, square, bulldog of a man in a stained T-shirt and dark green work pants, stomach hanging over his belt, open beer bottle in hand.

By late summer, the terrace is covered with neat, herringboned bricks. Henry's laying the last of them as a cement truck pulls up the hill, its mixer rotating. When it reaches the terrace, Frank directs the driver to circle around, back up to the terrace, and dump wet concrete onto the bricks. Henry jerks up, staring, his mouth shocked into an O. He runs to the truck driver, but Frank strides forward, pointing him back to the terrace, yelling at him to get a hoe and spread the concrete over the bricks.

In two days the brick is buried under a layer of dead, gray concrete, and the summer is gone.

—⁓—

I'm standing in Mother's small bedroom, her double bed taking up most of the rectangular room. There's a mirrored bureau against a wall, a closet beside that, and a bathroom at the end of the room. On the bureau is an electric orange-juice squeezer, and there's still orange bits of pulp from Mother's last breakfast. I'm reluctant to tackle it, the medicine chest, and the little boxes of hairpins and cosmetics on the bureau. These things are too concrete, too close.

I slide Mother's clothes down the rack of her closet toward me and start looking them over. Here's my grandmother's Quaker dress, along with her shawl and gray bonnet.

Quaker Meeting, spring morning, wood thrushes calling, the smell of lilacs wafting through screened windows. A Sunday school play in which Chippie Shay is Quaker founder George Fox, and I'm his wife. We sing hymns, then the teacher leads us into Meeting, where the adults are already seated, heads bowed. The silence is alive, swelling the air like a held breath. I clutch the shawl closer around my shoulders, then regret the scratch the stiff taffeta makes as adults near me raise their heads. I spread the quilted skirt of Grandmother's dress carefully on the hard, wooden seat before I sit down.

Once we're seated, kids on either side of me scrape one shoe over the other, make cat's cradles of rubber bands around their fingers, or pick at their nails. Lucky Jimmy Tolles snuck in his coonskin cap, and now he runs his fingers over it, making lines in the fur. We're settling in for the long haul, one stifling hour where some imp inside me keeps straining to jump up and scream or throw a fit.

I'm awakened from a daydream by a scratchy sound behind me, and the air stirs. I realize that lilac branches are sawing against the window screen, and the line of a hymn we just sang in Sunday school fills my mind: "In the rustling grass I hear Him pass." Suddenly I feel like I'm right where I should be, and the silence is no longer boring.

I lift the ancient dress out of the closet and lay it across the cardboard box addressed to my home in Maine. I look over the rest of the dresses and suits. Most of them have moth holes, stains, or ripped seams. A few look okay till I carry them to the window and find flaking linings or yellowed collars. I'm reminded how careless Mother was with her things. I'm amazed—thinking back—that we made it through childhood at all.

The last time I'd done this kind of work was when my Uncle James died in 1995. He was the widower of Peg Coe, Jim's only sibling. He wanted me to have the packet of letters my grandmother Phoebe Coe had written to her daughter Peg in December 1944, a year after Jim Coe had been declared missing in action but not yet officially dead by the navy. The words of Phoebe's recurring theme drift back to me as I sort through the clothes:

> Dear Peg:
>
> I was not surprised to hear that Rachel [my mother] is going to Florida in Feb., for she cannot stay long at home, even with her new interests [Frank] and does not seem to think it unusual just to pass her children out to be cared for by her friends. . . . I hope Rachel will settle down after she is married. The children need a permanent home and a mother who is not thinking of clothes, night clubs, and parties all the time and planning who she can leave the children with.

But then, moving an armful of clothes to the bed, I think about the letter's references to another Christmas without Jim and remember the struggle Christmases were for Mother when I was growing up. We kids literally fought for her attention throughout the season because she was preoccupied and sad. In this tender first year of his loss, maybe Mother needed to get away from the most immediate reminders of Jim: us kids. I can feel my eyes widen with this new take on my mother; I too have always seen her as shallow and flighty. But now I'm thinking about her in a new way, seeing her vulnerability. And I see my grandmother that way, too. Phoebe was also in mourning; as was plain in other letters in the sheaf, she resented Frank taking Jim's place before Jim had even been declared dead by the navy.

I turn back to the closet and lean in toward the end of the rack for more clothes. There's a dark shape against the wall. I pull aside the last few dresses and robes and see a man's overcoat.

My breath stops. I pull the coat down the rack. It's a heavy wool tweed, and it takes both hands to hoist it up to the other side of the bedroom door so that I can hang it in the light.

I stare at the heavy charcoal weave, nothing anyone would wear here in Southern California. It's got old-fashioned, pointy lapels. Turning up the collar and lapels to see no dust along its fold lines, I wonder if the coat just came from the cleaner's. Mother didn't have a man friend . . . did she?

I look over at the dresses on the bed, seams of dust along their hanger lines, moth holes in the folds of skirts. Mother must have taken this coat out regularly and whisked it. Aired it, at least.

Standing on tiptoes, I look in the back of the collar: E. H. Peterson, Philadelphia, the label says. Hmm, I think, Frank's territory.

But Mother shunned the very thought of Frank. I feel down the front facings of the coat, looking for more clues. There's nothing but a small, yellowed twill tag sewn in the seam. I turn it over: 41L, it says. I don't know a thing about men's sizes.

Why would she have it? Shrugging, I finger through the pockets. Nothing. I turn a small, two-finger-wide breast pocket in the lining inside out and find an ivory-colored woven cotton tag sewn into the seam with 1935 on it. I remember the ring with the same date on its inner curve.

I recall seeing Mother and Jim Coe's wedding pictures once at my brother Henry's. But there was no coat like this. Jim was in his white uniform.

I turn back to the coat, run the tweed between my thumb and fingers, squeezing the coarse wool. A surge of pity swells the back of my throat as I picture Mother—an old woman alone in the shadow of the half-closed closet door—doing the same thing. Could this be what she kept of Jim Coe, after throwing out his letters and not talking about him for all these years? Did she commune with him by touch? Had she risked Frank's jealousy by hiding this coat in their various closets throughout their fifteen years of hell? Had I misjudged her hasty remarriage, her silence about Jim? Had she loved and missed Jim so much that she wrapped her grief in this strong, sinewy tweed, a secret reminder of his touch?

I blink back tears, feeling for the first time what our silence about Daddy Jim cost Mother and me: a chance at shared loss, even consolation. I take the coat down from the door and fold it over my arm. I carry it over to the telephone and look up the number of Fred Niles, Mother's sister's son. He's out here in California, only an hour away. And he's thirteen or fourteen years older than me, old enough to remember Jim Coe.

Yes, Fred says when I get him, a 41 long would have been Jim Coe's size; he was tall—six-two—and lean, as opposed to Frank, five-ten and "built like a fireplug."

—∿—

A week later I'm saying goodbye to Juanita in the little Santa Barbara airport, giving her a one-armed hug as I hold the coat in a garment bag over my shoulder. "I'll call when I get home," I say, thanking her again. I feel her eyes on me all the way out to the plane, like I used to with Mother, and—yes—there she is, still waving, as I take a window seat.

A couple of hours later, when we have a long layover in Chicago, I find the nearest set of rental lockers to stash the coat. It's heavy, and I want to use this time to fast-walk, if I can find the space, to get the exercise I've missed during the long days of packing all last week. But as I put my purse and carry-on in the locker and start hanging the garment bag, I feel a sudden anxiety. What if someone breaks in and carts off this irreplaceable link to my father? I unzip the bag, take the coat off the hanger, and fold it over my arm. I put the rest of my things in the locker, and just before swinging the metal door shut, I fish my mother's little magenta beret—another sentimental relic that I can't bear to part with—out of my carry-on bag.

Outside the airport, the February wind whips down the concourse, hunching travelers into their collars as they flag down busses and cabs. I put on the coat and beret, smelling my mother's Chanel No. 5. The coat's so big I can lap the front over to double-thickness against the cold. I hold it closed against my side, pull the hat down further on my forehead, and lean into the wind.

II

The Search

3

A few days after I get back home to Maine, my brother Henry calls in tears. "That's the first time I've seen him with us," he says of the photo I sent. "It must have been right before he was lost."

And my sister, Jean, calls with "Flopsy and Mopsy!" naming the rabbits in the photo. She confirms that it was Easter in Portsmouth. "I remember walking to school there," she says. "The snowbanks were huge."

Over the next few weeks, I call Jean every Sunday, when rates to London are cheaper. I mine her memories of Daddy Jim, as the one child old enough to remember him. She tells me about going to school in Portsmouth, New Hampshire, and how the kids on the playground would pretend to fight the Germans and Japanese, how they would hide under their desks or file outside for air-raid drills, how Daddy Jim came home one night with lobsters and let them crawl around on the floor. And how he gave her a bright blue china elephant before saying goodbye for the last time. "Remember that elephant painting you did for Grandmother?" I say, thinking of the yellow, blue, and gray cubist painting that hung in our grandmother's den for years.

"No," she says, and I describe it to her. Although abstract and complex, it was the essence of elephant, rearranged to showcase trunk, tusks, and thick, wrinkled knees. But the only elephant she can remember is Daddy Jim's. I'm not surprised.

I sit at the breakfast table stirring raisins into my oatmeal. Henry sits across from me, and our baby brother crawls under the bench somewhere near my feet. Frank hunches over his orange juice across the table, his hairy forearms on either side as if guarding it. Mother stirs something on the stove. We're all quiet. Jean comes downstairs dressed for school, holding her books and notebook against her chest. She's fifteen or sixteen, and I look up, stop-

ping my spoon in mid-stir. She's beautiful, with soft reddish-brown hair, flawless skin, and wide-set blue eyes. Her clothes are sophisticated combinations of colors—today a spring-green pinafore over a gray- and green-striped shirtwaist dress. Her white socks are carefully folded at the tops, her oxfords freshly polished.

Mother turns from the stove, hands on hips. "You're not wearing that stupid crinoline!" she says.

Jean, head down, goes back upstairs to change.

She comes down again, her skirt now slack against her thighs. Clutching her books to her chest once more, she starts toward the door. "Stand up straight," Mother snaps.

"It's those damn books," Frank says, his words slow and slurred. "Of course she's going to be round-shouldered when she carries them that way, but she's a moron. She can't learn."

Jean, without turning, shifts the books to her side, looks at her feet, and walks out.

Jean, Henry, and I, over the next few weeks, call back and forth about the photograph, how sad and worn out our father looks, and wonder whether he somehow knew he was going down. We talk about the fact that World War II documents are now declassified, that the World War II vets are dying, that the time to learn about Daddy Jim is now. Jean and Henry tell me all they can remember about him, and then we agree to read *Pigboat 39*, a book by the wife of the last living officer of the *S-39*, Jim's first submarine command. Mother sent all of us copies of the book when it first came out, in the 1980s, but none of us read it. It took Mother's death and the photograph to break through a silence we're only now just becoming aware of.

When I read the book, I'm riveted at any mention of Jim Coe. I contact Guy Gugliotta, widower of the author, and find that most of the *S-39*ers have passed away. Again, I'm struck by the years of silence and wish that I had started the search earlier. I'm also filled with specific questions that I wish I could ask Mother.

But this late-blooming curiosity is typical, I find, by reading another book, *Lost in the Victory,* about others who lost fathers in World War II. The government calls us "orphans," and I get on the Internet, keying in the address in the book. It takes me to AWON, the American WWII Orphans Network, and suddenly I can't believe it: here are people like me! Most of them grew up in similar silence, confusion, and even shame about their lost fathers as we Coes did. And most don't overcome that silence until they're in their mid-fifties; with kids grown, careers winding down, and the sense of mortality quickening, war orphans finally start looking for their lost fathers.[1] A further way we Coes were part of a wider story is that most of these people had troubled mothers, and many had jealous stepfathers who—actively or inadvertently—enforced the silence around the lost hero. These similarities point up the uncounted costs of war that go way beyond the battlefield, reverberating for generations.

Once my siblings and I broke this traditional silence and started talking about Daddy Jim, the enormity of what we didn't know about him hit us hard. The paradox of the wartime loss—a lifetime of trying to see the loss as heroic when in truth we felt resentful and confused by it—had not only silenced us but also diminished our father. Like our AWON contemporaries, we Coes had no sense of Jim's character or what he had gone through. We had no idea what he achieved; what he meant to our mother; what their marriage was like; or how, where, or even why he died. We didn't know when his birthday was, what year he'd died, or how old he was when he was last heard from. We had no grave to go to, no idea whether he was ever missed, mourned, or memorialized. We never heard about a funeral, had no idea when or how to commemorate his loss. We never went to a Memorial Day service or Veterans Day parade, didn't speak or think of him on those or any other days. There were no friends who stopped by to reminisce about him, no war buddies who checked up on us, not even a picture displayed in our home to remind us of him.

Joining AWON helped me and my siblings over our initial guilt and shock for perpetuating this enormous void throughout our adulthood. AWON told us that we had adapted, at a formative age, to a wider cultural silence. The nation had been triumphant, and the message in the late forties and into the fifties was to not look back at losses, but move on, make up for lost time. The culture ignored widows and orphans, while glorifying their lost men into empty abstractions. No wonder I'd been confused!

———⟋⟍⟋———

A year after my mother died, when I finished settling her estate, I found that the small legacy she had left me would make it possible for me to semiretire. I cut down my teaching load and made plans to interview everyone still living who had known Jim Coe. Over the next few years, I tracked down most of the men still alive who had served with him, contacted the widows of his friends who had kept up with my mother until her death, and interviewed other veterans of World War II. I visited naval archives and researched declassified documents. I read about submarine warfare and toured several submarines, getting a context as well as a physical setting in which to place what I learned about my father.

I worked my way to a reasonable explanation, if not the answer, to his troubled face in the Easter photo with the rabbits. And I learned, through records of Japanese bomber pilots in the Tokyo Naval Archives, approximately where, why, and how deep my father lies.

Finally, I tried to resurrect Jim Coe on the page by arranging all this information chronologically, in the order that he lived it. This was the only way I could think of to make him real.

———⟋⟍⟋———

Jim Coe was born in Richmond, Indiana, in 1909, to Demas (short for Nicodemas) and Phoebe Wiggins Coe. Jim had one sibling, sister Peg, four years older. Demas Coe was vigorous and hardworking. A newspaper reporter and editor in Richmond and Indianapolis, he later—with his brother-in-law—ran his father's business, the J. M. Coe Printing Company. He continued to freelance on the side as a correspondent for newspapers in Indianapolis, Cincinnati, and New York until his death in 1934. The few samples of his writing that I could find, plus his civic affiliations, suggest that he had a keen social conscience plus a fascination with history. One series of articles highlights the dangerous, "patriotic, conscientious, and God-fearing" work of the abolitionists who built and ran the Underground Railroad along the Ohio/Indiana border.[2]

Demas's social conscience was shared by Phoebe, whose Quaker parents had raised her with two black "sisters." My brother Henry remembers Phoebe when he visited her once in the fifties, going to her screened-in back porch with a sandwich, milk, or leftover pork chop for the hoboes who passed through Richmond. They'd rake leaves, shovel snow, or fix a broken door or light fixture in return.

Phoebe Wiggins taught third grade at Richmond's Warner School before she married. She served on the board of directors of Richmond's Margaret Smith Home (for unwed mothers) for forty-eight years, thirty-five of them as president. After Demas's death, she became a director of the J. M. Coe Printing Company, working actively to protect and pass on to us Coe kids Jim's small financial legacy in the company.

The only firsthand memory I could find of Jim as a child was from Edward Wilson, one of Jim and Peg's schoolmates. Ed remembers Jim walking to school with a flute up his sleeve. Its tip peeked out of his cuff, and he cupped it in his hand as he walked. Music became his lifetime companion, as he later played flute in high school and the U.S. Naval Academy's gymkhana band, and his academy yearbook write-up says, "His renditions on the fife are unsuppressed emotion."[3] My mother told me that he played by ear, and at least one shipmate in the early forties watched him fashion a crude stringed instrument out of string and sticks to pluck pick-up percussion at a deck party in Tsingtao, China. Jim Coe had music in his bones.

He was also mischievous. Grandmother Phoebe told my sister a story about him as a little boy cracking raw eggs on the floor and skating around the kitchen on them. She also told of catching him peering intently in the mirror at himself one day: "Do I have a pleasing personality?" he said. Evidently, someone had told him he had, and Jimmy thought it might show up in the mirror.

Demas loved the circus, performing with it each year when it came to town. In top hat and tails, Demas was trainer of "Dewey, the famous talking elephant" (two men in an elephant costume).[4] My aunt Peg remembered her father taking her and little brother Jim to see the circus. Demas walked up to a balloon man and paid him for the whole bunch of helium balloons he was holding. Demas then whisked out his pocketknife and cut the man's fistful of strings with a flourish. The balloons flew up and away, and Jim and Peg raced under them, trying to follow. They shaded their eyes to track the diminishing dots of color into the clouds. Demas probably figured that the kids were like him, preferring the drama and surprise of these few soaring moments to a tamer afternoon of a single balloon tied to the wrist.

Jim didn't show himself as a scholar at Richmond's Morton High School, but this may be because he followed his gregarious nature (like Demas before him) into a wide range of extracurricular activities. Despite the fact that he was a year younger than most of his classmates, Jim played three sports, acted in plays, played flute in the band and orchestra, and sang in the Boy's Glee Club. He was in citizenship, business, and church clubs.

Jim was known on the basketball and football teams as "Dog-ears"— because of his flanged-out ears—and also as "Red." The latter may have originated not only from his fiery hair but also because of the basketball team's title, "The Red Devils," as in "Morton's Red Devils drive Centerville Bull Dogs into kennel, 37-33." The nickname "Red" stuck to Jim for life.

Jim's yearbook picture pegs him as a cutup. The style of the day seemed to be for men to look stern in their photographs and for women to smile demurely. Jim, by contrast, looks like he's guffawing. He stands out from the somber young men as a real goof—either not quite all there or the class clown.

In July of 1926, Jim was accepted to the U.S. Naval Academy. He was only sixteen. He undoubtedly shared his era's fascination with transportation; he'd always slept with a toy locomotive engine under his pillow as a boy. The navy was a young man's path not only to ships but also to cars, tanks, trains, and planes.

And it is clear from his many activities and sociability that Jim was outgoing and adventurous. The chance to see the world, plus the opportunity for close companionship, as well as duty to a higher cause, would have appealed to this gregarious and idealistic young man.

He also had a keen sense of duty around money. Jim wrote his parents on his first assignment to submarines that he would use the promotion to pay them back all of what they'd spent on him. He thus might have welcomed the chance to get an education that wouldn't cost his family much more than his transportation.

Also, a career as a naval officer, to a middle-class family in the patriotic heartland of America in the late twenties, was a mark of some prestige. Being close to the media of the day, Demas would have known that the most advanced technology existed in the armed services. It was a place for a young man to get cutting-edge skills in the exciting new fields of radio, electronics, hydraulics, sonar, and—later—radar.

I was proud that Jim had made it into the Naval Academy at such a young age. "The Naval Academy was not easy to get into," says Jack Lee, a retired rear admiral from Jim's class of 1930 whom I interviewed. "I believe the ratio of applicants to admissions was about the same as it is today: about ten to one. When I received my acceptance, I was on cloud nine. I believe that most of my classmates considered it an enormous privilege to become a midshipman."

Jim appears to have felt this way, too, because he kept his acceptance letter, which made it down to me seventy years later. It marks the end of his childhood and made his life like a meteor, brighter because of the higher cause it served, but straighter—no room for wobbling or second-guessing—and shorter.

4

In the late nineties, I arranged to tour the Naval Academy campus so that I could try to picture the young Jim Coe among the stately brick buildings and green lawns seventy years earlier. My brother Henry came with me. I'd contacted retired captain Guy Gugliotta, the last living officer of the *S39*. Guy generously arranged to take us around the academy. Henry and I thought we were well prepared to meet Guy, our first submarine veteran, because we'd read *Pigboat 39*.

But the rush of pride I felt at his first words took me by surprise: "I can see Red Coe in you," he said, looking from Henry to me. He was looking up at us, a slight, bald man in his eighties, with beautiful posture, as if he did tai chi every morning. He was dapper in his brown suit, and he had deep-set, penetrating eyes. They drew my gaze, causing a jolt of empathy or sadness. I hoped my reaction wasn't because I saw pity in them; I didn't like AWON's designation of us as "war orphans" and hoped Guy didn't see Henry and me that way. Even though it was early in my research, I'd changed considerably from the girl who had blithely told people she didn't care about her lost father. Now I had a stake in Jim Coe, proved by the delight I felt when Guy added, "I see some red in your hair."

I thanked him, with some tentativeness, feeling newly vulnerable. Although I felt a growing urgency to find out who my father was, I was not sure what I'd discover.

Guy drove us in his big late-model car to the Naval Academy, graciously telling us he'd been counting the days since he first got my letter. When we got out of the car, Henry and I soon found ourselves hurrying to keep up as Guy struck out across the campus. He was like a man on springs as he led us from the chapel up Stribling Walk to Tecumseh's statue and on into Bancroft Hall. Here, we found our father's name carved in polished granite high up on a wall, along with all the other graduates who had fallen in war. Again, I felt the new stake I had in Jim Coe when relief flooded me at seeing "Cmdr." before his name. In some listings of lost submarines, this hard-won rank that he was awarded only a day before leaving on his last patrol isn't noted. I told Guy and Henry this, and Guy said the navy had to be extra careful about every detail before chiseling a name in stone. Then he discreetly wandered down to the other end of the long hall, letting Henry and me linger under Jim's name.

We then went to an outside memorial of several walls of white marble facing the Severn River. We found Jim Coe's name topping the fallen alumni from the class of 1930, and Guy tactfully left Henry and me to absorb this, our first outdoor memorial to Jim. Something clicked into place in my mind, a new feeling of normalcy, that we too now had something like a grave to visit. We'd tried to give ourselves that when we'd ordered our mother's grave-stone inscribed to include Jim—with "Wife of James W. Coe, lost at sea." But here was something that had already been standing for decades. Like so much else about Jim, we hadn't known it existed.

"We can always come here," I said, and Henry nodded. "It's beautiful," he murmured. Then we turned and saw Guy standing in another section of lower marble walls, which turned out to be a columbarium. He was wiping his eyes, and later we learned that his wife's ashes were there. I realized that that's what I'd seen earlier in his eyes, a still-fresh grief for his wife.

———

When we arrived home from our trip, Henry lent me a scrapbook that Jim Coe had compiled at the Naval Academy. I'd never known of its existence, and Henry told me that that was because it hadn't been in the attic of our childhood, where Jim's other mementoes were stored. Mother had given it to Henry at an early age, and he'd hidden it in his closet, knowing that Frank sometimes used Henry's room to nurse his whiskey in private while Henry was at school. So, as a hidden link to his father, the scrapbook had a deep in-fluence on Henry, making him aspire to the Naval Academy himself. But Mother wouldn't allow it, saying she had already given enough to the navy. Henry went to Brown University instead.

The man who emerged from the scrapbook in Henry's young mind had a profound effect on him growing up. "I missed him intensely," he wrote me. "I missed not having him as a father whenever I saw a positive or a loving interaction between father and son . . . no matter their age, no matter my age as observer. I still observe intensely the interaction of fathers and sons."

Jim Coe could hardly have known the deep, lasting impression he would make with this scrapbook, but just the act of buying and compiling it shows extraordinary self-confidence for a sixteen-year-old. He was saying in effect: "These years are going to be important enough for me to record meticulously."

A coffee-table–sized album bound in black leather with a worn gold Naval Academy insignia on the front, the scrapbook shows a tradition of marking personal history that is stronger in the Midwest than in other parts of the country; I didn't meet any other World War II veterans with scrapbooks. So Henry and I feel incredibly lucky to have this record of Jim's early years.

Its tawny pages have a thick nap, so I can almost feel indentations of Jim's fingers. I see a ruddy-faced, jug-eared boy laying out photographs, announcements, and letters on the pages, gluing everything down carefully to last seventy years.

His priority is clearly fun, not academics. A telegram he sent in his sophomore (or "youngster") year, notifying his father about an impending Christmas visit home says, "Expect to see you Sunday. Fooled them again today," about passing his end-of-term exams.

Old sepia photographs show Jim bent over, hands on knees, about to get a swat from a midshipman wielding a broom behind him. Already playing to the audience, a habit that will mark his photographs throughout his life, Jim—despite his awkward crouch—grins up at the camera.

Group pictures show him mugging, grinning, smirking, making bug eyes (like my aunt Peg's, his eyes were slightly protuberant), or waving from his peers' midsections as they hold him horizontally like a battering ram. Even when a classmate is leapfrogging over him on the beach, Jim bracing his bent back against the boy's weight, his grinning face is lifted to the camera. His academy yearbook write-up shows his childhood exposure to his father's circus hobby: "We believe [Jim] left a good carnival job to join the Navy. Whenever a good laugh is needed to cheer things up, Red is the doctor."[1]

Jim Coe being leap-frogged by Naval Academy classmate.

I pick out his body easily from a group of midshipmen frolicking on a beach; they're all in dark, old-fashioned tank tops and matching briefs. Jim, in contrast to the other boys, is tall and thin and looks hairless, his skin pale and smooth as Sheetrock. "You could say he was as funny looking as homemade sin," said retired admiral John Tyree when I interviewed him and other Naval Academy graduates at a submarine veterans' convention in the late nineties. Tyree had been Jim's old plebe (a freshman at the academy under Jim as a senior). Plebes were assigned to rooms full of seniors (or "first classmen") for the ritual of hazing. When I asked whether Jim was mean in the hazing process, John said no, that Jim had been delightful, easier on him than Jim's roommates had been.

But a witness to that interview remarked afterward that he had been embarrassed at Tyree's candid assessment of Jim's looks. I assured him that I took it differently, certain enough of Jim's character as laid out on the pages of the scrapbook to feel that Jim himself would have found Tyree's description—as I did—funny. This was a surprising, new, buoyant feeling; I felt as if I'd almost shared—across fifty-six years—a chuckle with Jim.

Corroboration of this view of Jim's looks was given by Roberta McCain, widow of the late John S. McCain, Jr., Jim's classmate at submarine school, and mother of Arizona senator John McCain. "He had slightly bulging eyes," Roberta told me in a phone interview, "and he only had to roll them to make people laugh. And that *pink* hair! Well, all he had to do was be anywhere within a city block to make me laugh."

In a later phone call, Lil Nelson, widow of Jim's best man at his wedding, agreed: "Jim wasn't as good-looking or smart as my husband, but oh, that personality!"

Jim indeed seemed to have developed the "pleasing personality" that he'd been looking for in the mirror as a child. "He was one of the most popular men in our class," Jim's classmate, retired admiral Bill Snead, told one of my correspondents. This sociability became, as we'll see later, what he was known for. But a close second characteristic showing up in the scrapbook is loyalty. Numerous telegrams, notes, and letters to his family attest to Jim's devotion and gratitude. He talks of how much they've done for him, how he would rather take a loan from a bank than put them under financial strain. One particularly telling page has a large photograph of a mass of rubble in what looks to be a warehouse. It is the J. M. Coe Printing Company, and an announcement carefully pasted below the photo tells that a fire gutted the building on the night of September 12, 1928. A notation in pencil shows that Jim got leave to go back to Richmond to help his father rebound from the tragedy. The building was repaired, equipment was replaced, and the company resumed its business November 15. A telegram to Demas from Annapolis after Jim returned to the academy, dated November 1, says: *Happy Birthday Dad Old Boy. Today starts real success. Jim.*

Henry laughed with pleasure when we discovered this, and I knew what he was feeling. With highly developed antennae for father-son relationships, Henry was delighting in Jim's easy affection for his father, resolving our conflicted sense of "father" in the wake of having Frank as our stepfather. Certainty clicked inside my chest like a hatch cover dogged into place. Yes, I agreed; *this* is the way things should be between fathers and sons—and fathers and daughters, too.

—◁◊◊▷—

The culmination of Jim's Naval Academy scrapbook is his graduation in June of 1930. White-uniformed midshipmen lounge on the lawns beside their visiting parents in some shots, with the Severn River in the background; others sit on the grass in front of dormitory buildings, their suitcases and trunks scattered around. The graduating class, in dress whites, sits in the middle of cavernous Dahlgren Hall, flanked on either side by parents and visitors; in the next shot, midshipmen are standing, arms upstretched at their white officer's plank caps they've flung into the air. Knowing what these boys would face in another decade, the caps look to me like puny circles of hope against a dark abyss; but looking at it from their point of view, trained for a brilliant future with their proud parents looking on, there's pure triumph in the upstretched hands. I was to feel this new, poignant mix of sad hindsight along with the eagerness and hope of the young, newly minted ensign Jim Coe many times over the course of my search.

But it's easy to feel Jim's unmitigated happiness at the scrapbook's photos of a tall, slim, smiling girl, Jim's date for his graduation (June Week) festivities. Jane Rohe was a Richmond girl, just graduated from Jim's old Morton High School in the same year as this academy graduation: 1930. Her daughters, whom I tracked down through the Morton High School Alumnae Association, said Jane played violin, sang soprano, and loved to dance. Besides music, Jim and Jane shared a love of laughter. In every scrapbook photo, Jane is laughing, either at Jim who is probably mugging behind the camera or at him standing next to her, tilting his head toward her ear. Jane has a natural

Midshipmen and guests for the Farewell Ball, U.S. Naval Academy, 1930 (Jim is second from left; his date, Jane Rohe, is in the middle).

ease and vitality in front of the camera. Unlike the other young women in Jim's scrapbook, who are frozen in tight smiles, Jane seems remarkably self-possessed. It speaks of a rare rapport in which the two are simultaneously thrilled yet comfortable with each other. I'm not surprised later to find that this is the girl Jim wants to spend his life with.

But that's a few years off. In 1930, twenty-year-old Jim is pledged, as are all midshipmen, to wait two years before he can marry. This was a new rule, instigated by Naval Academy administrators who wanted to save the young ensigns from getting married before they knew where they were to be assigned. If they did marry, they would have to resign from the navy.[2] This waiting period is usually spent fashioning a military specialty. A newspaper clipping from the *Richmond Palladium* in the scrapbook announces Jim's postgraduation assignment to the aviation division of the navy, where he purportedly would train in San Diego for part of the summer of 1930. His yearbook write-up underscores these flying ambitions: "Jim aspires to be the boy aviator of Richmond. His weird imitations of a wing-over, zoom, and a loop in succession as displayed on the diving board should be good practice for his future career."[3] Jane Rohe's daughter Sara Shute told me of her mother and father collapsing in laughter at memories of Jim's antics with an umbrella on the Richmond diving board.

However, Jim's navy personnel record shows that he didn't qualify for flight training because of poor circulation. There is no evidence of this failure in Jim's scrapbook or his few existing letters; perhaps this omission signaled a wish to put negatives behind him and move on, although he did—to his credit—keep a letter from the faculty of the Naval Academy warning him to get his grades up.

Jim was then assigned to the surface fleet. He reported to Port Angeles, Washington, on July 16, 1930, for duty on the battleship USS *Nevada*. At that time, the navy centered all its strategic thinking on the battleship; smaller ships such as destroyers and submarines were seen only as support or as forward scouts to battleship fleets. It was standard practice for academy graduates to serve on these bigger ships for at least a year before being sent to more-specialized craft like submarines.

Jim's first ship was in the Pacific Fleet, and all through the thirties, the fleet conducted exercises on how to fight the Japanese in a future conflict. Jim learned the *Nevada*'s fourteen-inch main guns, its five-inch secondary guns, and its four torpedo tubes. He was then transferred, in January 1931, to the new ship, USS *Chicago,* at Mare Island, California.

The *Chicago* was still under construction. She was a heavy cruiser, differentiated from light cruisers by her eight-inch guns, as opposed to six-inch ones. She could move at thirty-two knots (a little over thirty-five miles per hour), being a scout for the battle fleet and an enemy of smaller, less-powerful ships such as destroyers.

She was commissioned on March 9, 1931, in a ceremony, Jim says in a letter of that date to his family, that gave him quite a thrill. He explains the flag raising and then the watch system. He goes on to tell his family that he invited a Doris Devlin as his guest to the commissioning lunch. "Doris is really something. She graduated from California last June and has a Masters degree in Philosophy—she's a mighty smart girl."

As one of the first letters of my father's I've ever read, I'm struck by the gullibility of the heartland in his tone. There is none of the doubt, cynicism, or irony that characterizes our present Northeast, the region where I've spent most of my life. Jim expresses a wide-eyed belief in not only the individuals he encounters but also the systems they work for: the navy and the university. This impressionability will change in the war years, but the didactic tendency to explain things will remain, making me think that the urge to teach is a permanent part of Jim's character. I see teaching as what he might have gone on to had he lived.

Jim sailed on the *Chicago*'s shakedown cruise to Honolulu, Tahiti, and American Samoa, then divided his time for the rest of his two-year stint on her between the East and West coasts. The newsletters he kept from this period are rallying cries for teamwork: "The athletic ship is the happy ship. No reason exists for the men of the leading athletic ship to hang their heads in any company, and it is surprising how this feeling grips everyone from the Captain down. Your ship then acquires a soul to go with its husky body and the life of the ship becomes active, purposeful, and delightful."[4]

This philosophy of plenty of extracurricular activity and competition would pay off later for Jim on his submarine commands in high crew morale and loyalty.

The newsletter also shows the glaring difference between attitudes then and now around drinking, a fact with dire effects on my family in my formative years. In the celebration of Prohibition's repeal in 1933, there is none of our caution about addiction, drunk driving, and family dissolution. *Chicago*'s *Big Shot* newsletter points up drinking as humorous proof of one's manhood, competence, and inventiveness. A hero of a poem with a "blonde-headed lass and a whiskey glass" is eulogized for his thirst:

As for booze, he could truck it
from a ten gallon bucket
Or take it in shots at a bar.
There's a ring that shows on the bridge
of his nose
How he drank from an old fruit jar.[5]

In this climate of approval, it's surprising that more navy men didn't end up like my stepfather. The repeal of Prohibition linked drinking inextrica-

Jim on the USS *Chicago,* circa 1932.

bly with freedom in the minds of Jim's generation, and the navy's stark contrast of daytime adherence to rule and rank with nighttime's inebriated release among the bars and officers' clubs cemented this association.

But I didn't know all this when I visited Jim's sister, my beloved aunt Peg,
one vacation after fifth grade. Our mother would occasionally let us Coe
kids visit, one at a time, this closest link to our father. Part of the adventure was getting to ride the train all alone from Philly to Washington, D.C.,

where Peg and her husband, James, lived. They were childless, so they doted on us.

My aunt Peg was a writer, first for the *Richmond Palladium,* then for Norcross Publishing Company in New York, and then for the *Washington Post.* She wrote a children's book about my brother, called *Henry's Wagon,* and dabbled in genealogy. But when I came to visit, she gave herself over to entertaining me, taking me around to all the museums and the Washington Monument.

One morning, when Peg was getting ready to drive me to the Smithsonian Institution, I picked up her orange-juice glass by mistake and took a swig. The taste hurtled me to the sink to spit out the bitter, medicinal liquid before Peg emerged from the bathroom. I later matched it by smell to a bottle of vodka stashed under the sink. But although I managed to keep this slipup from her, I punished her for it in my ten-year-old fashion, self-righteously clamming up in the car on the way to the city. As she asked me over and over what was wrong, I turned away, pushing my forehead hard up against the passenger window. I stared down at the streaming pavement, struggling to get up the nerve to say what fouled my mind: "You shouldn't drink! I hate it! Bad enough that I have it at home, but now *you!*"

But I was a coward, silenced by my stepfather's curses and swats when my mother confronted him with the same thing. To this day I kick myself for not having the presence of mind or the charity to conjure up a polite lie— an "Oh, I'm just tired"—that would have let Peg off the hook. In hindsight I recognize the festering guilt of the alcoholic as she peered at me and questioned, hurt rising in her voice. "If you don't tell me what's wrong, how can I fix it?" Finally, she sighed and said, "Well, I just don't know."

That visit began a vague distrust of her, which grew into avoidance and then became a gulf in my twenties and thirties. Now, when I think back on the few times I visited her as an adult, I realize how dark and still her houses were. The windows were heavily curtained, and the end tables had countless water rings from her uncoastered cocktail glasses, and I picture Peg sitting for endless hours in growing darkness and isolation.

As I gathered information about Jim Coe, her only sibling, I began to see

Peg with new eyes. With no kids of her own, Peg had an unusual stake in her younger brother, the last of their father's line. She'd shepherded Jim in their formative years, walking him to school and helping him with his algebra. As an adult, Peg followed her brother's career closely, proudly pasting pictures of him and the navy's latest ships into a scrapbook devoted to him. I've never come across anyone since who's documented a sibling's career this way.

I began to sense, for the first time, the enormity of her loss and realized that she was like Mother in this way. News articles of Jim's loss mention Peg speeding down to Annapolis to be with Mother, and perhaps that's when the conviction took root in both women not to sully our childhood with mourning. Both women struggled—for the rest of their lives—to silence the pain of their loss.

Sometime in the late seventies, two years before Peg died of lung cancer, Uncle James wrote me, saying that Peg had some family stories that she wanted to pass on. He urged me to come down with my typewriter. I said no, feeling I was too busy between work and mothering. Now I deeply regret it, knowing that I'd let the long-ago fear of my stepfather's drinking drive a permanent wedge between Peg and me.

She was a precious link to my father and could have told me who he really was. But I was still asleep in those years, deaf to the call of my ancestors.

I had ordered Jim's service record from the navy, and when I received it, I tried to flesh out the terse, chronological entries with research. When Jim had a choice, as he did in his next assignment after the *Chicago,* I tried to learn his motives.

What made him go into submarines? It was particularly dangerous duty; I needed to know why he'd done it. I couldn't find any direct statement from him. His Naval Academy scrapbook didn't mention it and showed no reference to any early interest in subs, as he'd had in planes. All I could come up with in the generic research I was then forced to were some similarities to the specialty he'd preferred: flying.

Submarine service had undergone a major shift in status from the twenties, when it was widely believed in both the British and American navies that submarines were vulnerable and ineffective. Better listening devices to locate submarines, longer-range aircraft, and better weapons to sink boats had made submarine service seem like a risky dead end.

Congress responded to this perception in 1928 by deeming submarine duty as dangerous and thus worthy of extra pay. Jim's classmate Jack Lee remembers the pay as being 25 percent more than that of other assignments. This was a similarity with Jim's first choice, flying, and may have influenced him.

By 1930, submarines were improved in speed, comfort, and underwater endurance. Sonar proved to be as effective a weapon in submarines hunting the enemy as it had been in submarine detection. These strides enhanced the desirability of submarine service, gaining enough prestige to be fully voluntary. By 1933, the year Jim entered, applicants for sub training far outweighed openings.[1]

There was also an attractive mystique to submariners, perhaps because of the sheer wonder of humans living and moving beneath the sea. Navy tradition embellished this image by proclaiming that only the most intelligent and fearless applicants were selected for submarine duty and that only the strong survived.[2] And because submarines were small milieus compared to the surface ships that Jim had just come from, young officers had more of a chance to make their mark. Submarines had only 40 to 75 men, compared to the 621 men on the *Chicago*.

Jim went to submarine school in Groton, Connecticut, from July through December 1933, and I was thrilled that it was in New England, where I'd have a chance to drive to research sites. I began by traveling to Portsmouth Naval Shipyard each week to brown-bag it with a contingent of World War II submarine veterans who volunteered in the museum there. They graciously fleshed out all the rigors of sub school.

It was grueling academically and a harsh test of men's ability to withstand life submerged for long periods of time in a cigar-shaped tube of air. It also required learning how to operate and repair all parts of a submarine. An additional hurdle was dealing with simulated underwater catastrophes, such as escaping from the submarine at one hundred feet down and swimming to the surface without getting the bends. Days were long, with class time devoted to mastering all mechanical, electrical, and pressurized systems in a sub, taking apart and putting back together all parts of the boats and their torpedoes, and practicing approach and avoidance maneuvers on the school's fleet of old World War I submarines. Nights were spent poring over systems manuals, memorizing every part of the boat, and drawing them onto charts. Author Herman Wouk's protagonist in his World War II saga tells his son of submarine school, "It's the toughest school in the Navy," and he was probably right.[3]

New Hampshire submarine veteran George Watson remembers the trials of sub school well, although he attended it more than fifty-five years ago. As I followed Watson's brilliant white hair through the dark interior of the *Albacore*, a 1950s submarine that's now a museum in Portsmouth, he noted the parts—such as the double hull, fuel and ballast tanks, and berths—that corresponded to World War II subs. I kept checking the oval shell surrounding us and shifting my feet, seeking solidity. I wanted to get out and leaned into Watson's voice, trying to distract myself from claustrophobia. We paused inside the control room, and he described an array of tests designed to weed out men who couldn't acclimate to submarine life even before they started classes.

One test was held in a dark room simulating the bridge of a submarine at night. A planetarium-like ceiling made it look like stars drifted overhead. On the horizon were gray outlines of ships at various distances and levels of obscurity. Students who couldn't pick these out and identify them were sent back to surface ships.

Another test weeded out anyone with respiratory weakness or what I was feeling: that the curved walls were coming closer, that the space was shrinking. Watson gestured at the rounded interior of the *Albacore*. The men were packed into one of two connected cigar-shaped compartments smaller than the one we were in. This mock sub had benches on either side, the two rows so close that men were knee to knee as they faced each other. Then the air pressure inside the compartment was increased to fifty pounds per square inch, what it would be inside a submarine more than one hundred feet beneath the surface. This is about three times the atmospheric pressure at sea level. The men had to hold their noses and push out their lungs to "crack" the pressure on their eardrums. They watched the thermometer climb past one hundred degrees; heat and sweat made it difficult to breathe, and the men had to fight down a natural instinct to panic and run. The pressure reached a peak, and, with it, the temperature soared to 130 degrees. An instructor studied the students, looking for signs of panic or other frailty that could jeopardize a submarine. Finally, he let air out of the compartment, slowly bringing the pressure back down to normal. Watson described condensation building up on the walls of the mock sub as the instructor let the air out of the compartment, causing fog so thick that Watson couldn't see the man across from him.

Bill Tebo, another Portsmouth Shipyard Museum regular, told me that men whose systems couldn't take the increased air pressure would bleed from the ears. And then there were those who couldn't stand it psychologically, who became claustrophobic or jumpy or froze under the stress. They raised their hands during pressurization and were taken out to the adjoining tube, where pressure was gradually equalized. They were then sent packing.

Tebo, a wiry enlisted man who had served in World War II subs but looked like he was still in his sixties, told me about the ultimate test. It was the escape tower, a ladderlike structure submerged in a tank of water more than one hundred feet deep. To simulate an escape from a submerged sub, the men first had to strap on a Momsen lung, a device inflated with oxygen that lay on the chest like a hot-water bottle. A breathing tube snaked up from it, which the swimmer would activate through a mouthpiece. A canister of carbon dioxide absorbent connected to the breathing tube purified the air that the swimmer would breathe. A nose clip ensured that the men would not breathe in water on the ascent and that they could readily equalize the pressure in their eardrums. After donning the device, the men would wriggle through an escape hatch and climb the tower. Officers had to climb the full one hundred feet; enlisted men came up from fifty feet below.

Tebo remembers being put through this test in stages. First, the men had to ascend through only twelve feet of water, then twenty-five, and—finally—fifty feet. The final test was having to ascend the full fifty feet twice.

George Watson was still surprised, more than fifty years later, at how long a gulp of oxygen taken in at a depth of fifty feet lasts. "All you have to do is breathe out the whole way up," he said. "That one breath will last you." This is counterintuitive; instinctively, we want to hold on to our precious lungful of air or breathe in more through the Momsen lung. But the oxygen you take in at fifty feet under is greatly compressed by water pressure, and it expands on the way up as pressure decreases. This can burst your lungs if you don't get rid of it at a regular and controlled pace as you ascend.

This controlled ascent, of course, is also counterintuitive. It's natural to bolt and flail for the surface. But "you have to make sure you don't come up faster than the bubbles floating up from your Momsen lung," Watson said. The submarine school instructors made the men stop when they came to periodic knots in the rope they guided themselves up with and count to ten. In this way, they avoided the bends, the scourge of deep sea divers who decompress too rapidly (causing bubbles to form in the veins).

Bill Tebo remembered submarine service as highly competitive. Perhaps having heard of how tough it was to qualify, only twenty out of ten thousand men in Tebo's boot camp volunteered for submarine training. Of these twenty, only three went on to graduate from sub school. Submarine author Carl LaVo echoes this: "Every Monday [in sub school] the men took written tests; any who failed two exams were returned quietly to the surface fleet. 'Every Monday morning, someone would be missing,' said Keller [an enlisted man]. 'You'd be told he went to a minesweeper; he went to a destroyer.'"[4]

But the men who went through submarine school as officers are more modest in their assessment. "I don't know how 'elite' we were," Guy Gugliotta told me when I used the word. "We were mainly just trying to learn how to save our skins."

Jack Lee agrees. "While it wasn't easy, I believe all of us that were selected completed the course at New London."

Perhaps Naval Academy preparation was what made the difference. Whatever it was, submarine school grads had to have skills that went beyond mechanical aptitude and good recall. Admiral Charles A. Lockwood, in a postwar memoir, describes it as what today we'd call emotional intelligence: "They must be alert without being brittle, . . . interested in their shipmates without being nosy; they must appreciate food without being gluttons; they must respect privacy without being seclusive; they must be talkers without being gabby; and they must be friendly without being tail-waggers. . . . The wrong kind of a man aboard a sub, on a long cruise, can become an insufferable thorn in the sides of shipmates. He can, emotionally, cause almost as much damage as an enemy depth bomb."[5]

A sense of humor helps immeasurably. Jim's sub school classmate John Davidson, who—along with his wife—was a good friend to Mother in Annapolis after Jim was lost, remembers Jim and his Naval Academy classmate Dudley "Mushmouth" Morton as the two clowns of their sub school class. Jim and Mush shared a "snake ranch," as off-base bachelor digs were called in those days. Their place was across the river on the New London side and had a reputation as a great place for a party. Davidson tells of Jim's arriving late to their eight a.m. "juice" class (on electricity) one morning.

Lieutenants and ensigns host party for instructors at submarine school,
57 Mott Avenue, New London, Connecticut, June 1933. *Left to right:* Jim
Coe, Vernon Lowrance, Arthur Wilson, Dudley "Mush" Morton, Arnold H.
Holtz, Walter C. Bailey, unknown housekeeper, James C. Dempsey, and
William B. Sieglaff.

He wandered in about eight thirty or twenty to nine, and the instructor
said, "Well Mr. Coe, what excuse do you have today?"

And Red said, "You know that road coming out here along the river,
coming out to the submarine base from the big bridge? You know that
curve there that has a great big tree on the right? I was coming around that
curve just as carefully as I could, when suddenly that tree moved out and
just knocked the hell out of my car."[6]

When I first came on this story in my research and delightedly told my
husband about it, he said gently, "That's an old joke." But that didn't dampen
my spirits; the man I was getting to know had a personality, and it was totally the opposite of silence, sadness, and loss, the association we had with
him when we were growing up. This guy was able to enjoy himself and
amuse others even in the midst of the most demanding drudgery. I was enor-
mously grateful for this compensation for the shortness of his life. Now, in-

stead of moping around or avoiding thoughts of him as I had growing up, I was starting to smile at the thought of him, even picturing him grinning back at me, saying, "Yup, kiddo, it was swell."

—◦◦◦—

Jim graduated from submarine school in December 1933. After Christmas leave home, he set off in the last days of 1933 by car for San Francisco, en route to Pearl Harbor, Honolulu, his next assignment.

In a letter home January 11, 1934, Jim tells about his trip from Richmond to St. Louis, where he'd picked up a friend, "Ike," to drive on to Big Springs and then El Paso, Texas. New Year's Eve found them in Globe, Arizona:

> We decided to have a bit of jollity. Globe is a little town of 6,000, and all the ranchers were in. We went over to the public dance hall where they were all congregated and in about 10 minutes I met a brother of 'Pablo' De Vos who was a very good friend of mine and a classmate at the Academy. I met him because he looked so much like 'Pablo' that I just upped and asked him.
>
> He introduced us to what he termed the five nice girls of Globe, and we had a fine time dancing. However, we didn't get to bed until 3AM and so started at 11 Monday morning.

I'm struck by Jim's gregarious nature, and as I read, I get a sense of the profound absence that Mother must have felt in our house: the lack of wonder and adventure, of confident assurance that people outside one's walls, even strangers, are friendly and welcoming. Jim was exactly what our family needed. He would have made the world seem safe and wonderful to us kids. But I'm also struck with the sense that this very reaction might be why Mother hardly ever talked about him. She didn't want us to know what we'd lost.

Jim then goes on to describe getting caught in a gale and the subsequent flooding of Los Angeles, waiting out the storm there in a hotel, and then driving the inland "Ridge Route" to San Francisco. He negotiated mountain passes where the roads were full of mud and rocks, with bridges half carried away by swollen streams. "However, they had been working these CWA [President Roosevelt's work-relief program] people all night on cleaning out the mud and so we got through in good shape."

After getting to San Francisco, Jim drove up to Mare Island and spent an afternoon with his old ship, the *Chicago*, which was being repaired after an accident. He then boarded the steamship for Honolulu, where twenty-five of the ninety passengers "are Navy and we really have taken control of this ship."

The letter ends with a financial accounting: the whole trip by car cost $45, and passage on the steamer to Honolulu, with car, cost $60. He thanks his father for all his financial assistance up till then and asks him to tote up all that Jim owes him so that he can start paying it back out of his sub duty pay.

Jim's steamer reached Honolulu on January 12, 1934. Another first-time traveler on the Dollar Lines of that day attempts to fill in the aesthetics: "Arrival in Honolulu in those days was a traveler's delight. Small canoes filled with diving boys hoping for small coins dropped by the passengers, leis, and those magnificent flower wreaths in great quantities, the Royal Hawaiian Orchestra, Diamond Head, the overwhelming beauty of the vegetation dispersing perfumes in the air."[7]

Jim's service record has him reporting for duty on the submarine *S-27* January 12, the day he arrived. I couldn't find anyone who had served with him for the year and a half he was on *S-27*, so I went to the literature to get a sense of what life was like on these "S-boats."

"Pigboats," as they were christened because of their poor handling on the surface, causing them to continually dive and resurface like porpoises or "sea pigs," were coastal submarines, unlike their later transoceanic counterparts. S-boats were built in the decade following World War I and were used for maneuvers off Panama and Hawaii in the twenties. In the thirties, as newer, more habitable subs—called "fleet" boats—were developed, S-boats—though declared obsolete—were still used. Unlike the fleet boats, S-boats had no radar, sonar, or vapor-compression systems to distill saltwater. While submerged, the interior of the boat—without air-conditioning—

En route to Hawaii (Jim Coe in middle).

became covered with condensed moisture, making everything, including the boat's complement of about thirty-nine crewmen and four officers, sopping wet. Along with this was a pervasive odor of battery gas, diesel oil, and body and cooking odors, which—the submariner's wives could attest—permeated the men's clothing long after they came ashore.[8]

Besides these poor living conditions, S-boats were mechanically restricted compared to the newer subs. Whereas fleet boats could submerge to three hundred feet and more, S-boats were good only to two hundred feet at most. Their engines were heavy and slow compared to the newer boats' engines—high-speed ones akin to the diesel locomotive's. S-boats had a surface speed of fifteen knots at most—more like twelve—which they could sustain only for short periods of time, and had a top submerged speed of eight knots or less. The fleet boats could go faster (twenty-one knots on the surface, nine submerged for up to an hour) and further (a cruising radius of twelve thousand miles), in considerably more comfort (with air-conditioning and supplies to last fifty-one or more days at sea). But even so, twenty-three of these S-boats were pressed into service for lack of better equipment at the onset of World War II.[9] They rose to the occasion with surprising strength and endurance, and my father did the same.

6

Jim served on three S-boats out of Pearl Harbor from 1934 to 1937. These were tense years with Japan, when President Roosevelt and Congress built up the navy to treaty strength. That meant an increase in ships and material, but not manpower, and ships were operated with only about 80 percent of their full complement of crew.[1] This was to Jim's advantage; within the even smaller pool of submarines, and aboard the clunky S-boats to boot, where mechanical know-how and common sense were highly valued, he moved up fast: from communication officer, to first lieutenant and commissary officer, then gunnery and torpedo officer, engineer and electrical officer, and finally to executive officer and navigator. In the beginning of this climb to his own command, he had to learn not only his own job but also that of every other officer and enlisted man on board. This was a requirement of every officer on submarines.

The enormity of this task is immediately evident to anyone who visits a World War II submarine. I toured subs in Fall River, Massachusetts, and Portsmouth, New Hampshire, and I was overwhelmed by what seemed a chaos of machinery, with every wall surface covered with dials, valves, levers, gauges, buttons, and blinking lights. The tour guide explained some of these as engine and motor controls, speed indicators and sounding gear, electrical meters and fuse boards, compressed-air manifolds and pump controls, vents and valves, and compasses and cables. Red, green, and white lights in different compartments of the sub gave the rooms an eerie glow, and the metal gleamed with the splendor of an operating room in a modern hospital. It was the most intellectually daunting place I've ever seen, completely beyond my comprehension. Yet young men—some without any formal education— had to master this environment in a short time, at risk of life and limb. Enlisted men had to know the jobs of all other enlisted men, and both officers

The control room of the USS *Lionfish*.

and enlisted men were tested on this knowledge to qualify to serve on submarines.

In his book *Battle Below*, World War II reporter Robert Casey voiced the reason for this shared knowledge: "If I muff my play, you'll muff yours," a crewman summed it up. "You muff yours, and curtains for everybody." This vital interdependence fosters an egalitarian spirit that isn't encountered in other parts of the service. "Any man's mistake is as good as the next man's, and on a submarine no mistake is unimportant," one skipper told Casey. The author goes on to describe a submarine crew as "the most nondescript mob ever assembled in the hold of a ship—lads in dungarees or skivvies or college sweaters moving about with no semblance of military order. . . . They converse with their officers as equals—even argue with them."[2]

And this populism, in turn, engenders tolerance, both on and off the ship. Casey again is surprised at submariners because, in them, familiarity seems to breed respect and camaraderie rather than contempt. "Yet here were men who lived virtually in each other's laps for months on end . . . and ashore, where they had every opportunity to separate and enjoy a few hours of privacy, were seldom out of one another's company. Where you saw one of them you seldom saw less than half a dozen. And while they would fight willingly—individually or collectively—with members of the lesser services, they seldom so much as raised their voices to any of their own kind."[3]

This strengthened my impression of Jim's gregariousness, his ability to get along with people. I thought wistfully that after life on a submarine, Jim would have found life at our house—in peacetime with wife and small children as "crew"—a piece of cake.

In Casey's account, not only is each submariner dependent on all others' mastery of their jobs, he is also dependent on their split-second timing. "Every man has to be able to do his job in all circumstances in the same unvarying fraction of a second," said an officer. "If he doesn't do it he dies and so, very likely, does everybody else. There can never be any such thing as a seventy-five-percent-efficient submarine. . . . Not for very long."[4]

Along with this interdependence, split-second timing, and the knowledge to take over any other job on the boat in an emergency, submariners—especially those on the old S-boats—had to know how to take virtually every system apart and put it back together. Once they were under way, there were no repair facilities. So submarine crews had to be inventive, able to jerry-rig solutions—sometimes with shoelaces and chewing gum when parts were scarce. S-boats were always breaking down. One sailor summed it up this way: "The men of the submarines have always had a hard job without much glory. In peacetimes they were the hardest-worked crews in the navy. At sea we were doing our maneuvers just as the other ships did. In port we were always tearing down engines or refitting or something. Other ships got holidays—the pig boats, no."[5]

Undoubtedly, Jim was stretched to the limit in his initiation to sub duty. So I was surprised to find he had time to keep in touch with his family and to make significant life changes during this period. In his scrapbook is a telegram to his sister at 29 Bank Street, New York City, dated September 28, 1934, wishing her the greatest happiness on her upcoming marriage to Uncle

James: "Would certainly like to be there in body to lend a helping hand but know you'll get swell start despite this handicap. No flinching at the altar. Don't forget ring. Love, Jim."

In an effort to learn more about this period of my father's life, I wrote letters to submarine and naval magazines and to Web site bulletin boards, asking them to post queries to their readers for information on James "Red" Coe. I also scoured my mother's address book, looking for names of naval people or other old friends Mother had mentioned to me through the years. I wrote to the names I recognized. Mrs. William Nelson was one of them, and she called me from her retirement home in Maryland soon after she got my letter. I was thrilled at her quick response and told her how good it was to hear her voice. "Well, I was glad to get your letter," she said. Her voice wasn't the thin, quavery one I expected of a widow in her eighties, but strong and resolute, the voice of a woman who knows her own worth. She turned mock-accusatory: "Especially since I'd gotten my Christmas card to your mother back with "Deceased" scrawled across the front. That was none too pleasant!"

I apologized for apparently missing her when I sent out notices of Mother's death. And then, "You knew my father?" I asked.

"We were *close*," Lil said, adding that she had even dated Jim in Honolulu in the midthirties, until she met future husband, Bill Nelson, Jim's classmate from Annapolis and sub school. "He loved people," Lil said of Jim. "And he was going with so dang many girls before he met your mother!" She filled me in on Jim's crowd: fellow submarine officers Bill Nelson, Dudley "Mush" Morton, Jim Davis, David Hurt (with his wife, Connie), Wreford "Moon" Chapple, Corbin "Bang-bang" Shute, Jim Dempsey, and John McCain, Jr. Lil remembered them and the young women they went with—some of them, such as Ruth Steele (to become Mrs. Jim Davis) and Margaret Clifton (later Mrs. Corbin Shute), from military families stationed in Honolulu. Lil remembered them all going to the beautiful Royal Hawaiian Hotel regularly to dance. Jim was a wonderful dancer, she recalled, very outgoing, funny, and always cheerful, with a penchant for cocktail-napkin jokes. He played word games like "How do you write the word that is pronounced 'peep-ay-oh-leen-ay' in Hawaiian?" "Pipeline" is the answer. (Yes, I'd have to concede again to my husband, it isn't funny, but it shows me a bit more about Jim:

that he had absorbed language differences of the Hawaiian culture, that he liked word games—as I do—and that he dutifully kept the conversation away from the classified subject of submarines.)

A more prurient and adolescent example of this group's cocktail-napkin riddlery is one I found tucked away in Jim's scrapbook and probably not meant for mixed company. It goes: How do you draw the following baseball situation: One out, nobody on, bottom of the fifth? The answer is three crude line drawings: a woman with one breast bared, a toilet with the seat up, and an open liquor bottle on its side, with an S-line of fumes coming out.

As if reading my mind, Lil Nelson tells me that their crowd was looking mainly for fun in those days. To my questions about values, tastes, and any ideas of a future beyond the navy, she replied—somewhat testily—"What were *you* thinking about at that age?" She reiterated that they were all young and not thinking beyond the next party or promotion in rank.

So this was the perfect milieu for my mother—the quintessential party girl—to enter, sometime in 1934. I forgot to ask Lil when that was, but I like to believe it was after June of that year, when one of Peg's letters shows that Jim still had serious intentions toward Jane Rohe. Peg first writes Uncle James about it on May 15, 1934:

> Well, it seems that when [Jim] was home Christmas at two-o-clock on the night before he had to leave for California, at a dance he got [Jane] to admit that she was in love with him. He had no money then, so could do nothing much about it. . . . About two months after he went to Honolulu, she wrote to him and said they'd have to stop writing because she would always be doubting him when he was away. . . . He told her all right if that was the way she felt about it, and he has been rewarded with stony silence ever since. Now he has his pay raised and can ask her to marry him, which he already has by mail the same boat that my letter left on, and he wants me to play Cupid in his cause.

In a following letter of June 19, Peg reports having a letter from Jim telling her that Jane Rohe thinks they haven't "seen enough of each other on peaceful terms recently to contemplate getting married right away" and that

Jane may come out to Hawaii to visit. Peg advised Jim to "plaster her with letters for a couple of months and ship off an occasional gardenia."

A letter probably resulting from this advice survives, kindly sent on to me by the late Jane Rohe Shute's daughter Sara:

2 July 1934

My darling Jane:

I've just come home from another date—and it's no use—I've met some pretty swell gals over here and meet new ones who come over to visit from time to time but I always think of the same things when I'm with them— how much nicer it would all be if you were the girl. My thoughts are so wrapped up in you darling that I can't seem to click even out on the boat as I should.

Jane, why don't you come on out here. I know we'll be able to see things the same way then. I get so provoked when I think that I came off last Xmas without you. I know I should have brought you and I realized it then too, but I didn't have the courage to ask you to start out sharing the grim financial outlook that I had then. I wish to God I had now, for knowing you as I do, I know we'd have made a go of it and been much happier—at least I would have. These six months have been hell, Jane. But now I can ask you and here you're not sure—oh, be sure, Sweetheart— we'll be so happy. It's heavenly out here and we won't have to worry about the finances much either with the economy act over.

Jane, dearest, don't wait any longer. I love you and always shall. Do what your heart says to and tell me you'll come.

Always yours,

Jim

Two months after Jim wrote this letter, there was a fire in his parents' living room. In the course of beating it out of the curtains, Demas inhaled smoke and was hospitalized. His lungs, already weak from a childhood bout with pleurisy, gave out, and he died on September 5, 1934, at age sixty-four. There is no report of whether Jim made it home from Honolulu for the funeral. If he did, perhaps he saw Jane and they had an altercation—maybe over another "Jim" that she was reportedly dating. Jane told Sara years later that her mother, Muriel Rohe, had hidden Jim Coe's letters from Jane because Muriel wanted Jane to marry Jim Weston, a college beau.

A little over a year later, Jane did. And Jim married my mother. Their marriages were within a few weeks of each other: Jane's in September and Jim's in October of 1935.

It seems sad because the photos of Jim and Jane together, and the letter above, show that Jim was smitten with Jane Rohe—and vice versa. "My mother carried a torch for him forever," Sara told me on one of our long walks. (Sara retired only an hour away from my home here in Maine, and when we get together, we share the intimacy of that long-ago road-not-taken of our parents.) "I knew he had red hair," Sara said, "because my mother talked about it and automatically liked men with red hair. When she saw red highlights in my hair, she would remark approvingly on it because Jim Coe had red hair."

Both Jim and Jane, then, probably married on the rebound. Jane married the Jim she went to college with; the marriage produced three children but didn't last. In 1947, she and her children came back to Richmond. Jane remarried a few years later and had two more children. Two of her daughters tell me that she talked about Jim Coe all her life. "I think that both my mother's husbands were and are jealous of Jim and my mother," eldest daughter Jane Weston wrote me.

I have to admit that I was gratified to find that Jim Coe had haunted another family besides my own. Jim's early death and what he died for undoubtedly made him a larger-than-life rival to Jane's spouses, as it did to my stepfather. Although I'm not happy that Jim was a divisive influence, the fact that he has been remembered with passion means that he's had a kind of life all these years and gives me a more personal bridge to him.

7

When I think of how many times my own daughter asked me to tell her the story of how I met her dad and of how many holiday dinners my husband's parents tell assembled family and friends the story of their first meeting (nearly sixty years ago now), I realize that there's a big hole in the Coe family history. The silence around Jim Coe when I was growing up prevented me from asking my mother the simple question: "How did you and Jim meet?"

Seeing the importance to other families of this part of their history made me realize that the silence shrouding Jim Coe was more than just never knowing what became of him. It was like pricked flesh hardening around a hidden splinter. The silence festered under the surface, irritating and haunting us and, in my case at least, keeping me on the outside of the shared lore of marriage.

And so I now choose to create some of that lore myself, starting with those moments in my parents' lives that account for my very existence. I'll cast the lovers in present tense to help bring them to life.

But first, some background. When did Jim meet Mother? Most likely sometime in 1934, on Waikiki, Oahu, where Rachel had moved in the winter of 1933–34. She'd followed her sister Helen, who had a job in Honolulu and had set the precedent for moving a continent away from their strict Quaker parents. Rachel had recently been laid off from her job as a buyer-in-training at Macy's in Depression-wracked Manhattan. She was now twenty-four, and—with Helen's help—had landed a secretarial job with Pan American Airways in Honolulu, the beflowered, aquamarine paradise of her dreams.

It's a day in fall, say late October. Rachel Gawthrop—nicknamed Ray—gives up on sleep and throws off her bedclothes. It's 5:30 a.m., still dark, with another hour before she has to stir for work, but she can't stand it any more. Adrenalin pulses through her brain, pushing her thoughts like arrows, faster and faster. Mondays are always like this, when she can't wait to get to the beautiful new glass-fronted office building of Pan Am. For the first time in her life, she's part of something big, a great surge toward the first passenger flights from the U.S. mainland to Hawaii. Even though she just answers the phone and types up Mr. Bunson's letters, she's helping to make aviation history. Well, at least she's paving the way for friends to visit her in only a few hours' hop from San Francisco.

She swings out of bed, washes up, puts on lipstick. She doesn't need powder or rouge because her natural color is so high; sometimes she intensifies it by massaging her cheeks with the bristles of her hairbrush just before descending the stairs to meet a date. She leans toward the mirror and smacks her lips, then smiles, checking her large, straight white teeth for lipstick stains. "Movie-star teeth," she calls the showy white caps that her father had her fitted for as a graduation present from college.

Ray feels energy surging up from the balls of her feet, prickling the backs of her long, lean calves. She thinks of the girls in Reception at Pan Am trying not to gawk at her legs when she'll walk through the door a few hours from now. She'll wear her new silklike stockings, one of the few pairs in all Honolulu. Francis I. Dupont gave them to her father as a gift for finishing the fountain plumbing at Longwood Gardens outside of Wilmington, Delaware, and Ray's dad had raved, in his letter accompanying them, of ones even better to come. Dupont was experimenting with a new sheer, see-through fabric. Ray scratches her head, turns from the mirror: What was it called? Oh, *nylon!* She snaps her fingers. Yeah, that's it, not even patented yet, but in come-hither taupe to show off her tan. Cider vinegar, that's her secret. She takes a bottle with her whenever she goes to the beach, rubbing it on her legs. Smelly but swell.

She pulls on shorts and a white cotton blouse, pats her pocket to make sure her cigarettes are there, and tiptoes down the hallway to the front stairs of the rooming house, carrying her sandals. The dark stairwell reminds her of the Depression, how it came along and spoiled everything, and she knows she's lucky to have a job at all, much less one in the forefront of the travel industry. Ray loves to travel, and fastest is best. This was also the first job she could tell her parents about. When she arrived here in February 1934, the only job she could find was for a liquor distributor, work her Quaker tee-totaler parents wouldn't have allowed.

As Ray sneaks down the stairs, the squeak of the old wooden floorboards sounds her excitement, and she pauses, listening for answering rustles behind the doors of other roomers. But mynas and honeycreepers calling through the open screens of the front parlor cover her steps, and she grins, tiptoeing to the front door. Mrs. Seward, her landlady, is overprotective of her "girls," and Ray knows that she would disapprove of any young lady walking the neighborhood alone at this hour, just as her parents would. That's why her mother gave the nod to her living here in the first place. Mary Gawthrop and Mrs. Seward forged fast bonds when Mary visited last March. They sat over iced tea at the picnic table under the palm tree in the backyard, and Ray found them digging around in their handbags to compare their Women's Christian Temperance Union pledge cards. Mary had tried to get Ray to sign one before going off to college; if it had just been panther sweat— the kind of moonshine the boys used to sneak in to the fraternity houses at Bucknell—it would have been a snap, because Ray hates the taste of whiskey. But tobacco? Not a chance! Ray had simply pointed at the word "never" in the pledge and said, "Only for snakes would I say *that.*" And turned to her mother, a hand raised, the other over her heart: "I pledge *never* to drink or smoke a snake."

"Oh Rachie, thee's so cheeky!" said Mary, her mouth pulling at the corners in spite of herself. Rachel, with her impetuous energy and her teasing, mischievous nature, made Mary Gawthrop—old at almost forty when she had her—feel young again.

Now, Ray strides quickly down the front walk of the rooming house to the sidewalk. She ducks into bushes, avoiding pools of light from the streetlamps, and turns in the direction of surf sounds. They remind her of the soft brush of cymbals in the jazz joint she went to the other night. She hears the catchy rhythm in her head and does the Lindy down Beach Walk, prancing, shuffling, twisting, with a little jump at the end. She sniffs in the heavenly clovelike scent of spent carnations that blankets Oahu and celebrates her freedom from view of the rooming house with the jig-walk, then bops on into the Shorty George as she reaches Kalia Road. She tries a round-the-back as she crosses the street, looping an arm in the air to fall away from an imaginary partner—always tall, always in uniform. Okay, so she's khaki-wacky, but so what? Her sister Helen, who's the bee's knees to their parents, is the same way. She up and married a career army officer, for gosh sakes. Her Quaker parents were trying to make the best of it by overfeeding their new son-in-law, probably hoping he'd be too fat for maneuvers. Ray pictures the heavy roasts and slimy vegetables that Chloe, their cook, brought to the table and gives thanks once again that she's out of there.

Now at Gray's Beach, Ray swivels left, where the distant lights of the Halekulani and Royal Hawaiian hotels pale the sand sugar-white. She strides along a boardwalk edging the beach. The sky behind the hotels' flood lamps is black. Ray pauses to kick off her sandals, then pulls a flattened pack of Camels out of her shorts. She sits down on the sand facing the water, resting elbows on her knees. The water is black in front of her as she strikes a match, the dark waves breaking on the sand like snare drums. The chilly scene reminds her of her father, how he messed up her chances at the last place she'd tried to live on her own. It was an even better job than this one; she was fresh out of college and lucky to get anything in 1931's New York. A buyer's training course at Macy's got her into the store's "Peasant Shop," a department where she occasionally used the French she had majored in at Bucknell. But Fred Gawthrop came down to New York to check on her and immediately made her move out of the cozy Greenwich Village apartment she shared with two other girls. His objection wasn't the location as she'd expected, but that the building she lived in was made of *wood* rather than brick or stone! To overprotective Fred, it was a fire hazard.

Ray shakes her head. She can't wait till she's married and out from under him, in charge of her very own home. Meanwhile, she's hit the jackpot here, where her father will never come. He hates to travel.

The rising sun spreads a pale pink wash over Diamond Head in the distance. Ray finishes her cigarette, plants it in the sand, and gets up, brushing off her sit bones. She strikes out east across the sand toward the growing light, proud to feel her spine straight, stomach sucked in, and chin tilted up

to her full height, despite the sand shifting under her bare feet. Perfect posture is now second nature, *her* walk, without having to do any more of the
calisthenics the women in the Peasant Shop taught her, those awful early
morning stretches and sit-ups and pacing back and forth with a book on her
head. She'd much rather spend early mornings like this, striding down the
beach smoking like a gent. She looks around to make sure she's alone, then
stops and lights up a fresh cigarette.

She walks fast, narrowing her eyes against the silky air. The sky over the
water is pearly now, like the inside of the oyster shells she had the other night
at the Queen Kapiolani Restaurant. On her left is the dark-leaved hibiscus
hedge that encloses the Halekulani Hotel's garden. Floodlights underneath
the foliage illuminate the white veins of straplike bird-of-paradise leaves that
line the stone steps up to the hotel. Red heart-shaped anthuriums fill niches
in the stone, the lamps lighting up their stamens like silver fire pokers. Ray
wishes suddenly that Mother could be here to see it; last March when Mary
visited, the best of Oahu's flowers weren't yet in bloom.

—◦◦◦—

Meanwhile, a rumpled Jim Coe splashes water on his face in the men's room
of the Halekulani Hotel. He lifts his face to the mirror, groans, and again
cups water in his hands. He leans over the sink and immerses first one eye,
blinking in the clear water, then the other. Raising his head, he sees that his
eyes are still pink as a rabbit's; he blinks some more. He's ashamed of his eyes;
they're bulgy, and when he's burning with a blue flame like he was last night,
they pink up like an albino's. He dries his face with a hand towel. The red
will go away, but damned if he can remember how it got there.

He slicks water into his hair to activate last night's brilliantine. He combs
it straight back in copper-colored grooves, then goes through a swinging
door to the anteroom, turning down his shirt sleeves as he walks. He feels in
back of the quilt-patterned cushions on the mahogany couch. His imprint
is still there, and after making sure his change is all in his pants, he smoothes
the cushions. At least he didn't shoot his supper and make a mess, thank
God. He looks around for his uniform jacket. There's no coatrack here, so he
must have left it in the bar. Like other submarine officers, he's mastered the

art of the rumple-free catnap, and—just as he trusts his eyes to come clear in a few minutes—he trusts his coat will be hanging neatly on a hanger somewhere. Here in Oahu, the locals take care of navy men.

He leaves the men's room and walks into the lobby. Under a high, paneled ceiling are muraled walls with scenes of surfboarders in dark, tank-topped bathing suits riding bright blue waves into shore, while fishermen cast out nets with backhanded gestures, as if sowing grain. A huge stone fireplace framed with potted palms is at one end of the room. The floor is polished slate of muted pink and smokey blue, and more dark mahogany benches with bright quilted cushions line the walls.

Jim looks around for his friends, then remembers that only he and Catty Adkins and—um, let's see—Bill—oh yeah, Bill Nelson were there. Jim remembers them at a table in the empty bar, beating their gums about flyboys and floozies and how their old pal Mush Morton was making out with the girls. But what happened after that?

Jim finds his black uniform jacket on a hanger behind the empty bar. He shrugs it on before knocking on the open door that he assumes goes into the kitchen. "Anyone here?" he says, craving coffee. The walk inland to a cab or bus will be much easier with some joe pumping through his veins.

A form crosses the beach in front of the hotel. Jim steps through the front door, blinking to adjust to the pearly half-light of the predawn beach. It isn't a waiter with coffee, but he's not disappointed. He stares after the woman, noting a trim, long-waisted chassis, slim legs, a sleek head held high, crowned in a circlet of dark braids. What's this choice bit of calico doing all by herself? He looks at his wrist, then remembers he left his watch on the boat. He peers after the woman as she recedes down the beach. With that walk, she must be a model for one of those swank magazines that his sister thinks is the gnat's eyebrows: *Harper's Bazaar* or something, at a helluva price. No ordinary dame could carry off that height. He thinks of poor Edna Sawyer, the tallest girl at Richmond High, slouched in shame. Her eyes were always down, her head to one side as if peering for indentations where she could stand and try to look normal, casual. He feels a lilt in his chest; this girl down the beach has some kinda guts.

Fingering a small box in his pocket, he hears Catty Adkins's advice: "Once they pass the looks test, weed out the ones with no sense of humor." He pulls out his wallet. Yes, here's one of his last calling cards. Running fingers over the raised type, he tells himself again that he'll have to order a new supply. He looks up the beach. If she comes back this way, he'll be ready. He walks down the stone stairway and sits on the bottom step, closest to the beach. He pulls out his pipe. It's a new habit, an attempt to avoid cigarettes. He promised Jane he'd stop—oh no, *Jane!* The thought tightens his knees in readiness to get up, go back to his ship. What am I doing? he thinks. Then the woman in the distance turns, the dawn pinking her long arms as she glides down the beach toward him.

"She hasn't written back," he counters, thinking of the empty weeks since he proposed. August, the latest Jane would have gotten his letter, then September, and now October almost gone. Two months of nothing even after his last letter saying he'd always love her.

He rises, brushing off the back of his pants, and walks down the sand to the water's edge. He puts his plank hat on, pulling the bill down to shield his eyes. Lime-green light shines off the breakers. It's already getting hot.

He turns, and the woman, now nearing the stone steps where he's just been sitting, slows. She sees him eyeing her from the water and puts a hand behind her back.

"I won't tell," he says, smiling.

"Oh no," she says, shifting something into the other hand behind her back. "I don't see any Emily Post out here" and brings out the cigarette. She puts something in her pocket, then takes a drag and walks on past the steps.

He walks parallel to her, keeping to the water's edge. "You're at the hotel?" he calls.

"Maybe," she says, walking on.

"Well, I just thought," he stops, takes out his pipe.

She slows, glances back, sees the low sun's glint on his sleeve as he shakes the pipe's bowl over the waves. Ray stops, lifting a foot as if to check her sandal, eyeing his stripes. A wide one and a skinny one, with a gold star above.

Hmmm. She puts down her foot and pulls at her chin. Jim fishes in his coat for tobacco. He's got to be at least a baby lieutenant, Ray thinks. J.g. it's called. And tall, too.

"If I," Jim points the pipe stem at his chest, "stayed *there*," he points at the hotel, "I'd demand room service," he turns down the stem at the sand, pumps it up and down, "now!"

"Yeah?" She faces him, puts hands on her hips.

"And that would be java, hundred proof." He holds up a palm at the hotel, draws his head back as if warding off a blow. "Hold the cocoa."

She gives him a brief smile. He's dazzled by her flash of brilliant teeth in a rosy face. "Make mine a lime rickey," she says, then turns and walks on.

His eyes widen, and he follows, one part wanting to rush up the sand, the other—Jane's part perhaps—warning him to turn back toward Diamond Head now. This girl's trouble; much too pretty, and sassy to boot. But the little caps on her sleeves, the way they flange her shoulders out like she's about to lift off, the whole effect slimming her torso, while the curves of her braided crown glint coral in the rising sun: it's the most elegant engineering he's ever seen. "Oh well," he shrugs, following her off the beach to Kalia Road. "Hair of the dog. Can I buy you a drink?"

She stops again to adjust her sandal, propping herself against a palm. "You can hold this," she gives him her smoking cigarette, "before I do a Galloping Gertrude and land on my face."

A light sweat glistens on the nape of her neck as she pokes at her foot. His knees go gluey. "Walk you home?" he says.

"Maybe." She pushes off from the tree and turns up Beach Walk. He walks at a respectful distance along the curb.

When they get to her rooming house, she stops and squats to put something in the grass. "Oh," he says, recognizing the ruby shell of Oahu's beautiful snail, now hunted almost to extinction. "An achatinella."

"What?" she says.

He fishes out a stub of pencil and his calling card from his wallet. On the back of the card, he writes the snail genus phonetically: ah-kah-teen-ay-lah. He shows it to her. "That's how it's pronounced in Hawaiian, next time you hear it." He leans forward, holds up a scolding finger, looks her in the eye:

Jim Coe, circa 1935.

"Next time you pass the Halekulani and hear the gardener say 'Where is that achateen-ay-la, the ruby-coh-loh-d one?'"

She casts her eyes down, her cheeks and neck flushing, then kneels to the snail.

"Oh no," he says, his chest tightening as he crouches beside her. "I didn't mean . . ."

But, "Here," she says, looking away from him, putting it in his hand. "If you're going back that way."

"No, no," he says, snapping back up. He strides to the nearest palm tree, its lower trunk covered by a thick passion-flower vine. "You've *saved* it," he says, bending to put the snail deep under the vine. "The darned *tourists* are making these things extinct." He comes back to her. "This one will be just folks here, and it's our secret."

She rises, still flushed, looking questioningly at him.

"It's the straight dope," he says and nods toward the tree. "That little bunny'll love you for it. You deserve a reward." He whips out a tiny black jewelry box.

She pulls her head back to look askance at him, then says, "It's not a snake, is it?"

Rachel Gawthrop on beach in Honolulu.

He gives a startled laugh, then tries to get a deeper look at her eyes. But she's looking at the box.

"It's a diamond clip," he says, putting it in her hand and closing her fingers around it. "I can't resist."

"But no," she says, holding out the box. "We've only just met." Still, a smile plays at the edges of her mouth.

He holds up his palms. "No, go ahead. Open it, see what you think."

Uncertain, she slowly takes the top off. Her eyes widen over a dime en-

cased in a paper clip, all sitting on a square of cotton. Suddenly a loud "hah!"
explodes as she doubles over, slapping her knee and then holding her stomach. She laughs a series of deep guttural "hah-haaah" sounds. Jim gives a
startled hoot. This paroxysm is beyond a belly laugh and so at odds with her
cinched-in, elegant appearance that there's no way he can't give way with her,
doubling over with total delight.

"Oh, me!" she straightens back up, wiping away tears. "Stop it, or I'll cast
a kitten!" She slips the box into his jacket pocket, then snaps around and
runs up the walk.

"I didn't get your name!" he calls after her.

She turns on the front steps, puts a finger to her lips to signal "Shhh!"
gives a quick wave, and disappears into the house.

He pencils the house number on his thumbnail, a saying from childhood
coming into his mind. "She is gentle, she is shy, but there's mischief in her
eye." He starts back to the ship, thinking he'll *have* to call her tonight while
the memory's fresh. "Ask for Miss Achatinella, see if she wants to go for a
ride in my breezer." Turning down Kalakaua Avenue, he looks back, adding
the corner to his mental compass to navigate the shortest way back to this
glorious girl with mischief in her eye.

8

In November of 2000, I went to the national conference of the American WWII Orphans' Network to give a presentation about researching my father. This proved to be a great way to get to know other "orphans," a name I still wasn't comfortable with. After my talk, attendees kept coming up and telling me their stories. At least two of them, in researching their fathers, had found out things that they would rather not have known. One's father had been accused by his military unit of stealing, and another's had died on the Bataan Death March from trying to carry too much, an act that his son interpreted as greedy and shortsighted. I told them both that their fathers' acts could be read any number of ways in hindsight, but that it's impossible for us to know what shaped their behavior at the time. I added that I had to remind myself of this fact every single day: that there are always at least two angles to see things from.

To add to my own angles, I used a free afternoon at the conference to call on one of my mother's old friends whose name I'd found in her address book. Mary McGregor, widow of submarine skipper Rob Roy McGregor, had known my parents in Honolulu in the thirties. As we sat overlooking Mary's beautiful Japanese garden in the Point Loma section of San Diego, Mary remembered Jim as the funniest person she'd ever known. "He could get any group of people laughing," she said, adding that Ray would stand clear and watch in awe of how Jim could win people over. Later, Ray learned to play off Jim, and they were a kind of dog-and-pony show, each taking turns holding the floor. Ray loved characters, collecting stories and anecdotes about anyone she found strange or eccentric.

As Mary reminisced, I could see how Ray was drawn to Jim's outgoing, exuberant wit and his musicality on the dance floor and how Jim was drawn to Ray's giddy enthusiasm, her long-limbed beauty, and her full-bore, chesty laugh. Another trait that I can see bringing them together was their shared energy. Ray lived in the future; she was always looking forward or making plans. Being a navy wife let her travel, one of her dreams. Mary McGregor filled me in on the life of an officer's wife; Mother could almost endlessly stay on the go packing for trips to Shanghai, Tsingtao, or Hong Kong, entertaining other officers' wives, riding horses and playing tennis at the ubiquitous officers' clubs, and going out dancing several nights a week.

I thought about this as I drove back to the conference. A memory came and joined what Mary had told me. Mother had said, when I pressed her about who Jim was, "He always was up for something. I would be in an old housedress, on my knees in the garden, and he would come home and say, 'Let's go out!' I'd say that I couldn't, looked awful, had nothing to wear, but he'd say, 'No, you look great. Let's go dancing!'"

But the best thing Mary gave me was the idea that Mother was a different person from the woman I grew up with. "Your mother was not herself," she said of the first time she saw Mother after her remarriage to Frank. "She was nervous, sad, on edge. I said, 'What about this,'" meaning the new marriage. "Her eyes filled, and she looked away." Mary conjectured that Ray must have figured she'd made her bed, that now she just had to stick it out.

Because Mary had witnessed this, it made it easier to ask her what had been on my mind since I first started researching Jim Coe: was he faithful to my mother? Knowing how difficult it would have been for anyone to answer in the negative, I told Mary why I was asking: "This was one of the ways our stepfather badmouthed our father to us. He said that Jim 'chased every skirt in Sydney.' He also said that Jim was planning to divorce Mother because *she* was running around on *him*."

Mary erupted, "What a wicked man!" then went on to tell me that Jim was "a man's man. He'd just as soon hang out with his crew than go with women," she said. And as for my mother: "Word got around fast." She named a few wives who were known for running around on their husbands in the small world of submarine officers. "But your mother wasn't one; she stayed home with her kids."

I thanked Mary; her reaction had been instantaneous and heartfelt. As I drove back to my hotel, I reconsidered those times in my childhood when Frank paced the basement complaining about Mother when I was down

To Be Bride of Navy Lieutenant

Mr. and Mrs. Frederic H. Gawthrop, 2211 Shallcross avenue, announce the engagement of their daughter, Miss Rachel H. Gawthrop, to Lieutenant James W. Coe, U. S. N., of Richmond, Indiana, now stationed at Pearl Harbor, Hawaii. The wedding will take place on October 7 in Honolulu.

Announcement from *Honolulu Advertiser* of Ray and Jim's engagement, August 25, 1935.

there practicing the piano. It wasn't just drunken talk; he was trying to shape my thinking, to drive a wedge between me and my parents. He'd almost succeeded.

After I came back from San Diego, I found an old yellowed newspaper clipping in my mother's papers. It was an announcement in the August 25, 1935, *Honolulu Advertiser* of her and Jim's engagement. A letter of August 16, 1935, from Ray to Phoebe Coe, also in Mother's papers, tries to persuade her future mother-in-law to come to the wedding. "My family says they can't possibly come for the wedding. I have a very strange father who does not like to travel and just won't. . . . It just seems too bad we are so far away from people we love when Jim and I are so happy."

She goes on to tell Phoebe about her job at Pan American Airways, which she hopes to continue after they are married. "Also, I am a brunette and very tall—about 5'9"—I weigh about 135." This description and the job are all Ray tells Phoebe about herself. But the letter clearly shows her lifetime priority: what comes next. So she tells Phoebe when Jim will come back from the Big Island; when they will announce their engagement; when they'll go to see the minister; and when she'll send Phoebe a picture of herself. This gives her letters—like herself—a forward momentum, but leaves the reader or observer knowing little of the woman behind the blur of movement.

Jim and Ray were married on October 26, 1935, in Honolulu's Episcopal St. Andrews Cathedral. Ray's matron of honor, aptly called "Wings" Eddy, wife of Jim's Naval Academy classmate Ian Eddy, wrote Ray's parents to tell them about the wedding, as Jim and Ray flew immediately to Kauai, an island without mail service, for their honeymoon. "As you'd know without my telling you," Wings writes, "Rachel looked perfectly beautiful. Of course she was radiant and happy, and in her lovely simple wedding gown and exquisite veil, she was a joy to see."

In my mother's effects, I found two wedding portraits, but they were too damaged to reproduce here. In one of her pictured alone, Ray looks uncharacteristically shy, her smile uncertain, her head tilted downward slightly as if she's hiding something of herself. She stands ramrod straight, but she doesn't look confident. In the other portrait, however, beside her matron of honor, her smile is more relaxed, her head higher, and her body more composed. "Good for you!" I think to her photograph. The only adornment on her plain satin gown is a full-length necklace of pikaki blossoms in four delicate strands looping down to her ankles. A simple layer of chiffon forms a small halo around Ray's black hair, worn up off her neck. The halo, suggestive of a baby's bonnet, accentuates the childlike wideness of her eyes and her high, clear forehead. She looks like a young woman fully protected from the world. Sadly, I think about a formula she later fastened on for life's fickle timing: "If you had a happy childhood, you go through trouble later on," she warned, "and vice versa." She was trying to cheer me up in my tough college years, trying to convince me that given what came before, I'd have life knocked as an adult. She was also trying to talk me out of doing anything foolish, like going to a therapist to talk about my problems. She didn't want the family's dirty linen aired, even six states west of Pennsylvania.

It's obvious that she got this view of life's timing straight from her own experience and that Frank, even in long and ample retrospect, was just something that happened, part of the inevitable downturn in life's schedule. In light of that concept of her own powerlessness, it's impossible to look at these wedding pictures, Ray's radiant innocence, and not shudder. She's like a rudderless ship, with Jim giving her happy direction for a while and then drifting (sometimes wallowing and pitching) ever since.

Ray and Jim and their guests attended a reception dinner-dance after the wedding ceremony at the Halekulani Hotel. The new Mr. and Mrs. Coe then flew to Kauai, the most undeveloped of Hawaii's islands, where they honeymooned for two weeks. I found pictures from this trip in Aunt Peg's scrapbook, and although the photos are in the old sepia tones of the time, it's obvious why this island is called the "Garden Island." It is mountainous and lush, with waterfalls plunging off steep cliffs into rivered gorges far below. My mother and father ride horses along the mountain paths, and many shots are posed at high lookout points with layers of mountains in the distance. My parents wear white shirts, dark riding breeches, and the boots that I recognize from the attic of my childhood.

These years in Honolulu, from 1935 to 1937, look idyllic, according to the pictures in Peg's scrapbook. Jim and Ray are in flowered shirts, sandals, shorts, and straw hats, sipping drinks on various beaches with friends. Or in grass skirts and sunglasses, doing the hula under palm trees. Or arriving or departing from various docks, their necks strewn with leis. Or looking out the rear window of their black roadster, their Scottie, "Kilts," clutched in Mother's arms or perched on the car roof.

Roberta McCain confirmed what Mary McGregor told me in San Diego: my parents had a good marriage. "You just know these things," she said

Jim and Ray honeymooning on Kauai, October 1935.

when she called in answer to the letter I'd sent her asking about Jim Coe. "You could tell." Her voice was resolute, definite. I believed her, and this overcame Frank's message and the letters of Jim's mother, Phoebe, complaining of Ray's remarrying so soon after Jim was lost. I believed Roberta and Mary and could now take the pictures of Jim and Ray at face value: they were happy.

In this process, I realized that Mary McGregor was right about the change she witnessed in my mother. In the midthirties, Ray has none of the taut, tight-lipped wariness of my childhood. She is relaxed and radiant, proud of who she is. She looks like someone I want to know, especially in one picture where a pair of clunky brown-and-white oxfords with low, cuffed white socks peek out of a long denim skirt as she sits on the beach with Jim and friends. She looks like a schoolgirl, but unlike the real girlhood picture I have

Relaxing on the beach. Jim Coe is third from left; Ray Coe is farthest right.

of her, she doesn't look mischievous or itching to be elsewhere. She is just happy to be where she is: beside Jim.

The people I've interviewed who were there in Hawaii in the midthirties confirm that these were great times. Lil Nelson and Margaret Shute told me about how my parents and their crowd would dance regularly at the Royal Hawaiian Hotel. Mother loved to dress up, and I can picture her in some of the long silk gowns she saved from those days. Roberta McCain went on to say, in our phone interview, that for day wear, Mother wore tailored clothes that made her look like a British lady en route to a foxhunt. She said that Jim had a hand in picking Mother's wardrobe and that he was extremely proud of her. And Mother confirmed that they had the money to set styles; her father gave her a clothing allowance of $6,000 a year. That was big money in the thirties, and I was wowed. "My god!" I remember saying. "You could have *lived* on that!" Mother replied, "Well, Dad said that a young man just starting out shouldn't be expected to keep his wife in clothes." Fred Gawthrop had a degree from Swarthmore College in engineering, building a firm that designed the vast network of fountains in Pierre Dupont's Longwood Gardens. Fred plowed some of those revenues into real estate in Wilmington, Delaware, thus sheltering his profits from the Depression. So Mother and her sister grew up as indulged, albeit restricted, children.

Roberta McCain remembers a phone conversation Mother had with her teetotaling mother. They were at a party, and Mother let Roberta listen in on the phone extension. Roberta said, "Ray talked Quaker [thee and thy] to her mother for a while, then told her she was drinking champagne at that very moment. 'Rachie, thee isn't!'" Mary Gawthrop exclaimed in horror.

A 1936 Christmas card from Jim, Ray, and "Clipper Coe," their German shorthaired pointer, shows Ray fashionable even in pregnancy, her stomach softly swelling a three-quarter-length coat with a white mandarin collar and wide sleeves. Under the coat is a long flowered skirt. Jim is dressed in a wool tweed blazer and checked pants, and they both wear white shoes. They stand under palm trees with a cozy wooden house in the background, its bamboo window shades wafting outward on a gentle breeze. Ray proudly holds Jim's arm, while Jim cradles Clipper's front paws in his palms. They look settled and happy, yet alert to the future and poised to move on. Their beautiful clothes make them look as if they're just setting off on a cruise.

My sister, their first child, was born in March of 1937. Jim telegraphed his sister Peg: "Mother's, Daughter's health excellent. Father says fair chance." Photos from this period, again from Peg's scrapbook, show that both parents are thrilled with Jean; she is frequently swathed in frangipani leis, and Jim reads to her or crouches behind her, his big hand protectively across her stomach. However, something Mother said stands out in my memory. When I was brimming over with new feminism in the late sixties, I told my mother

Jim, Ray, and "Clipper" Coe.

about the women's movement in a futile attempt to reform her preference for men over women. The one assent she gave to my tirade was when she said, "Yes, I remember when Jean was born, some crewmen from Jim's ship called on us. After they looked in the cradle, they told Jim, 'Better luck next time.'"

After Jean's birth, Jim was transferred from sub duty in Pearl Harbor to the Naval Academy, where he began teaching navigation in September of 1937. He and Ray left Honolulu for the long trip to the States in July, Jim

Jim with daughter
Jean, circa 1939.

aboard the *S-33*, one of the World War I–vintage subs. Ray and Jean took
a steamship to San Francisco, then boarded a train to the East Coast. Jim
writes to his mother July 16, after she met Ray for the first time:

Dearest Mother:
    First let me thank you so much for meeting Ray and Jean in St. Louis
and making their changing [of trains] so pleasant. . . . I was only too glad
that you did it all Mother dear, and it's about the first time that I've ever

Rachel with Jean, circa 1937, boarding ship to go back to the States.

been able to do anything for you—so please don't ever think about repaying me for the ticket again. . . . Ray had a hard trip and meeting you and having that nice visit pepped her up a lot. I'm glad you got along so well together Mother dear and I'm sure that when we come to Richmond next month and you really get to know her that you'll be crazy about her.

Jim's letter goes on about the poor conditions on the S-boat. An engine broke down in San Diego, and they are limping to Panama on one engine, averaging only about seven knots (eight miles per hour) on the surface.

It is about 95 degrees hot down here and pretty sticky inside this cigar but the weather has kindly allowed us to rig a shower topside which is very refreshing. I have been kept fairly busy navigating and that has helped to pass the time but still 18 days in one of these things at sea is stretching things a bit and I'll be glad to step ashore for a few days even if it's in Panama. Our poor ice box couldn't stand the heat and all of our remaining meat spoiled about a week ago necessitating its disposal in the sea but the potatoes and canned beans are holding out and so no one will starve. This trip is a valuable experience for a naval officer but one which I hope never to have to repeat.

Jim knows how to focus on the good. He might have learned it in high school when he won a public-speaking award in which the assignment was to find a sad event in history that turned out to have some positive effect. Jim spoke about the death of Christ fostering Christianity. It appears that he's generalized this lesson to S-boats, where looking past immediate sacrifice to the long-term good was a necessary outlook.

In September 1937, Jim and Ray settled in at Annapolis, where Jim taught navigation for the next two years. Jack Lee wrote me that Jim had probably applied for this assignment: "In 1937 we were assigned to shore duty generally in accordance with our request. The instructors were largely from the upper half of the class, and the Academy was a popular duty station."

I was proud that Jim got this assignment and happy to find that he and Ray moved forward in their lives, seizing this opportunity to put down roots. They bought a small piece of land on the eastern shore of Maryland, where they picnicked and went crabbing, intending to build there eventually. They also bought a city lot in Annapolis and started having plans drawn up for a small house. A photo from this period—again from Peg's collection—shows Jim and his family sitting on the stairs of the Gawthrops' house in Wilmington with Ray's parents. Jim seems delighted with three-year-old Jean.

Another Jean, Jean Noyes, a distant cousin by marriage, remembers meeting Jim during these years: "When I was a lowly freshman at Goucher College in Baltimore, your father was stationed at Annapolis. He invited me over one day and arranged a date for a game. I remember him as a warm, friendly, handsome man who made a gawky young girl feel really special and

Jim and Ray Coe (at back) with Ray's parents, sister, and toddler Jean Coe at
Gawthrop house, Wilmington, Delaware.

provided a day that her fellow students greatly envied. I am sure it could not
have been anything but a chore for him, but this was in no way apparent to
me at the time."

Jim's sister, still in New York, had asked Jim to show this shy young cousin
of her husband James some attention. To someone like me, who grew up
fighting with siblings and not able to make peace with them until well into
my thirties, this affectionate cooperation between Jim and Peg is poignant.
It shows me that my Coe grandparents must have modeled this kind of mu-
tual support and respect.

This incident also reminded me of how serendipitous history is. Here was
a small kindness, a favor that Jim did for his sister, but it was so significant
to this distant cousin of mine that it stood out in her mind all these years
later. And because of that, I got a glimpse into Jim's character that I wouldn't
have otherwise. He had no idea at the time that he was doing something that
would give him precious definition to one of his children more than sixty
years later.

My cousins Pat and Fred Niles, Mother's sister's kids, were old enough
to remember the family gatherings in Wilmington, Delaware, during these

years. Cousin Fred remembers Jim giving the kids an Australian gadget—a pocket-watch–shaped puzzle featuring a pirate whose head you could try to cut off by pushing a dial. Fred and his sister couldn't do it, though, and after trying for an hour, the kids gave it back to Jim. As Fred recalls, "He teasingly scolded us and opined to the room that he didn't know what would ever happen to us if we couldn't figure out something that simple. Then he passed it around to the adults, and nobody could cut the head off! We didn't mind at all that the adults were as dumb as we were, and maybe that was your dad's way of including us kids in his world."

Jim made a big impression on my cousin Fred; a few years later, when Fred heard the news on the radio that the Japanese had bombed Pearl Harbor, he knelt at his bedside and prayed that nothing had happened to his dear uncle Jim.

9

Jim finished his tour as an instructor at Annapolis at the end of May 1939. In July he was ordered to Submarine Squadron Five in Manila, Philippines. This squad, made up of six ancient S-boats, was part of the small Asiatic Fleet, a group of boats long neglected for fleets nearer the states, such as Pearl Harbor, San Diego, and Groton, Connecticut.

Despite these inferior boats, duty in the Asiatic Fleet was desirable, known for its ample recreation, very affordable living conditions, and exotic ports. Navy men were treated like kings in regular stops such as Shanghai, Hong Kong, Singapore, and Tsingtao, a port on East China's Yellow Sea, north of Shanghai, established by Germans at the turn of the century. A famous saying in the fleet was that bringing a wife to the China station was like bringing a ham sandwich to a banquet.[1] This set my feminist hackles up, and I prefer the other saying, which applied to all members of navy families: "No strain in Asia," meaning that living was easy because domestic help was affordable.

However, the era of U.S. Navy personnel being catered to in the Far East was coming to an end. There was increasing Asian resentment toward this pattern, Japan's being the most intense. After its invasion of Manchuria in 1931, Japan assaulted American churches, hospitals, universities, and other outposts in China throughout the thirties. But when the United States retaliated with the threat of economic sanctions, Japan would quickly apologize. It did this after bombing the *Panay*, a U.S. ship on China's Yangtze River, in 1937, saying that it was a mistake—an explanation that the United States was glad to accept to avoid war. This incident was part of Japan's brutal occupation of Nanking, which resulted in an estimated two hundred thousand deaths.

As the world recoiled from this and other Japanese aggression, Japan continually publicized its desire for peace, causing many well-meaning Americans to believe it. Historian Samuel Eliot Morison says this talk of peace was not hypocrisy; rather, Japan had a different definition of peace than we Westerners did. Japan's "peace" meant complete control of all Asian countries by a Japanese ruling class.[2]

Reading about this road to war was a revelation to me. Heavily influenced in my formative years by our Quaker Sunday school and youth-group teachers, who turn out to be the only people I've ever heard object to our involvement in World War II, my pacifist bias runs deep. Add to that losing my father to war and coming of age in the Vietnam era, and it is understandable that I was skeptical of all military solutions. I had learned to be suspicious of all us-versus-them statements that demonize the enemy, as well as to always ask what I would do in a threatening situation, thus making the political personal in any kind of analysis. So I read the historical reports of the Japanese talk of peace as a possibility that war could have been averted because, after all, *I* would have sat down at the bargaining table and listened to them, wouldn't I?

Fortunately, these last few years of research have made me painfully aware of my ignorance. My pacifist bias kept me from learning about any war, and my resulting ignorance of World War II caused some intellectual and spiritual double takes as I tried to fathom my father's motives for going to war.

I learned that Roosevelt—astute politician that he was—played to the firm pacifist and isolationist voice in America. He concentrated for two years on diplomatic efforts to stop Japan's assault on China. He heeded Gallup polls of the day showing that no one was willing to go to war over China, despite Japanese assaults on Americans there.

I also came to see that Japan's military elite had a deep stake in conflict. Not only did they regard war and conquest as life's highest good, but they solidified their power by provoking U.S. hostility. So even if we had tried to liberalize our policies toward Japan, its imperialistic forces would have continued their aggression. Pacifist scenarios such as a more liberal U.S. immigration policy toward the Japanese in the twenties and thirties, allowing Japan to further expand its navy, withdrawing all U.S. interests—including the Asiatic Fleet—from China, or not curtailing U.S. oil supplies to Japan would not have assuaged the militaristic influences on Japan's government.

I learned that unlike the Vietnam War, World War II was not a result of suspect policies by U.S. leaders. American citizens themselves gradually turned against Japan. Having seen the destruction of British shipping by German U-boats in the Atlantic, we were not easily going to trust any country that had joined with Hitler. Japan's signing of the Tripartite Pact with Germany and Italy in September 1940 put American opinion firmly against Japan, making negotiations with it that much harder. Even before the attack on Pearl Harbor, the majority of Americans wanted their leaders— short of war—to prevent Japan from expanding its power.

So gradually I had to drop my pacifist assumptions that we could have avoided war. This opened my mind to the possibility that Jim's service was not wasted, that he may not have died needlessly. Fortunately, almost everyone I contacted during this project was way ahead of me and so could fortify my new attitude about our part in the war. David Jones, an Australian submarine author, typifies this view, telling me in e-mail that his parents' generation throughout Australia believed that Japan would invade them after expanding into Manchuria, China, Indo-China, Thailand, and on into the East Indies. Australians "were very grateful to America, as an elder brother, for coming to our rescue. Our best armed forces were overseas fighting Germany and Italy; much of what was left was in Malaya and was swallowed up in the Japanese advance which seemed unstoppable. There was very little left to resist them, so for us at least, the Pacific was a struggle for survival."

By the end of the thirties, Japan's army held the entire coast of China and looked toward bringing all the colonies of the Far East under its rule. Japan strengthened its naval bases in the (formerly German-controlled) islands of the Marianas, the Carolines, and the Marshalls, which it had been allotted by the British at the end of World War I. Although Japan was allied with Britain in World War I, Japan's military leaders hoped that the Western powers would be weakened and distracted by fighting among themselves so that they couldn't oppose Japan's goal, even then, to control all of Asia. Japan wanted the Russians out of northern Manchuria, the Germans out of Tsingtao, and the Dutch out of the Dutch East Indies (now Indonesia). These objectives clearly anticipated Japan's expansion of the late 1930s.[3]

In response, the American navy strengthened its Asiatic Fleet with seven newer submarines called fleet boats. Together with the S-boats, this expanded my father's Squadron Five to thirteen submarines, the strongest arm of the Asiatic Fleet by the end of 1939. The fleet's surface boats consisted of the cruisers *Houston* and *Marblehead,* thirteen old destroyers, and the ships' tender *Canopus.*

Jim's first assignment in the Asiatic Fleet was to the *S-36* as its executive officer. Robert Norton, a crewman at that time, remembers Jim coming aboard. "We had just transferred our executive officer, who was not very well liked, back to the States. We were wondering what our new exec would be like; he turned out to be Lt. James Coe. We were soon pleased with the change. He was fair and friendly and soon fit in very well with the crew."

This kind of adaptability was extremely valuable on the old "pigboats," where foul living conditions could make tempers flare. Like other S-boats, the *S-36* was an oven when submerged. The engine room was 120 degrees. The uniform for everyone—officers and crew—was shorts and sandals. "Sandals," says Robert Norton, "because we perspired so much our shoes would fill with water." The decks ran and squished underfoot with the men's sweat. Crews were covered with heat rash or with tiny white "Guam blisters," and when they surfaced, mosquitoes and flies would feast on the men, especially at night. There were no showers and no laundry. Another sub vet remembers that the men couldn't even go to the bathroom: "Using the heads during the hour before sunrise to an hour after sunset during all-day dives would give our position away. As the temperature rose to over a hundred, the air became contaminated with body gas, diesel, hydraulic, lub-oil fumes and whatever escaped from the batteries. Meals became tasteless. Cigarettes would not stay lighted because the inside air lacked oxygen. Machinery broke down randomly. . . . The drinking water tasted like copper."[4]

Clothes, in addition to bodies, took a beating, especially when old batteries had to be removed from the boat. At these times, fumes from the battery acid were so strong that the men's clothes were quickly riddled with small holes. Batteries were a hazard at any time because S-boats, with their old, riveted hulls, tended to leak, and wet batteries released deadly chlorine gas. Therefore, chlorine drills—necessitating instant surfacing and ventilation— had to be practiced frequently.

Any man who asked to leave these harsh conditions was let go immediately, no questions asked. In these close quarters, with work that required such instant response and precise synchronization of tasks, a hostile or alienated personality could literally bring down the whole ship.[5]

Submarines, in these prewar days, were seen only as adjuncts to the navy's surface ships. Subs hadn't yet proved themselves as weapons. They were slow compared to surface ships and vulnerable to aircraft in clear waters, where their outlines were visible at depths down to one hundred feet. And they were prey at most depths to destroyers equipped with sonar. Because of these problems, submarine skippers were taught to be highly cautious, thereby further detracting from the submarine's potential as a warship. Subs were thus relegated to the role of scouts, charged with reporting Japanese fleet movements; they also screened territory ahead of the fleet, standing ready to torpedo combat ships if necessary. Under the Treaty of London, U.S. submarines were forbidden to attack noncombat ships.

This scouting and screening activity extended to the Yellow Sea, where the Asiatic Fleet traveled at least once a year to the waters off Shanghai and Tsingtao. Navy wives and children joined the men there and stayed in the International Settlement—the area of Shanghai ceded to the United States and Great Britain in 1863. Sometime during the fall of 1939, in what must have been an addition to the usual spring fleet visit, Jim and my mother and Jean, then just two years old, stayed in the settlement's Park Hotel. While Jim was aboard ship, Mother left Jean in the care of the hotel amah and took a rickshaw to shop and sightsee. A photo of that period shows her grinning—as if she'd just snagged a bargain—outside Jelly Belly the Tailor's shop. She's clutching a shopping package under her arm as if to say, "Boy, what a deal!" With my mother's love of Chinese silk and embroidery, and with the rock-bottom buys in exquisite tailoring and hand finishing, she must have been in heaven.

Rachel Coe in Shanghai, circa 1939.

But such luxury was ending. In May and June of 1939, the Japanese army had entered Shanghai's International Settlement, threatening the American and European residents there. By the next year, they occupied Tsingtao; that year—1940—would mark the last of the Asiatic Fleet's peaceful visits to those waters.

My mother told me about a time during her visit in 1939 that foreshadowed the darkness that was to come. She was in a rickshaw on Shanghai's crowded streets, still shocked at the citizens' poverty in contrast to the way she and other Americans and Europeans lived back at the Park Hotel, when her rickshaw came to a sudden stop. The man who pulled the rickshaw had fallen and now lay motionless in the traces while traffic flowed swiftly on around them. Then a horde of men suddenly swarmed around the shafts, pushing and shoving each other to take over the job, while others hauled the fallen man by his ankles to the curb, his head bouncing along the cobblestones. Ray realized with horror that the man was dead. Another man lifted the shafts of the rickshaw and continued to pull Ray onward. All of this took only seconds. When she told me this story some thirty years later, she still had trouble getting the words out.

Back in Manila, Ray's and Jim's lives were in striking contrast to the kind of mortal poverty they witnessed on the streets of Shanghai. In Pasay, a new suburb near Manila Bay, they lived in a two-story single-family house built on stilts above the ubiquitous rice fields. Household help was only pennies a day, so they were able to have a cook, a laundress, a gardener, and a nurse for Jean. The Manila Hotel, the Army-Navy Club, and the Polo Club were all nearby, where my mother had a busy social life of tennis, bridge games, and luncheons with other navy wives. She went horseback riding at Clark Airfield, where the navy had stables, and she kept her legs darkly tanned by going regularly to the beach. At night my parents went dancing, my mother excelling at the gymnastic moves of the jitterbug and shag. I remember Mother delighting me with the names of other dances when I was little: the Big Apple and the Flat-Foot Floogey with the Floy Floy. Despite the heat, mosquitoes, flies, lizards slinking into empty slippers and shoes, and occasional poisonous snakes in the garden, my mother loved life in Manila, and I can see why. "No strain in Asia" was especially true for an officer's wife with an ample clothing allowance in U.S. dollars.

In January of 1940, Jim was given his first command as skipper of the *S-39*. Submarine author James DeRose wrote to tell me that Jim, at only thirty, was exceptionally young for a command at that time in naval history. It shows his prowess with people. From his first days as skipper, he tried to offset the constant mechanical breakdowns and foul living conditions of the S-boat by boosting morale. Early in my research, I was lucky enough to find the Web site of Tom Parks, one of the most articulate and voluble enlisted men of the *S-39*, who describes Jim as the finest skipper he served under in World War II. Tom wrote me,

> When I went aboard S-39 in 1940 I was a Fireman third class, not long out of boot camp. I was introduced to your father and I stood in awe of him. I had only seen commanding officers at a distance and I ranked them right up there with God. Captain Coe actually smiled and welcomed me

Jim Coe in Hono-
lulu, off *S-39,* circa
1934.

aboard. He was strict but fair and, unlike some captains, he made sure that
his crew had high morale.

His running mate was Wreford "Moon" Chapple, Commanding Officer of the S-38. When the 39 and 38 boats were operating together, the
two captains would engage in games of chess by blinker light. The stakes
were always the same: twenty cases of beer. The beer was consumed during a softball game between the two crews.

He [Jim Coe] organized excursions to such places [around Manila] as the San Miguel Brewery (great beer), the Magnolia ice cream plant, and the Tabacalera cigar factory. When the 39-boat made its 2000th dive (not many by today's standards) he arranged a ship's party to celebrate the occasion.

Add to this all kinds of improvised races between the *S-38* and *S-39*. Guy Gugliotta remembered a relay race that Jim dreamed up that must have harked back to his track team experience at the Naval Academy. Members of the two crews rowed to an island, and a signalman from each crew would carry a sealed message to the top of a nearby mountain. On reaching the summit, each man would have to send the message by semaphore (hand flags) to his oarsman, who would then row back to his submarine with the message. Tom Parks remembers this race: "Speed counted but accuracy in transmission and reception counted also. As I recall, the 38 boat won but actually we all won. We cheered our team as if it were the regatta at Henley, but it was also good for the morale of the captains. Commanding a man of war is a tough job and they deserved some fun too. We also saw them as human beings. Your father and Moon were two of the best."

The men loved to gamble, and Jim used this to his advantage by creating competitions within the boat to relieve tension and boredom. The stepped-up security that came with increased hostility from the Japanese kept submarine movements secret until the last minute before the boats left the docks. Jim invented a "Where are we going?" pool, where raffle tickets with possible destinations sold for pennies each. He also instigated a "What time do we anchor?" pool.[6] Revenues from these and other popular pools went into the ship's recreation fund, which built up fast and afforded all kinds of shore parties. Jim fortified this account by creating a slush fund that the crew could borrow from at 10 percent interest until payday. This saved the men from the usurious rates of Manila loan sharks.[7]

One suspects that only a gambler could set up such systems, and at least two scenarios that I first came across in Bobette Gugliotta's book *Pigboat 39* suggest that Jim was one. He was playing poker when Larry Bernard, the *S-39*'s new ensign, first walked in to the officers' quarters in Olangapo on Subic Bay, just northwest of Manila Bay, where the *S-39* was being overhauled. Bernard remembers Jim clad in only shorts and sandals, and he told Larry to pull up a chair as he fished him out a cold beer from the ice bucket under the table. This took the place of the formal reporting-in that Bernard had feared.[8] Later, new ensign Guy Gugliotta received much the same treatment. Guy was particularly nervous because he had just suffered through submarine school, where the leaders had stripped him of all his self-confidence. "I guess you could say I had low self-esteem," he said of this period in his life. Added to that was resentment for having to leave his new bride, Bobette, at home.

Jim was playing liar's dice at the bar when Guy met him in the Army-Navy Club in Manila. Jim shook Gugliotta's hand, passed him the whiskey bottle, and motioned him to remove his tie. Guy—like Larry Bernard and Tom Parks before him—was soon feeling comfortable and welcome.

Even with this informal style, however, Jim was strict. He had his crew work hard on drills to make the boat compensate for the poor reputation S-boats had. Every day the crew would practice trim dives (submerging quickly to the desired depth and working to stay there by taking in or pumping out seawater), work at battle stations, and run through such emergency exercises as man overboard, fire, collision, and chlorine release.[9]

Jim had them practice these drills on the four-day trip from Manila to Shanghai in the spring of 1940. The crew looked forward to the cooler waters and the increased leave the men always enjoyed in the Far East. They would be there for three months, with wives joining them. However, my mother couldn't go this year, because she was too far along in her second pregnancy; instead, she journeyed to the mountain resort of Baguio outside Manila to escape the city's heat.

An officer from another S-boat remembers my father during this visit. Captain Bill Hazzard, a tall, handsome ex-skipper whom I met at a submarine veterans' convention in 1999, told me that he'd just gotten out of submarine school and was an ensign on the S-37 when my father was assigned to test him for qualification as a submariner. Walking through one's submarine with a visiting skipper and answering his questions about all parts and tasks of the submarine qualified a man to wear the dolphins—the coveted insignia of the submariner. Hazzard remembered going through the

S-37 with Jim, hoping that this tall, copper-haired skipper would not ask him about material Hazzard was shaky on. Jim did, but quickly taking in Hazzard's hesitation, glossed over it. (Hazzard later became one of the outstanding sub skippers of World War II.) "Somebody else might have flunked me easily," Hazzard said, "but he kind of sized me up and decided I was suitable, and I was very fortunate in that. He was known for his affability; he was always smiling and generous and genial with people." Hazzard ran into Jim again in Tsingtao, the small port city north of Shanghai. Established long ago by Germans, the city had been recently taken over by the Japanese. Hazzard and others from his boat and their wives had rented a house from a German, one Herr Bruder, a wool and rug dealer who had lived in Tsingtao since World War I. He and other Tsingtao Germans had to get along with the occupying Japanese, and they knew how to do it.

One night they had a party at Herr Bruder's house; Japanese naval officers were invited. "Their assignment, I'm sure, was to learn about the character of the American military man and submariners in particular," Bill Hazzard said. That was the evening Jim fashioned a makeshift banjo out of a long, hollow piece of wood and a string. "I remember your dad was beating percussion on this thing and smiling broadly," said Hazzard.

But Tsingtao's mixture of Germans, complete with Nazi youth groups, and the occupying Japanese army and navy were a prelude of things to come. With news of German U-boat attacks in the Atlantic, and Japanese cruelty to the Chinese abundantly obvious, Americans were glad to leave China. Jim had an added impetus: worry about my mother making it down from the mountains in time to reach the naval hospital in Cavite. As it was, Mother waited until the last possible minute, not wanting to go back to the sweltering July heat in Manila. There was a fierce storm; Ray felt the baby drop, and knowing she didn't have time to negotiate the 130 miles of winding, stormy road down from Baguio, she chartered a small private plane. The plane was buffeted by heavy winds and rain, three-year-old Jean was scared and crying the whole way, and her amah was throwing up, but they finally landed in Manila. They raced in a cab to Cavite, where nine-pound Henry was born almost as soon as my mother was wheeled in to the Canacao Naval Hospital's emergency room.[10]

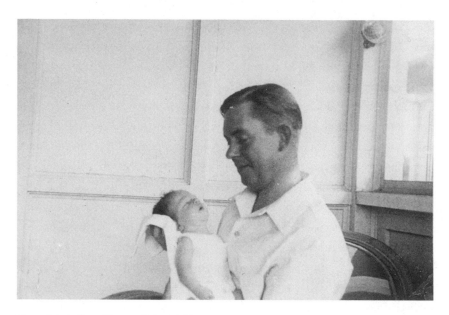

Jim with infant Henry, July 1940.

Among the photographs I inherited from my mother is a rare one of Jim with newborn Henry in August of 1940, so the *S-39* must have made it back to Manila from China in late July. My father's face is in profile as he holds Henry, supporting the baby's head with his hand covered by a white towel. Henry's hair is dark and stringy, in contrast to the thick blond of his youth. Jim makes a contrast, too, his face softened by its rapt expression, his eyes almost closed despite his fascination, as if he's in prayer. Jim and Ray, reunited after separate adventures in exotic and unknown territory, with the threats from Japan sharp in the air, must have felt doubly blessed with Henry. Perhaps they realized that such moments of adoration were precious and fleeting. Jim looks as if he does.

I like to think of this as the time that Jim's men leaned off the *S-39* somewhere in Manila Bay to scoop up the beautiful glass fishing ball that Henry would inherit sixty years later. The men presented it to Jim, and I'm sure they were proud of its size. Mother told me that it was one of the biggest ever found.

This was the last chance for such celebratory gestures, as the rest of the world heated up, threatening to explode into war. Roosevelt beefed up the Asiatic Fleet in the person of flinty, no-nonsense admiral Thomas Hart. Hart swept into Manila, rounded up all the Asiatic Fleet's ships, then ordered all navy wives and children back to the States. He was convinced that the Japanese were about to invade the Philippines.

This possibility, however, seemed far-fetched to most navy families, lulled by the easy living in Manila. When Hart called for the two thousand navy dependents to be shipped back to the United States, there was great protest. David Hurt, Jr., whose father was skipper of the fleet submarine *Perch,* was fourteen at the time. "The evacuation of Navy families in November 1940 was a bitter pill for us since the Army families stayed on," he wrote. (The army families left about six months later.) "Hart wanted no dependent distractions for his force." In further correspondence, Hurt elaborated: "My state of mind during the evacuation was concern for my dad, distress at the separation, and extreme distrust of the Japanese."

Carolyn Bernard, widow of *S-39*'s executive officer, seconded this when I reached her by phone in the spring of 1999. She vividly remembered almost sixty years ago standing with the rest of the wives, many with small children in tow, on the crowded pier in Manila, waiting to board the SS *United States* for the long, unhappy trip back to the States. They were trying to prolong the final moments with their husbands, whom they weren't sure they'd ever see again.

Carolyn saw my parents saying goodbye. Then my mother, with baby Henry in arms and toddler Jean in tow, was forced up the gangplank by the surging crowd. Carolyn watched her look over the ship's rail at Jim: "I have never seen such a mournful, heart-wrenching expression as your mother's face. I can't describe it. It was almost like a deeply hurt animal, just dumbstruck with grief. She was a very sensitive woman."

Having known my mother to show grief only two or three times in her life, and never having thought of her as "sensitive," I was startled at this description. Again I recalled the letters of my grandmother Coe, who felt that Mother had been disloyal to Jim in remarrying so soon after he was declared missing, and I recalled the slurs from my stepfather on my parents' marriage. I told Carolyn gently that not having known my mother at this time, having heard very few words from her about my father over the years, and then of course being aware of her hasty remarriage, I had trouble imagining this. Carolyn's voice lowered and became gravelly with conviction: "He [Jim] was the love of her life! Your mother loved him till the day she died!"

When I got off the phone, I started to consider again what had first occurred to me at the door of my mother's closet when I found what probably was Jim's coat. Had Mother adored Jim (the way she appeared to in the early Hawaii pictures) and never stopped loving him—but kept quiet about it for the rest of her life? Again, I was overcome with regret that I had never considered this possibility when Mother was alive and thus never asked her the right questions. The convincing part of Carolyn Bernard's message, besides her voice, was her image of my mother as a hurt animal. Mother was not articulate and never questioned her strict training against showing grief. I remember her crying only a couple of times in her life, and then it was when she was in physical pain from toothaches. Could she have been too "sensitive," someone without the nerves or constitution, to bear grief or sadness? I thought of two postcards I uncovered in her papers; they were written to her father and sister from Pine Tree summer camp in the Pocono Mountains when Rachel was a child of eleven:

Dear Dad,
    I am not a bit home sick and haven't cried once since I have been here. One girl is homesick. Darnit. I didn't want any girl to be homesick.
[After one more sentence about the lovely time she's having, she closes.]

The one to her sister is similar, but with the "Not a bit homesick" triumphantly underscored twice. She had obviously been trained against expressing sadness and was proud of being up to the task on her first visit away from home.

My talk with Carolyn Bernard was thus a turning point in the way I thought about my mother. I realized I had probably misread her all these years as "insensitive" about Jim's death. This is a common complaint among the fellow orphans of World War II at the conferences I've attended: that

Jim and Ray happy
in Manila.

the widows never expressed grief over the lost fathers, that they simply
moved on.

But now I wondered what I or any of us would have done differently. The
entire culture was living this message: we won the war, so get on with it. And
would open grief have been good for young children? I don't think so.

And so when Roberta McCain called a few months later to tell me that my parents had a good marriage, that "it's one of those things you just know," I took what she said at face value and was grateful to think of my mother and father happy in their few short years together. Other navy wives—Margaret Clifton Shute, Mary McGregor, and Lil Nelson—confirmed this happiness in subsequent interviews. Again, the conviction in their voices persuaded me to sweep aside the nagging voice that said that no one would tell an inquiring daughter anything bad about her deceased parents anyway. I trusted their enthusiasm over Jim and Ray's union and became a believer.

Like all converts, I then made a shrine. I gathered all the photographs that pictured my parents happy, most of them from their years in Hawaii and Manila, and made a collage—the first of my life. I hung it on our living room wall, and one of my friends even said, "Gee, your mom is quite dishy. I hope you don't mind."

"On the contrary," I said. I'm proud of my mother now, for the first time. I now see all the pains she took to look perfect for the camera as the proud work of a woman in love. I'm grateful to her for loving Jim in his brief time on earth. He deserved it, and—judging from their pictures and their friends' accounts—she did a good job.

10

The trip back to the States in the winter of 1940 turned out to be baptism by fire in full-time child care for my mother, who had had help from Filipino maids and amahs up to that point. On the crowded SS *United States,* she was allowed little more than baby bottles, formula, and diapers for the journey, as luggage was restricted. All bassinettes and cradles were already taken, so she had an orange crate nailed to the floor of her cabin at the foot of her bed, and this was where she stowed baby Henry while trying to tend to Jean. The trip was rough, with high seas slamming furniture against walls. In the ballroom, a grand piano careened across the floor and rammed into a stewardess, breaking her leg.

Navy wives and children were packed like sardines into the few available cabins. Caroline Bernard shared two small rooms with six other women and a baby, a clothesline for drying diapers bisecting their space. My mother was luckier; as a skipper's wife, she got two rooms to herself. Even so, it was a nightmare. Jean was seasick day and night, would eat nothing but lettuce, and grew dangerously thin. Everyone was terrified. Rachel thought the ship would surely break apart in the enormous waves.

Dave Hurt, Jr., aboard the SS *Washington* with his stepmother and younger brothers for the same journey, thought so, too. "We took the 'great circle' route," he wrote. "Actually, that is the shortest distance overall but requires that one go North initially. Consequently, it was a cold, rainy, rough trip. So rough at one point that we had to turn around and head into the seas for six hours. This was necessary because some of the waves had crashed over the stern and smashed in the doors to the aft cabin area."

Back in Manila, Jim, eager to prove himself worthy of his first command, worked his crew hard in dives, submerged attack drills, and deck gun practice. But another trait besides rigorous practice began to show itself in Jim's leadership style. Crewman Tom Parks remembers Jim learning from his crew in the person of "Pop" Bridges, their chief of the boat, who had been a submariner in World War I. "One time in Olangapo in dry dock your father was anxious to get the boat out and back in service. He had us working 16 hours a day. Finally, Chief Bridges went to him and said, 'Captain, you have never done a day's work in your life, so you don't know how much work a man can take in a day. You're working the men too hard!' Captain Coe never said a word, but the next day he cut back our hours."

As spring of 1941 approached, the maneuvers became more warlike. Faster dives on shorter notice were effected by a reduced number of crewmen—only those on watch—rather than the whole crew that usually dove the boat in peacetime conditions. The *S-39* also practiced all-day submergence and received the bone-rattling experience of depth charges dropped from a nearby destroyer. The crew performed these drills with all torpedo tubes full.

To offset the growing tension from a threatening Japan, Jim and Moon Chapple stepped up the recreational competitions between their two boats. They had boxing matches, liar's contests to see who could tell the most dramatic sea stories, and field days. One field day consisted of a softball game, a pig roast, and a poetry contest (with men reciting their own sea ditties). The softball game was memorable because of sideshow ringer Howie Rice, *S-39*'s radioman. Jim had become desperate because Moon's boys had beaten them many times. Rice, whom I met at a 1999 submarine veterans convention, remembered it well. He'd been a high school tumbler and could walk two blocks on his hands. On hearing this, Jim challenged the *S-38* to a walk-on-hands contest. Rice, now a wiry seventy-nine-year-old who swims daily and looks like he could still walk on his hands, said, "Somehow the word got out, and as I was normally a nondrinker, members of the *S-38* somehow got me to drink some beer." Rice shook his head. "Well, when the time came for the contest, I couldn't even find the *ground* with my hands, much less *walk* on them. So Moon Chapple won again."

Tom Parks wrote me that when they didn't have ship competitions, Jim and Moon could often be seen, after a few drinks, on the Army-Navy Club's lawn in Manila riding bikes at each other while swinging golf clubs at a soccer ball in makeshift polo games. They were also known to love their beer, and after being in various dives in Manila, they would challenge each other to fistfights, most of which Moon, who had boxed at the Naval Academy, won. Allyn Christopher, an *S-39* crewman, remembers once when the two S-boats were departing from port, Moon yelled over to Jim: "Where'd you get the black eye?"

"Hit it on the bedpost, you S.O.B.," Jim yelled back. Moon chuckled because he'd been the one who had done the damage.[1]

It's easy to see why young men with such exhausting responsibilities had to let off steam under the growing tensions of Manila in 1941. These skippers were responsible for every important decision on their boats, and one mistake could ruin their careers. "In no other type of vessel," writes submariner Ned Beach, "is the Commanding Officer so personally responsible for the actual handling of his ship as in a submarine. . . . Not content with the mere reports of progress from junior officers and crewmen working below, the Captain has to be personally sure that they are not making mistakes." When Beach became a commander himself, he articulated what Jim and Moon undoubtedly felt: "Where before I had made suggestions and then loyally carried out the skipper's wishes, now it was up to me to make the decisions. Frequently they were hard to make and harder to stick to. In all of them I held the sack if anything went wrong."[2]

One can add to this the decrepit condition of the S-boats. By July of 1941, Jim had increased inspections of the *S-39* to one a week to stave off the constant leaks and mechanical breakdowns. *Pigboat 39* tells about a leak springing between the main motors. Machinist mate James Pennell and his crew started slowly lifting up the metal floor plates, knowing that one of the men would have to wriggle down into the greasy, smelly bilgewater below to feel around for the source of the leak. Suddenly, Jim appeared. "Hold my ankles," he told Pennell, then lay on his stomach and eased head and shoulders below deck, feeling around in bilgewater till he located and then staunched the leak.[3]

When I read this, I was reminded of my brother Henry, who told me about his flight home from Washington, D.C., in March of 1999 after helping me research Jim's patrol reports in the naval archives. Henry, as outgoing as his father was, said he complimented a janitor in the airport restroom on how clean the place was. The janitor looked so stunned that Henry explained his belief that no job is more important than any other, that all work is honorable. The janitor said that was the first time anyone had even noticed his work. Because Mother and Frank raised us to act and think like elitists, with status a main priority, I like to think that Henry's egalitarianism came straight from Jim.

Robert Norton, who, as mentioned in the previous chapter, had first met Jim when they served together on the *S-36,* confirmed the view that Jim didn't hold himself above his men.

> One thing I learned about your father was that he was a tolerant person. . . . Being at sea on a ship with no laundry or bathing facilities or air conditioning meant a big change in living conditions. Our daily uniform for officers and crew became shorts and sandals. . . . Since we ran on the surface at night, your father stretched canvas across the rails on the cigarette deck aft of the conning tower. Here he often slept at night to be readily available if needed. I had lookout duties on the surface and since we couldn't smoke, I chewed tobacco. I would scan and spit. One night a figure came out of the dark, your father wrapped in a blanket well decorated with tobacco juice. He never said a word, but I never chewed tobacco again.

Besides being tolerant, Jim was a shrewd teacher. "He could take a wayward sailor and make him love him," *S-39* electrician's mate Charles Witt told me in a phone interview. Witt was referring to a man who had a habit of going ashore and drinking too much, then coming back late to the ship. Usually this and other infractions were handled in captain's mast, where the skipper would mete out such punishments as extra work details, cancelled leaves, or demotions in rank.

But Charlie witnessed a variation on this as he stood on the fantail of the ship one Monday morning around ten o'clock. "Captain Coe was standing on the bridge in his clean whites when this wayward sailor, all grungy and disheveled, staggered aboard. He'd been out drinking all weekend and knew he was in for it. 'Weeell, aren't you a purty thing,' Captain Coe said [putting on a Hoosier drawl]. Then he told the sailor to go to the tender (the USS

Canopus) and take a shower and shave, clean himself up, and meet him back on the bridge."

During this interval, Charlie said, all the guys thought, "Now he's *really* gonna get it!" Charlie made sure he was up on the fantail again when the sailor came back from his shower. He was clean but hungover as he tried to steady himself in front of Jim.

"You got any money?" Jim said.

"No, sir," said the sailor.

Jim told him to go back to the *Canopus* and get an advance on his pay from the paymaster. Then he was to go ashore and back into town, get everything out of his system, and come back in time to start work at eight o'clock sharp the next morning. Charlie said that after that day, the guy followed Jim around like a puppy and was never AWOL again.

Tom Parks contrasted the types of leadership he witnessed in the six commanding officers he served under in World War II. "'Sundowner' is an old sailor's term for a harsh disciplinarian who, in granting liberty, would demand that the liberty party be back aboard by sundown," wrote Tom. "It came to mean a very strict, by-the-book captain." Such people rule by intimidation, are more feared than respected by their crews, and are "the exact opposite of your father. . . . He was quiet, self-assured, but never pompous. He had a wonderful sense of humor, a trait not found in company of pomposity. . . . Captain Coe had that very special quality of leadership. The military academies can teach the principles of good leadership but they can't instill the quality. You have to be born with it. . . . His crew would do everything he asked and more if necessary and never complain."

Guy Gugliotta told me that when he was new to the boat and lacking in self-confidence, Jim threatened to strap him up to the periscope and keep the boat just below the surface so that Guy would stick out above the waves to "con the boat in" (guide it) to harbor. Guy believed his new skipper and started shaking inside at the thought of all the water snakes teeming in Philippine waters. He pictured himself clinging to the pitching periscope with his feet tucked as close under him as he could get, the electric-blue- and green-backed snakes writhing below. But he kept his cool until Jim started laughing, and Guy realized he was off the hook.

David Hurt, Jr., a teenager when he met Jim, never forgot this trait. "People enjoyed being around him because he was fun to be with."

But meanwhile, things were far from funny among the higher-ups. Admiral Hart was skittish enough about what he thought were imminent Japanese air attacks to withdraw all naval forces from vulnerable Manila Bay in the spring of 1941. He sent the fleet to the southern Philippine islands. When the suspected attack didn't materialize, he returned the ships to Manila. This was a pattern he would repeat throughout 1941 as failed negotiations between Japan and the United States increased tension. Japan, for its part, had many years' stake in China and wanted free rein there; it also needed U.S. embargoes of oil and other strategic materials against it lifted. It wanted to keep its bases in French Indochina and refused to discuss its support of Hitler. The United States, on the other hand, supported the sovereignty of all countries, noninterference in those countries' internal affairs, equal economic opportunity, and no change in the Pacific except by peaceful means. But this would mean that Japan would have to roll back its expansion and reexamine the purpose of its empire.

The result of this stalemate made leaders dig in their heels in the Philippines. General MacArthur, leader of the army's ground forces there, wanted to "stand and fight."[4] Approval of this policy necessitated a buildup of Admiral Hart's navy, which received twelve more fleet submarines in October 1941, plus a new tender, the *Holland*. This swelled the Asiatic submarine force to twenty-nine boats. Only six of these were antique S-boats, with hardworking crews determined to prove as worthy as the newer fleet boats.

By early December, again certain that the Japanese would attack the Philippines, Admiral Hart sent most of his Asiatic Fleet well south of Manila Bay waters. Only five destroyers, plus most of his submarines, were kept to cruise the area. Before the *S-39* left Manila proper, the men knew something was up. Jim was in a foul mood because his two-and-one-half-year tour of duty was to end on December 20, and he'd made plans to go home for Christmas and new orders. But he'd just received word that his leave had been cancelled because the man who was scheduled to take over command of the *S-39* had become ill.[5] Now with war in the wind, everything had changed, and who knew when—or if—Jim would ever get off the old boat and see his family again.

Radioman Howie Rice wrote me about the Tuesday before the attack on Pearl Harbor: "There was a call for all commanding officers to report to the Flag Ship immediately. Your dad came topside dressed in whites, wearing a fore and aft hat and a sword and white gloves, as this was a very official call. He came back about an hour and a half later and called the heads of departments together and told them to 'Get the exercise heads off the two exercise torpedoes, put the war heads on them, make them ready for war and load them in the tubes.' We also went to Sangley Point to fill the torpedo room."

After getting thirty days' worth of provisions, the S-39 steamed off toward the San Bernardino Strait, their patrol area. En route, they stopped at the island of Masbate, just south of Luzon, where they let off steam with some softball on Saturday and Sunday. After the games, they pulled away from the island and anchored in the bay. That night, December 8, Jim and most of the crew slept on deck because of the heat. Rice, on the midnight to 4 a.m. shift, received a cataclysmic message from the radio station at Cavite: "Japan has started hostilities, govern yourselves accordingly."

Rice scrambled up the hatch and over the sleeping men to Jim, who read the message and ordered the crew up and under way. By the time they got below deck, another message had come on the radio, this one to "put operation order 46 into effect." Jim opened his safe and took out an envelope with the number 46 on it. I see him open it in the dim light of his wardroom, peer at it, then turn away, rubbing his eyes. "Conduct unrestricted war against Japan," it reads.

11

How did Jim Coe feel when he read the famous operation order 46? Guy Gugliotta said that a feeling of unreality pervaded the *S-39*, that the men thought, "It can't be true!" This sense must have been ubiquitous throughout the forces; an airman over Manila's Clark Field described not believing he would ever be in a real shooting war: "It may seem incredible that anyone could have been in such an abstracted condition eight hours after Pearl Harbor but I accepted the fact of war only when it hit me in the face, and there were many like me."[1]

In trying to imagine Jim's feelings, I again had to confront the pacifist stance I grew up with. When my Quaker teachers of the fifties would herald the latest conscientious objector to jump in front of a submarine to prevent its launching, they added that if everyone behaved that way, there would be no war. So I, with a child's literal logic, assumed the reverse was true. Because conscientious objectors didn't want war and did what they could to prevent it, then military men must *want* war and served to make war happen.

This actually became the prevailing countercultural opinion during the Vietnam years, when returning soldiers were reviled by hippies and war protesters (like myself). In holding all participants accountable for the war, we were implicitly accusing them of wanting war. It was a slippage of logic that allowed us to reduce a highly complex situation to simple black and white and to take out our frustration over a seemingly interminable conflict on an easily identifiable scapegoat: those in uniform. It also spared us any grief over those who died; they had *chosen* to make war, after all. I didn't realize what a high stake I had in this stereotyping; if I could see my father as simply a trigger-happy young man who had fallen for the bloody myth of patriotism, I didn't have to grieve him. I was actually proud of my "objectivity" during the Vietnam era in dismissing Jim from the calculus. I used clichés such as "Live by the sword, die by the sword," "You reap what you sow," and "Better Red than dead" (which I callously told my aunt Peg once when I was railing against the Vietnam War; she said I was dishonoring my father and almost threw me out of her house). The clichés lulled me, standing in for thinking, learning history, or even facing the truth of who I was: a girl with a hole in her heart.

So when I started looking into my father's reactions to the opening of World War II, I was stunned with what I found. Because no letters of Jim's from this period survived, I phoned Charles Witt again. He told me that *S-39* submerged at dawn on December 9 and started listening for ships, Radioman Howie Rice using a near-obsolete piece of equipment called a hydrophone to pick up the sound of distant propellers. "We were at about 100 feet," Witt recalled. The *S-39* crept along until the sound man heard something, then followed. Jim peered through the periscope and ordered them up to forty feet. From this depth he saw a cargo ship off their starboard bow. He ordered the crew to surface for battle stations. "I was first gunner," said Witt. "Captain Coe had range and everything figured out to fire on her." The ship flew no flag. In keeping with the gentlemanly conventions of the Treaty of London, Jim warned the ship. Prewar submarine training had taught commanders to obey treaty regulations scrupulously, forbidding attacks on noncombatant ships. "Captain Coe got on the megaphone and also blew whistles," said Witt, "but the ship kept going. We then fired a four-inch gunshot across her bow. Then someone ran across the bow of the ship and signaled to us not to shoot." They hoisted a flag, and it turned out to be a Philippine freighter.

This story shows that Jim and his crew were not trigger happy. In asking the ship to identify herself, Jim was conducting restricted warfare, rather than the unrestricted kind called for in operation order 46 just hours ago.

After I got off the phone with Witt, Jim's warning shot resounded in my mind. It was as if he were telling me, these sixty years later: "Back off with your peacenik judgments! They have no place here." I could no longer dismiss him as a warmonger. I had to stand up and take notice of who this guy really was. Skipper Eugene McKinney, a colleague of Jim's in the Asiatic Fleet, helped me. "When we came out there [to Manila] in the summer of

1941, we were expecting the war to break out any minute," McKinney tells Robert J. Casey in *Battle Below*. "No use kidding ourselves . . . , the situation was pretty rugged. *We didn't want war. The last thing that a professional in the Navy or Army wants is war because he's been taught to know what war is* [my emphasis]. But it's his job, no matter how tough it is."

McKinney goes on: "We're not indulging in any heroics when we say that we didn't expect to come home again if there should be a war. Our lives were already dedicated to this business and already forfeit, if you know what I mean. I had a wife and a couple of children back here, but I couldn't allow them to enter into the calculations and I guess they knew that. Navy families are brought up on that proposition."[2]

This is no warmonger talking, no impulsive kid itching for battle. This is a conflicted man thinking his way through life's most difficult questions: What is my duty? Is there anything more important to me than my own life, my family? (McKinney was later awarded the Navy Cross three times for his aggressive command during the war. Apparently, thinking one's life already "forfeit" and hating the advent of war worked just as well in his case as the glorification of war that pacifists decry.)

McKinney's words made me realize that my pacifism had circumvented the whole notion of duty, or sacrifice. Deeply thoughtful and conscientious people who made the military their career believed that they were patrolling the Pacific in the late thirties and early forties to guard *against* full-blown war with Japan. I now have no doubt that some of them despised war the way a policeman despises crime; they both act as preventatives, and as such, their work is indeed a service, a true sacrifice.

Certainly Jim had chosen this role by firing a warning shot rather than a torpedo that first day of war.

———⟨⟩———

Three days after the incident with the freighter, any crewmen still not able to believe they were really in a war quickly became convinced. The *S-39*, on the surface north of the San Bernardino Strait, making its way toward Rapu-Rapu Island, saw the masts of Japanese cargo and troop ships making their way toward Albay Gulf. The men soon started hearing depth charges—

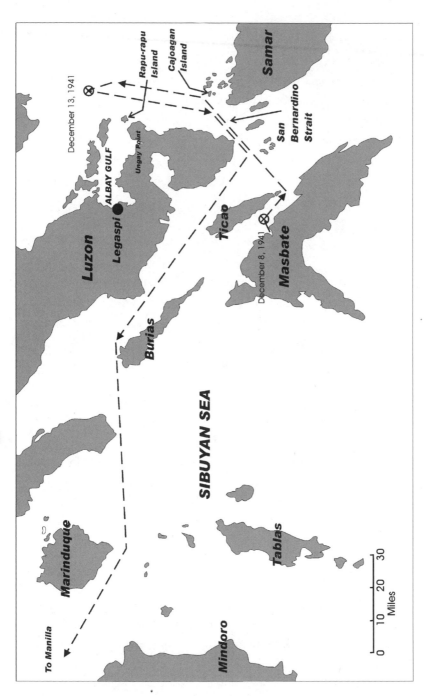

S-39's first patrol: ⊗ December 8, 1941: shot fired across bow of unidentified cargo ship; ⊗ December 13, 1941: attacked enemy freighter.

metal drums full of Torpex, a highly explosive gel—dropped overboard from destroyers escorting these ships. The depth charges seemed to be exploding all over the place, in a random pattern rather than the systematic pursuit of a target. The *S-39* was in water more than six hundred feet deep. Charlie Witt told me that they dove, careful not to take the old boat down deeper than her test depth of 210 feet. They waited soundlessly as the depth charges drew closer, holding the boat at ordered depth. If one of the depth charges were to explode close by, shock waves could send the boat past test depth, where millions of tons of seawater would crumple her hull inward, crushing the men.

While maintaining ordered depth, *S-39* had to creep along at two knots to minimize noise propagation. All her sea valves and hull fittings were closed against the deadly water pressure, and the men had to remain quiet, even taking their sandals off to prevent the scuff of soles against metal floor plates.

The crew quickly became familiar with the sounds of their stalkers: first, a click as the exploder in the depth charge functioned, then the sound of the explosion, then the hissing surge of water along the hull. Like thunder following lightning, the time between the initial click and the explosion signals the distance of the depth charge from the boat. Soon, click and wham came closer together, slamming concussive waves of water against the hull. The *S-39* bucked and plunged, flinging men around like rag dolls. The steel hull flexed in and out, vibrating all the gear. The air filled up with dust, paint chips, and bits of cork lining the inner walls; men ducked their heads against bolts and screws flying through the air like shrapnel. Lightbulbs smashed, leaving them blind. The temperature in the battened-down boat crept up over 110 degrees. Men tensed their stomach muscles against the powerful instinct of fight or flight, forcing themselves to huddle in soundless despair against the next charge.

Finally, the depth charges began to recede, and Radioman Rice reported to Jim that the sounds of the destroyers were fading into the distance. The men still hunkered in the dark, not daring to even whisper, growing lightheaded from thinning oxygen. Rice finally reported all sound of destroyers gone. Jim gave the order, and they surfaced. It was the night of December 12. The men gulped blessed fresh air, then tried to take a fix to locate exactly where they were. But before they could get a position, they saw a cigarlike shape slicing through the darkness. Thinking it was an enemy submarine, Jim ordered the men to fire two torpedoes. It was impossible to see through the darkness and drizzle, and they heard no explosion. Cautiously drawing closer to where they had seen the shape, Jim realized that they had fired on an island—Cajogan (off the north coast of Samar, in San Bernardino Strait).[3]

Stress and fear had replaced the *S-39*ers' former incredulity that they were really at war. Their first depth charging made them touchy and over-anxious. Meanwhile, Japanese merchant and naval ships continued steaming into Albay Gulf, with screens of destroyers coming out to meet them. The next night (December 13), the *S-39* was fully baptized into the lethal squeeze of war when it sighted another fishlike shape. This one was close enough to be sure: it was a Japanese submarine.

As they tried to creep away, the *S-39* suddenly picked up a target in the periscope. It was about twelve thousand yards off the port bow. Jim, sensing the excitement, awoke from a catnap and walked into the control room in only his Skivvies and a pair of disintegrating sandals. He ordered the men to battle stations submerged (which brought a third of the crew—the best and most experienced—into the control room) and started an approach at periscope depth.[4] This necessitated limiting speed to two knots to minimize telltale feathering as the water streamed around the periscope.

I imagine the small control room (sixteen by twenty feet) as dark, with the eerie glow of red, green, and yellow lights coming up from the plotting table and other controls. This is as far as I got, though, by myself. To grasp the technical details of an approach, I needed an expert—someone who had been there. In this I was lucky enough to find a veteran officer of eleven successive World War II patrols: retired admiral Mike Rindskopf. As torpedo data computer operator, the center of the fire control party, for the first nine patrols in the fleet submarine *Drum,* Mike had a hand in firing 125 torpedoes. After that, he was *Drum's* commanding officer for his two final patrols. *Drum* sank fifteen ships of eighty thousand tons and damaged eleven more, for which Mike won the Navy Cross, the Silver Star, the Bronze Star, and the Commendation Medal. Besides all this, Admiral Rindskopf is a wise and patient teacher, keying his expertise to a level his audience can grasp. He was thus the only man who could give me the precise details I needed to understand what went on in *S-39*'s control room on this first approach, and he graciously complied. After studying *S-39*'s patrol reports and the boat's biography, *Pigboat 39,* Mike visualized this scenario:

When Jim arrived in the control room, the normal submerged watch was on duty. It consisted of a helmsman for steering, a quartermaster for log keeping, a senior enlisted at the air and water manifolds, a diving officer with his bow and stern planesmen for depth control, a motor controller operator, and a telephone talker to maintain contact with all compartments. The approach party quickly relieved these watchstanders and added a plotting team and the officer assistants.

The team had at its fingertips several manual calculators to determine target range, course and speed, crucial to setting the torpedoes on their correct course. First, is the slide rule which converts the target observations (so many periscope graticule divisions subtended by the target mast) and estimated masthead height to range. Next is the ISWAS (this *is* where the target *was*) a circular plastic aid which helps determine target course and the courses the *S-39* should take to close the target. Then, the Angle Solver (nicknamed "banjo" because of its shape) determines the course to be set into the torpedoes and the target bearing on which they should be fired. The plotting party, under a junior officer, will add to the *S-39*'s instant positions target bearings and ranges which Jim and his assistant approach officer, Lieutenant Guy Gugliotta, announce. Finally, the sonar operator counts the target propeller revolutions which are directly convertible to target speed.

Jim stands with slightly bent knees, face forward as he peers into the periscope, gripping its handles which permit him to rotate the periscope, to change the magnification for general area survey or to ascertain target details, and to adjust the elevation to search for intruding aircraft. He can order the periscope raised or lowered, bending or straightening to stay with it. After some minutes observing the target, Jim seeks the assistance of Larry Bernard, his Executive Officer, as they study the Japanese Ship Identification book. He describes the target as a "Mast-Funnel-Mast freighter with cargo booms fore and aft." They select the likeliest maru [ship] and determine its masthead height. As *S-39* closes the target, Jim reports "Target 2 Divisions," then a bit later, "Target 2.5 Divisions." He also provides the target's "Angle on the Bow" as "Port 30 Degrees"—then "Port 35 degrees," and so on. Picture this as the angle between the target's course and the periscope as seen from the target. The calculated ranges are fed to Plot, and ultimately a best target course and speed is calculated.

From today's point of view, these calculations were rough. Submarine historian James DeRose says that American periscopes were inferior to those of most other navies. "They only had a graticule lens graduated in minutes of arc," says DeRose. "A stadimeter slide-rule was used for translating a comparatively rough angular reading into yards. Gross over-ranging as well as over-estimation of target length was unavoidably common."

But Jim has yet to learn this as he scans 360 degrees both on the horizon for enemy destroyers and in the sky for airplanes, with an eye to how he will escape them after firing on the ship. As he does so, the tension and temperature in the cramped room rise. Men shed their undershirts and tie them around their necks like scarves to catch the sweat before it can drip to the deck and make footing slippery.[5] All of them strain to concentrate and keep calm.

Maximum range for the Mark X torpedoes in the S-boats is thirty-six hundred yards. (The torpedo travels twelve hundred yards per minute.) Jim will try to get into an ideal firing range of about one thousand yards. With the *S-39* staying submerged at periscope depth of forty feet and having to be as quiet as possible to evade the enemy submarine, progress toward the target is frustratingly slow. Between looks into the periscope, Jim takes the boat down to one hundred feet to speed up for short spurts before coming up again for another look.

The target has been zigzagging. Jim reports when a zig or zag occurs, and Guy Gugliotta then plots an estimated pattern on which to base their own course. Then Jim gives data necessary to culminate the attack to the torpedo officer, who uses his angle solver to determine torpedo course, which he passes to the torpedo room for insertion into the torpedo prior to its loading into the tube, and concurrently tells Jim the bearing of the target on which he should shoot. He plots a new kind of torpedo spread from the one that they practiced in prewar training. Those drills had taught officers that the best chance of a hit came from firing a succession of three torpedoes. One was aimed forward of the target's bow, one at the middle of the hull, and one at the stern. This spread compensated for errors in approach calculations or target maneuvers, with the thought that two out of three would hit. But now that the war had started, the navy was short of torpedoes, and orders were to try to conserve them by using only two on most targets.

This first submerged approach of the war, slowed and intensified by its enforced silence, was baptism by fire for Jim. Another submarine skipper, Lew Parks of *Pompano,* speaks to what Jim saw through the periscope: segments of seascape like puzzle pieces that he must fit together in his mind: "It is never the same twice as he looks at it. When he is twisting, the target is also twisting. And while he is figuring all these details of the target's course and speed and his own course and speed, and the constantly changing relative positions, he has to make his run in, and keep from broaching [losing equilibrium and surfacing] all the times he's doing it."[6]

When the *S-39* finally closes the enemy freighter from twelve thousand to three thousand yards, Jim—afraid of losing the target if he waits any longer—gives the order to fire a two-torpedo spread. The torpedoes leave their tubes with an interval of eight seconds. The crew, having sweated out an interminable 21-minute approach, waits while the quartermaster observes his stopwatch approach the 2.5 minute predicted torpedo run. Just after that moment come two explosions. Jim looks through the periscope and says, "He's hit, going down by the stern and listing to port."

Pigboat-39 reports him as saying this quietly[7]—probably because of the possibility of the Japanese submarine still lurking about. But it's also likely, at this first blood, that he's filled with a complex mix of relief, triumph, awe, responsibility, and even empathy for the enemy seamen going down.

This is not just my pacifist wish fulfillment at work. My aunt's scrapbook eventually led me to this suggestion of a vast mix of emotions with which

Jim viewed his "hits." In the back of the scrapbook was a program from the memorial service that Peg and Phoebe held for Jim in Richmond, Indiana, in 1946 after the navy had declared him dead. In the program was a quote from Robert Casey's *Battle Below*. It was about Jim.

Holding my breath, I called all the used book stores in Portland and tracked down a copy. When I finally opened the book in the old musty shop, I quickly scanned the table of contents. No men's names here. But under the section "The Men" cited in the memorial service quote, I found a chapter titled "Portrait of a Letter Writer." I knew who it was immediately (you'll read Jim's famous letter later on in this book), and I blessed Robert Casey in my mind. He'd done a whole chapter on my father, quoting his words, his precious voice, to stand in for the letters that never made it down to me.

In a 1943 interview, Casey reports Jim saying that he was almost mesmerized by the spectacle of this first hit, the Japanese freighter, as it lifted out of the water under swirling smoke, then settled at the stern and backed down into the deep. Jim stood riveted to the periscope, unaware of destroyers setting out from the shore behind him.[8]

A good skipper must have an escape plan ready to execute immediately on firing because the steam torpedoes a sub fires leave a clear track of white bubbles and vapor on the surface in daytime, and phosphorescence at night, betraying their source. Enemy destroyers will charge straight down these wakes to depth charge the boat below. The diving officer in the control room, having held the boat precisely at periscope depth to maximize the skipper's vision while firing, has to then dive at a moment's notice.

And Diving Officer Larry Bernard was ready. Jim at last swept the periscope around behind them and reported that destroyers were on their tail, showering bullets around their periscope. "Rig for depth-charge attack!"

Bernard plunged them down to 150 feet, where they prepared for "silent running," a condition that necessitated turning off all noise-making machinery. The propellers and battery ventilation motors were slowed as much as possible, and the men sat down right where they were on the deck plates to conserve their energy and dwindling oxygen supply. They couldn't smoke, and they kept whispering to a minimum. Rudder (to steer) and bow and stern planes (to maintain a specific depth) had to now be operated by hand. In the eerie silence, Howie Rice could make out four destroyers ping-ing above them. (The Japanese sub seemed to have disappeared.) The little *S-39* hung in the water, defenseless except for the ability to zig right or left as a last resort.

They sat for hours, the men praying, while destroyers above them tracked them with the eerie pinging of their sonar. The enemy wasn't dropping depth charges; it was practicing something more like Chinese water torture. Jim and his officers wondered why. Maybe the Japanese—equally new at this game—were conserving weapons, as the American submarine skippers had to do.

As the hours dragged on, the men grew pale and headachy from lack of oxygen. Finally, Jim ordered Guy Gugliotta to gather all the *S-39*'s confiden-tial papers from the safe in preparation to surface. They were rapidly run-ning out of air. They would have to take their chances; if they came up near the destroyers, they would have to shoot it out with their deck guns or be captured. In the latter case, they would try to sink the boat first, along with the ship's papers, to keep them from the enemy.

Ensign Gugliotta packed the ship's documents into a canvas bag with some wrenches to weigh it down. Just then, Howie Rice reported that the pinging was growing fainter, indicating that the destroyers might be leav-ing the area. The crew waited, hardly daring to breathe, for interminable minutes. The pinging gradually subsided altogether, and Jim ordered the boat up.[9]

When they surfaced, the seas were empty. They stood aside and opened the hatch, and the ship's foul air (at higher pressure because of its compres-sion) blasted out of the opening. The boat then filled up with precious sea air. I picture the men gulping great draughts of what must have tasted and smelled like heaven itself. But George Grider, in his classic submarine book, *Warfish,* says otherwise: "Strangely enough, there was always a period when all hands had to get used to the fresh air. When it first came in, it smelled awful. For hours we had been accustomed to air impregnated with cook-ing odors and other smells, and the fresh air was almost disgusting for a few minutes."[10]

In the interview with Robert Casey two years later, Jim speculated that they'd been saved a vicious depth charging because of the Japanese submarine they'd glimpsed earlier in the area. The four destroyers above them had not dared to drop anything on what might turn out to be their own sub. So they waited the *S-39* out, pinning her under until she was forced to surface. But the *S-39* had won that game. "I didn't quarrel with my luck," Jim told Casey. "But it taught me one thing: it's bad policy to stay up admiring your own handiwork when destroyers are coming after you."[11]

Howie Rice told me he remembered hearing a broadcast later that evening after the destroyers had left the area: "Tokyo Rose said that the Japanese Navy had sunk an American Submarine off of Legaspi [*S-39*'s area]. We had heard a lot of depth charges going off in the distance."

So perhaps the *S-39* had been doubly lucky. The Japanese might have misread *S-39*'s silence as escape, left the area, picked up the track of their own sub, and—thinking it was *S-39*—made a fatal choice.

12

After their narrow escape with the inadvertent help of the Japanese sub, Jim and his men were ordered back to Manila. They had no idea that they—out dodging enemy subs and trapped two hundred feet under by destroyers—were the lucky ones. The Japanese had attacked Manila's Clark Airfield on Monday at noon (December 8 in the Philippines), only a few hours after radio reports were coming in with word of the Pearl Harbor bombing. MacArthur and other officers spent the five hours between the reports of Pearl Harbor and the attack on Clark Field debating whether to send photo reconnaissance flights out over Formosa (now Taiwan), a first step to retaliation. MacArthur figured the Japanese wouldn't attack the Philippines until April of 1942, and he doubted the news from Pearl Harbor when he first heard it. He was thus reluctant to attack without an official declaration of war by the Japanese, and his subsequent hesitation caused most of his air force to be caught on the ground when the Japanese bombed Clark Field.[1] The field and most of its aircraft were destroyed.

Admiral Hart, in stark contrast to MacArthur, had fully expected Japan to attack the Philippines since late 1940, when he evacuated my mother and all other navy dependents back to the United States. Consequently, only a few of his ships, including most submarines, were left in the area on December 10, when Japanese bombers swooped in on Manila. They first hit the waterfront, then the city proper, and, finally, Cavite Naval Yard. "They flattened it," said Lieutenant John Bulkeley, who was on a motor torpedo boat in Manila Bay at the time. "There isn't any other word. Here was the only American naval base in the Orient beyond Pearl Harbor pounded into bloody rubbish. . . . We began loading in the wounded to take them to Canacao Hospital. . . . There was half an inch of blood on the landing platform at Canacao—we could hardly keep on our feet, for blood is as slippery as crude oil—and the aprons of the hospital attendants were so blood-spattered they looked like butchers."[2]

When the *S-39* chugged into Manila on December 20, the men were stunned at the carnage. There was no more navy yard to help them, and they moved out to Mariveles Bay, across from Corregidor where the tender *Canopus* was tied up, to repair their boat themselves. Howie Rice said: "But the Japanese would fly over dropping bombs, so we had to move out into the harbor and sit on the bottom. Finally, your dad said enough of this. We got all the repair material that we could get from the *Canopus* and then moved into Manila Bay again and set on the bottom doing repair work. At night when we came alongside, the *Canopus* crew would tease us about being on a stinking pig boat. Well, they didn't know what was in store for them: the Death March."

Crewman Charles Witt added to this scene a sailor on hand with an axe when the *S-39* tied up to *Canopus*. On at least one occasion, the man had to cut the lines and dive as bombs started dropping around them.

On Christmas Day, Manila was declared an open city to save it from further destruction; the navy had to evacuate all personnel and equipment while ground troops withdrew to the Bataan peninsula. General MacArthur somehow "forgot" to tell his colleague, Admiral Hart, this until two days before the event.[3] This caused mayhem among the boats trying to leave.

Admiral Hart, ordered to leave, was lucky enough to catch one of these boats fleeing the Philippines. Captain John Wilkes was left in command and ordered all submarines out of Manila in the last days of December, but he decided that *Canopus* would be a sitting duck at sea. She thus stayed behind as part of the futile fight to save Bataan and Corregidor.

As the submarines and few surface boats left in the area fled Manila, the men felt deep regret and shame. They had failed to stop the Japanese and left behind many friends to certain death. Captured Manila gave the Japanese a base from which they quickly overran the Philippines and pushed southward. Historian Clay Blair, Jr., blames MacArthur and his air generals, but the submarine captains roundly blamed themselves.[4] In December they had fired ninety-six torpedoes and reported sinking only eleven ships. Postwar Japanese records were even more chary, confirming only three of these sinkings, and *S-39*'s torpedoed freighter wasn't among them.

Jim was ordered to patrol southward in the Philippines. "I was on the sound gear in the torpedo room," says Howie Rice, "when your dad scolded me for not picking up a target that he could barely see in the dark. I kept listening but nothing; he gave me heck for awhile, then he apologized, saying that it was a small sailboat." Tempers flared, and it was small wonder. The *S-39* suffered continual breakdowns, it was hot, everyone had heat rash or Guam blisters (itchy white pustules), and the Japanese were swarming over the East Indies, systematically shutting off ports to U.S. and Allied shipping. The *S-39* had escaped Manila, but where could it go?

And so the sub worked its way south toward Java. At one point, it ran aground on a rock, and Jim ordered the entire crew on deck to "sally ship." The crew gathered at one end of the boat and then ran to the other, slowly rocking the ship off the rock. One of the last American planes left in the Philippines saw them at this and—mistaking them for an enemy ship—swooped down for the kill. Jim charged up to the conning tower and grabbed the American flag, ran down to the deck, and waved it madly. The plane lifted out of its dive at the last minute and flew away. The men commenced running and rocking—with more haste now—and finally dislodged the old sub from the rock.[5]

S-39 suffered more breakdowns. After reporting these to headquarters, they were ordered into a repair yard in Surabaya, Java, one of the last friendly ports left. The crew staunched leaks and manned the pumps to get there, finally limping into the dock on January 22. The men were exhausted. They didn't know it then, but the Japanese had set their sights on Java and were about to swoop in to complete their stranglehold on the East Indies. By the end of February, southern Sumatra, Borneo, Celebes, Ambon, and Timor would fall, along with Singapore. Darwin, Australia, would also be attacked and consequently abandoned as an Allied naval base.

But by a stroke of luck, the *S-39* got to Surabaya in time for the men to go in shifts inland to a rest camp for a precious week of leave, while work on the *S-39* progressed at the shipyard. On February 4, air raids began, and *S-39* had to dive continually beside the dock—as it had in Manila—and sit on the bottom until the bombs stopped dropping. Then, still not fully repaired, she pulled out of port on February 14, just before the Japanese pounded Surabaya to rubble. The sub took on a stray American sailor inadvertently left on the dock during the rush from Java who would otherwise have ended up as a Japanese prisoner of war.[6]

S-39 was ordered north to Singapore, now under attack by Japanese troops, but en route she received orders to go on a special mission to Chebia, an island off Sumatra. There, a party of about forty downed British airmen—refugees from Singapore—had sent out an SOS that they were stranded. Some high-ranking officers—including Rear Admiral Ernest John Spooner and an air vice-marshal—were among them. Jim was ordered to pick them up from the uninhabited island before the Japanese discovered them.[7]

The crew, frustrated by having to flee Surabaya and jury-rig their own repairs, hurried to the island, gung ho to be of use. They sighted the island on the night of March 1, 1942, but saw that the waters swarmed with enemy boats and planes. In the distance, the shores of Chebia Island and the tops of its trees were bathed in bright moonlight. The *S-39* cautiously approached on the surface from the northeast, signaling the lost men by blinker light. "We could easily have been sighted from Chebia for at least one hour and from Kachangang [a neighboring island] for at least two hours prior to arrival," Jim wrote in his patrol report.[8]

No one responded. Jim asked for a volunteer to explore the island, and more than twenty men stepped up. Jim had to put names in a hat. Electrician's Mate Charles Petersen was the lucky pick, and he rowed a dinghy to the island. Petersen carried a blinker light, a simple code to communicate with the ship, and a service pistol.

He entered the jungle from the beach and found the remains of native shacks beaten to the ground. Pots and pans were scattered around; coconuts and even hanging plants had been chopped up. The cuts were fresh. After a lengthy search of the surrounding jungle and finding no sign of life, Petersen headed back to the dinghy, along the way discovering footprints leading to the sea but not returning. The prints were all at least one inch shorter in length than the size 6-1/2 shoes Petersen wore. The shape of the prints was military with square toes, indicating that a Japanese landing force had just left the island.

But despite this, when Petersen rejoined the boat, Jim decided to go completely around Chebia, sending messages from every angle. Having raised

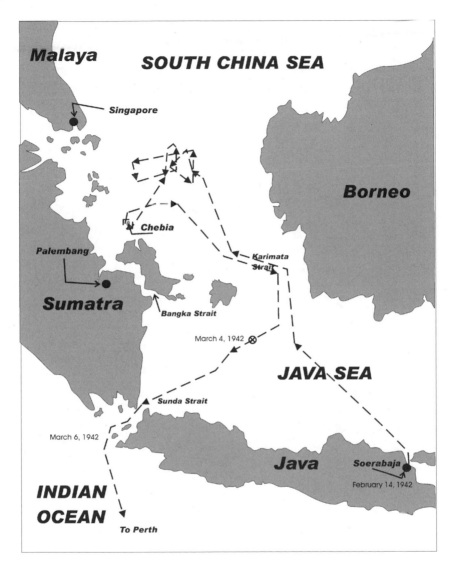

S-39's third patrol: ⊗ March 4, 1942, sinking of *Erimu*.

nothing, he then steamed three miles north to Kachangang Island and sent blinker messages to all parts of it while navigating a mean surf. Kachangang had fifty-foot cliffs dropping directly into the sea, so it wasn't possible to land the dinghy there. Even so, the *S-39* waited till daylight, submerged, and circled both islands again, watching for signs of habitation. No life of any sort was seen.

Jim speculates in his patrol report that either the British party was taken prisoner by the Japanese shortly before *S-39* arrived or the British escaped earlier by boat. His crewmen were disheartened and frustrated as they steamed away from the islands. But they had no time to complain. One or two enemy destroyers were nosing around the area, listening for submarines. Jim dove and started an approach on one of them but ultimately couldn't close to less than six thousand yards.[9]

Now that I was looking past my former pacifism by imagining myself in Jim's shoes, I was awed at his bravery. But his crew, eagerly throwing their names in the hat to scout the dangerous island, helped me understand why he risked everything to find the airmen. The men needed a morale booster. Rescuing the downed airmen would have restored their faith that goodness and justice still existed somewhere, despite seeing all their safe ports blasted to rubble.

———

Meanwhile, not far from Chebia, our navy's surface forces, plus Allied ships from Britain, Australia, and Holland, tried to hold off the Japanese navy in what later became known as the Battle of the Java Sea. Our heavy cruiser *Houston* and Australia's *Perth* were both sunk, and our *Marblehead* was gravely wounded in the five-hour battle, whereas the Japanese didn't lose a single ship. So the island of Java, last respite of the *S-39*, went down to the enemy.

U.S. submarines were then ordered to patrol the waters around Java to attack whatever Japanese invasion forces they could before withdrawing to the only remaining refuge, Perth, Australia. The *S-39* turned south from Chebia Island and steamed down past Sumatra, heading for the Sunda Strait between Sumatra and Java. In the middle of the Java Sea, Executive Officer Larry Bernard picked up some smudged shapes on the horizon. It was another bright, moonlit night, and the smudges at first looked only like smoke. Jim gave the order to follow them, and the *S-39* closed to about ten thousand yards—close enough to see smaller shapes peel off from a large one. They got closer and identified the silhouette of a tanker. The fact that it was lagging behind the ships it had been accompanying at first sight suggested that it was loaded with fuel, probably heading to refuel the forces invading Java.

Excitement grew in the cramped control room, but the approach party tried to keep their voices steady. After seventy minutes of maneuvering closer, Jim ordered the torpedomen to ready four torpedoes. The *S-39* bored in to an ideal position of one thousand yards, fired, then dropped the periscope to wait the crucial, agonizing moments.

In just under two and one-half minutes, the men heard three explosions. Jim squatted to the periscope and rose with it, his eye glued to the glass. "The tanker is heeling way over and settling down by the stern," he said, and a loud cheer went up.[10]

Jim, in the excitement, forgot or put aside his caution about watching a target sink. Charles Witt remembers: "It took 59 minutes to sink. Captain Coe called all of us—the whole crew—in to watch it going down. He called the two Filipino mess-attendants to look first, as revenge for what had been done to their homeland."

This peek through the periscope was the biggest morale booster, short of the downed airmen, Jim could give the men. War records were extremely strict; to get credit for a sinking, the target had to be seen or photographed going down, and the sinking had to be later verified by other ships or planes in the area or by Japanese reports and postwar records. Men in submarines were at an extreme disadvantage in this verification process. All they usually had was sound—if they were lucky. Only the captain, if fortunate enough to be unpursued, had the luxury of looking through the periscope and snapping pictures. So the men on the *S-39* had a rare experience that bright moonlit night of seeing with their own eyes the outcome of all their hard work, high tension, and heat rash.

After watching the ship (the 6,500-ton tanker *Erimu,* as it turned out) go down, the *S-39*'s soundman picked up three distant propellers coming toward them. The sub dove and was soon rocked by depth charges. She tried to slink away, but the destroyers followed her, dropping depth charges hour after hour that exploded just as close as the first ones had. The enemy was clinging to them, it seemed to the puzzled crew, by some weird luck or magic.[11] Jim was undoubtedly kicking himself for staying around watching his handiwork, no matter how much it helped his men's morale.

S-39 continued to get pounded. Along with depth charges, aerial bombs exploded close by. The destroyers had probably called in planes to finish the sub off. Jim ordered the boat down to the deepest level the chart showed: 130 feet. But the diving officer said that something was stopping them; the sub seemed to be wallowing in mud well short of that depth. Dutch charts for these waters were notoriously flawed, and Jim learned the hard way.

The S-39 must have been churning up mud for hours, inadvertently guiding the enemy destroyers and planes right to her. "The chart showed plenty of depth," Jim later told an interviewer. "But it just wasn't there."[12]

Once he realized this, Jim ordered a sharp burst of speed, which broke them loose from the bottom, and ordered the sub back up to ninety feet. The diving officer performed the ticklish operation of pumping some water out of a ballast tank along the inside of the hull, thus lightening the boat just enough to go up thirty or so feet. In the ancient S-boat, it was easy to blow too much, lose control, and pop to the surface—right in front of the Japanese. But Diving Officer Larry Bernard managed to keep the boat level, and they gradually crept off to the southeast, eluding their pursuers.

Scared and exhausted, with the boat in dire need of repair, the men stayed down for seven more hours. The air grew so stale that they had to spread a white powdered carbon-dioxide absorbent around the ship. It staved off headaches for a few more hours, but finally—all out of air—they had to surface.

The men found themselves near an uninhabited island. It was night, a seemingly safe time to stay on the surface long enough to recharge batteries. (Unlike a car battery that is constantly regenerated by the motor, a submarine battery is used up in powering the electric motor that turns the propeller to keep the submerged boat at its desired depth, along with charging lights, pumps, blowers, and other systems. So the boat has to come back up to the surface to recharge the batteries with the diesel engines, which need air as well as fuel to power them.) But well before they finished recharging, a Japanese destroyer came by and shined a searchlight on the island. The S-39 didn't have enough water to dive, so Jim could do nothing but turn the boat to face the destroyer, thus lessening the silhouette the S-39 made against the island. The men turned all sound off and waited like sitting ducks, standing by the deck gun—their only defense against the barrage to come. But by some miracle, the Japanese light played overhead and to either side of the sub, just missing it. Then the destroyer slowly pulled back, turned, and steamed away. When it had faded well into the distance, the *S-39* slipped back out into deep water.[13]

Thanking whatever island gods had saved them, the men set a course for the Sunda Strait, the narrow stretch of water between Sumatra and Java. They hadn't yet gotten word that Java had fallen and that Japanese boats would be thick in the waters around Java. But soon enough, Ensign Guy Gugliotta spotted a shape against the night sky north of the strait, and *S-39* dove. Radioman Howie Rice remembers: "I was on watch in the radio room, and had to pull the antenna plugs and close the antenna trunk, then go forward to the torpedo room and start up the sound gear, put on the headphones, make a sweep. As we reached 100 feet, I heard two torpedoes go right over us." Rice didn't say whether he shared the terror of this with anyone else.

But there was plenty of fear to go around. The *S-39* entered the Sunda Strait on March 5, 1942. Charles Witt remembers the horror of submerging in the narrow strait, with its strong currents and small islands making progress extremely dangerous. "We were 100 feet down, with a wicked current pulling us sideways, and Japs swarming above." Without propeller speed to offset the currents, it was a battle to control the boat. "Your dad was a good navigator, and he pulled us through hell," Witt said of their eventual escape from the strait. Crewmen Robert Norton and Frank Gierhart confirm this, but Gierhart brings up the lesson Jim should have learned: Captain Coe was a great navigator but shouldn't have sat around letting everyone look through the periscope as the tanker sunk. Some on the crew agreed, but others didn't, and they argued about it.[14] The men were cohesive enough to allow open disagreement.

Once through the harrowing Sunda Strait, they headed to Perth. The Japanese heavily guarded all routes south to Australia, which was now the only refuge for the whipped and exhausted Asiatic Fleet. Captains John Wilkes and Jimmy Fife (Admiral Hart, under pressure from Dutch commanders over the Battle of Java, had been removed from command) had set up a temporary submarine base in Perth/Fremantle, and most of the subs were now headed there, with or without orders.

As Java disappeared behind them and the *S-39*ers faced open ocean, progress was painstakingly slow in the old, damaged boat. They were at the end of their food rations and were forced to catch water in a rainwater barrel on deck. Skin rashes, blisters, and heat prostration were rampant, and the only thing that kept the men's hopes up was the knowledge that the west coast of Australia was just five days away.

Until the port engine blew. Then the engineers worked feverishly for three days on the glaring surface in scorching heat. But they couldn't get the thing going; they finally gave up and got under way on the starboard engine alone—with a worn-out clutch. For days they putted along at a dangerously slow and creaky seven knots.[15] Finally, weak with thirst and exhaustion, they limped into Fremantle.

But their ordeal wasn't yet over. Other crews gathered on the docks there filled in the *S-39*ers on the defeat of their Asiatic Fleet: Java had fallen, and the Japanese had taken a heavy toll on American ships. On top of all that, the U.S. submarine command was now criticizing fleet boat captains for not being aggressive enough.

Because I was no longer looking at these events through my old pacifist lens, I fully identified with *S-39*'s fate and was thus offended by this reception. Despite the fact that Jim and his fellow skippers had been *trained* by prewar dogma to be cautious, navy leaders now expected a 180-degree turnaround, and it sounded like sour grapes to me. I had to dig further into prewar submarine strategy to sort out the good and bad of this flip-flop.

Before the war, naval warfare was restricted by treaty to combat ships. So submarine skippers had to assume that every ship they pursued would be equipped—as our fleet's combat destroyers were—with active (pinging) sonar and the latest arsenals of depth charges, guns, and speed. Skippers were thus taught to be cautious, stay submerged during the day, and attack only from depths of one hundred feet or more where they were safer from aircraft and sonar detection. Because these depths were well below the level where one could use the periscope, skippers were virtually blind, reduced to pursuing targets only by sound (and on the old S-boats, with their antique sound equipment, this was a big handicap). But this restriction was absolutely drummed into skippers; in prewar drills, sub skippers in the Asiatic

Fleet who exposed their periscopes or were otherwise detected during torpedo practice were immediately relieved of command.[16]

Nevertheless, the "conduct unrestricted warfare" order of December 8 changed all this. It specifically allowed submarines and airplanes to attack more than just combat ships; all enemy ships except hospital ships were now targets. Submarine author Ned Beach summarizes the new wartime purpose of submarines this way: "Your submarine is primarily a commerce-destroyer. While it will attack any moderate-to-large warship it encounters, its principal objective is the lifeline of the enemy—its merchant carriers."[17]

This new wartime focus meant that sub captains, knowing that merchant ships weren't armed the way combat ships were, no longer had to stick to the cautious approach—that is, deeply submerged and thus blind. But this also meant that every sub captain had to think up his own attack and defense strategies—and do it quickly. Jim told Robert Casey that nobody in these early days knew much about submarine warfare. Skippers would have to make a lot of mistakes before getting things right.[18] But they also had to appear confident and decisive in front of their crews. If Jim was uncertain, hesitant, scared, doubtful of the war's purpose, or just plain homesick, he couldn't show it.

Now, after noting that prewar doctrine didn't fit the unrestricted warfare order of the day, I thought it doubly cruel of the deskbound brass to chew out the skippers creaking in from besieged Java and Manila. They were asking too much too fast and were probably letting their anger and frustration at having totally underestimated the enemy come out sideways: at their beleaguered sub captains, who were heroic just to make it back to port.

Nevertheless, although this injustice must have angered Jim for the sake of his men and colleagues, it also favored him and anyone else lucky enough to have sunk a ship with a decrepit S-boat. Clay Blair writes: "Coe, like two other S-boat captains who had sunk ships, Moon Chapple and Jim Dempsey, became something of a hero."[19] This might explain the sign in a Brisbane hotel that another officer of Jim's—Paul Loustaunau—told me about in an interview a few years ago. It sat on the bar in mid-1942 as people came in for drinks: "Hear no evil, see no evil, speak no evil," it said and then underneath each phrase was "Chapple," "Coe," and "Dempsey."

The *S-39*'s purported two sinkings got Jim moved up to a fleet boat command. He was transferred from *S-39* to *Skipjack* in the week that *S-39* was in Fremantle for repairs. (From there, *S-39* would sail to Brisbane, where S-boats were now headquartered.)

Before he left the *S-39*, Jim called his crew together one last time. Charles Witt remembers, "We had passed a hat and collected enough to buy him a nice watch. He shook hands, said thanks and goodbye to each one of us, and there wasn't a dry eye on deck."

13

The Battle of the Java Sea, which raged in early February 1942 while the S-39ers reconnoitered Chebia Island for the downed airmen, turned out to have a huge impact on my family. First of all, it was a resounding defeat of our Asiatic Fleet, necessitating the relocation and reconfiguration of our submarine force and spurring the submarine command to make its skippers more aggressive. Those commanders who weren't more forceful were consigned to desk jobs or worse.

But as the fallout from the Java Sea battle fueled Jim's rise through the ranks and his subsequent role in our family as hero, the battle itself took down my other father figure: our stepfather, Frank. As a ship's doctor on the *Marblehead,* Frank experienced hours of horrific bombing, which he must have been alluding to when he paced our childhood music room, half in the bag, talking about wounded men lurching around fiery decks. My mother told me he had frequent nightmares about the *Marblehead.*

When I found out that this period of the war was the intersection of the two fathers in my life, and the most likely beginning of their opposite trajectories, I scoured the literature of this battle. I also tracked down another war orphan whose family was shaped by this period. I'll take up his story momentarily. But first, I learned that in late January of 1942 the navy deactivated the Asiatic Fleet and put all its ships under the Southwest Pacific Force. The Allied naval forces in the Far East, headquartered in Java, were transferred from the command of Admiral Hart to a Dutch admiral, Admiral Helfrich. In the ensuing confusion of this political shift, our ships in Java were left without air cover. In the Battle of the Java Sea, February 27, 1942, both of our cruisers, *Marblehead* and *Houston,* were attacked by nine Japanese bombers each. The *Marblehead* was hit in the stern, knocking out the steering control and all interior communications. The decks caught fire, and the few doctors there rushed to get the wounded to safety while the defenseless ship lumbered around in slow circles. Enemy bombers continued the attack, tearing big chunks out of *Marblehead's* hull. She took on water.[1] Frank, who couldn't swim, operated on burned men until the ceiling of the ship's wardroom behind him collapsed, narrowly missing him.

The Japanese, meanwhile, seeing the boat low in the water and figuring she'd sink, left the area. The exhausted sailors then hand-steered her, all the while heroically pumping and manning bucket brigades. Forty-eight hours later she limped into Tjilatjap Harbor on Java's south coast, saved by a miracle of seamanship and spontaneous leadership.[2] And it left Frank permanently traumatized.

Another way the Java Sea battle touched my childhood was the fate of David Hurt, skipper of the fleet submarine *Perch*. His son was the fellow war orphan I tracked down. He became a particularly valuable source for this book because, as mentioned in an earlier chapter, he was a teenager at the outbreak of the war and remembered my father.

Lieutenant Commander David Hurt was one of Jim Coe's best friends. He and his family were posted in Hawaii with Jim and Ray, and the two families would get together for picnics and parties. My mother was so fond of Hurt that in the fifties, she broke through the wall of silence she'd erected around Jim and the subject of World War II to tell me Hurt's story. I was in seventh or eighth grade; it was gray and rainy, the kind of weather Mother would actively escape by going out shopping, often prolonging the experience by downing a six-pack of Hershey bars while pushing her grocery cart around the A&P supermarket. But on this gloomy afternoon at home, loneliness seemed to make her inert. She sat on the landing at the top of the stairs outside my room while I changed out of my school clothes, and she told me that the one thing she was thankful for about the loss of Jim was that he hadn't been captured by the "Japs." Then she told me about Skipper David Hurt, and the rare emotion in her voice, the sadness, anger, and awe for the man, made me come to the door of my room and gape at her. The story broke through her fifties' facade of cheerfulness, revealing her humanity. I sat down beside her on the stairs. She showed me, for the first time, a glimpse of the grief she must have carried for Jim. She couldn't talk about Jim directly; she deflected her sadness and anger onto the fate of Skipper Hurt. So I think of his story as part of Jim's.

Although considerably older than Jim, Lieutenant Commander David Hurt proved very different from the old-guard fleet boat skippers who clung to their cautious prewar training. Extremely intelligent, Hurt adapted immediately to the need for skipper innovation and aggression, attacking an enemy ship and then later a convoy in the first two weeks of war. He might well have sunk one of these early targets—a five-thousand-ton Japanese freighter—but this couldn't be verified (again, verification standards were stringent and extremely difficult in the heat of battle).[3] At one of these targets, "he fired four torpedoes," son David told me. "Three passed harmlessly under the enemy vessel, and the fourth did a U-turn and headed back to *Perch*. The only thing that saved them was that the torpedo porpoised out of the water about 100 yards off the sub's starboard quarter and exploded in the air, showering the deck and conning tower with shrapnel. Not an auspicious beginning, and it only got worse."

Then, in February of 1942, Hurt was ordered to the Java Sea.

In numerous e-mails, Skipper Hurt's son told me about political decisions of that period that must have made submariners feel abandoned by their country. For one thing, they hated to see Admiral Hart, one of their own kind, replaced by a Dutch bureaucrat, Admiral Conrad Helfrich. "His [Hart's] treatment was profoundly unjust and extremely political," Hurt, Jr., wrote. "In my view, the guy to be fired was MacArthur, not Hart. As it was, the Asiatic Fleet personnel thought they had been thrown to the wolves when they were put under Dutch control. Roosevelt also laid down the policy that only minimal support was to go to the Pacific, and that primary concentration of the war effort was to be in support of England." Historian Samuel Eliot Morison confirms this by showing that President Roosevelt, Secretary of the Navy Knox, and Admiral King all believed that Java could not be held much longer and relieved Admiral Hart so that a Dutch commander would take the rap for Java's fall.[4] So the submariners, most of them punchy from three months of unrelieved patrol in boats badly in need of repair, were set adrift in dangerous seas that their leaders had already judged a lost cause. They had no clear leadership; Helfrich ordered them to speed up their run to Java's defense by steaming on the surface by day. Admiral Hart's assistant, John Wilkes, who shared control of the fleet, countermanded this order as dangerous, and Helfrich ended up blaming the U.S. submarine force for being too cautious.[5] The sub force also was virtually naked and homeless; they had no base to retreat to for repairs or reinforcements. The inexperienced skippers were left on their own with dangerously inaccurate Dutch charts.

The *Perch*'s men had the added terror of the circling torpedo, which almost sank them in the first weeks of war, so Commander Hurt's rush to Java's defense in early February of 1942 was incredibly brave. The *Perch* aggressively approached a Japanese convoy in the Java Sea. Before the men could get off a shot, the enemy fired on them, hitting *Perch* with a shell that damaged her radio antenna. Still, Hurt was able to radio a message to Commanders Wilkes and Fife about the damage, then charged back into the fray as ordered by a leadership in the very act of abandoning its own forces. Historian W. G. Winslow elaborates: "With the island of Java now doomed, members of the Allied high command scrambled frantically to get out of Java. Coincident with the pandemonium ashore, communications went into a flat spin. The last radio contact the *Perch* had with Allied headquarters occurred on the night of 28 Feb., when the sub was ordered to attack transports at a landing point a few miles east of Surabaja. This irrational directive was probably tossed out by some distraught officer about to run for his life, for that portion of the Java Sea was much too shallow to permit effective submarine operations."[6]

Captain Hurt, by now apprised of the defeat of Allied forces and thus knowing the danger of these enemy-held waters, chose to obey orders rather than flee the stricken island. Depending on flawed Dutch charts to locate channels deep enough to hide, he cautiously approached Surabaja. Then, having to recharge batteries, Hurt surfaced twenty miles north of the designated landing point; he was spotted by two enemy destroyers. After diving and getting clear of them, Hurt ordered the boat back up to periscope depth. He scanned the destroyers and saw that one presented a potential target. He began an approach, but when he was within six hundred yards, the boat apparently spotted his periscope; it turned and started steaming toward *Perch* at high speed. Hurt ordered a dive to 180 feet; the chart showed that they were in 200 feet of water.

However, *Perch* hit bottom at 140 feet with the motors still turning over. This stuck her in heavy mud, which her propellers churned up, revealing her position. The destroyers dropped their lethal loads; depth charges were heavy and accurate, and the *Perch* could only lie there and take it, stuck firmly in deep mud. Forced to sit silently to escape Japanese listening devices and conserve oxygen, her men endured concussions that vibrated their bones and teeth, threatening to smash in the hull at any minute. They heard steel bulkheads shrink in and pop out, metal deck plates jump and clatter, and pipe and ventilation lines thump the walls. Everyone listened for the telltale hiss of leaks; everyone seized tables, pipes, ladders, doorways, or bunk edges at each concussion to keep from flying through the air. The whole ship shuddered and shook.

It's not surprising that men went crazy under these conditions. World War II veteran and author Paul Fussell tells of psychotic submariners having to be handcuffed to their bunks after a depth charging.[7] A son of a submariner who was badly depth charged on the submarine *Seahorse* tells me that his father never got over it. He was afraid of any loud noise in the house and could no longer relate to his family. One fleet boat captain, Morton Mumma, went crazy when *Sailfish* (the former *Squalus*) was depth charged off Vigan, Luzon, in the Philippines. Mumma was clearheaded enough to know he couldn't be trusted, and he ordered his executive officer to take command of the boat and to lock him in his stateroom until they could return to their sub tender. This was—paradoxically—an amazingly rational decision; Mumma was relieved of duty when he got to port but was eventually awarded the Navy Cross for his stellar career up to that point.

S-39 crewman Tom Parks tells a very different story about a later depth charging on the *Sailfish,* which Parks was assigned to after the *S-39:* "Our commander, [J. R.] 'Dinty' Moore, was a great skipper, cut from the same cloth as your father. I remember one time we were being subjected to a depth-charging that seemed to go on forever. My battle station was in the control room where I watched 'Dinty' direct our maneuvers. He was giving orders coolly and calmly and I was more than a little scared. He looked up from the plotting board, grinned at me, and gave me a big wink. Right then I knew that we were going to be okay."

I think of *Perch*'s David Hurt having similar grace under fire; he'd have to, to have done what he did. Under the barrage of depth charges, he put the men to work rocking the boat and turning the propeller just enough to finally pop them out of the mud. They then moved *Perch* slowly and quietly through the water, trying to discern a directional pattern to the attack so that they could evade further strings of depth charges. After two hours of this stealthy movement, the depth charges grew fainter; finally, the sound of the destroyer's propellers faded away. Years later, Japanese records showed that air bubbles and oil surfacing from the damaged *Perch* had convinced the destroyers' crews that the sub had been destroyed.

Perch waited longer, then finally surfaced. Assessing the damage, the men found that only one of their four engines worked; periscopes were flooded; and all antenna insulators—plus all engine-room gauges and the crew's toilet bowl—were broken. There were many leaks throughout the boat, and the conning tower had been flattened. But instead of retreating, Commander Hurt followed orders, heading *Perch* back in toward the Japanese landing on Java.

Two more enemy destroyers spotted him just after dawn. *Perch* dove again for the bottom, this time reaching it in two hundred feet of water. There she sat quietly in hopes of evading the destroyers. Submarine historian Theodore Roscoe cites this as a necessity, because *Perch*'s damage would have required nearly continuous operation of the noisy trim pumps, which, combined with leaking oil and air supplies, would have rendered an undetected withdrawal impossible.[8] But Clay Blair differs, calling Hurt's order to stay on the bottom "the same tactic he used off Formosa on his first patrol."[9] This makes it sound like a deliberate and preferred strategy rather than the desperate lesser of two evils that Hurt was faced with. I see this as an unfortunate misreading or dismissal of the aggressive choices and courage Hurt showed up to that point.

As the *Perch* lay on the bottom this time, depth charges fell with amazing precision, and the destroyers stuck to them for hours. "The only thing that saved us," recalls crewman Myron "Turk" Turner, "was mud; they just kept on beatin' us into the mud. As long as you don't get a depth charge under that submarine, it doesn't hurt. If it's on top, it just will jar you and all that, but all the pressure just about goes up; seven-eighths of the explosion goes up and one eighth goes down. It just kept drivin' us down into the mud."

Be that as it may, the *Perch* sustained major damage this time. "Her hatches were badly twisted; her propeller shafts were bent and her engines loose from their moorings," reports crewman Sam Simpson. "The acrid smoke from torpedoes that had run in their skids didn't help. It was the chlorine gas and steady build-up of water in several bilges that was to seal her fate."[10]

Finally, giving up the *Perch* for dead, the destroyers steamed away. Down under, jammed deep into the mud, the men again took stock. The ballast tanks were cracked, so air could only partially be blown into them to replace the heavier water and thus get the boat to the surface. When the blowers were turned on, compressed air could be heard blowing along the hull, revealing the fact that it couldn't help them. The men now faced the probability of slow suffocation. But Captain Hurt went all through the boat, reassuring the men with calm words. As usual, he gave them a plan to hold onto and tasks to keep them busy: they would wait out the rest of the day on the bottom (they couldn't risk surfacing until nightfall anyway), making repairs before trying to unstick themselves from the mud. So the men went to work pumping out bilges and patching up ballast tanks, engines, and the electrical system as best they could.

That night they tried to break the battered sub from the mud. "What the captain would do would be blow ballast and at the same time rock the ship back and forth," says Turk Turner. "We had one main engine that was workin' on the screws [propeller]. We rocked it back and forth and we was down to our last tank of air, and finally broke loose and come to the surface."

Only one engine worked, vibrating dangerously, and *Perch* miraculously got under way. Leaking oil (thus laying a clear trail for the enemy), she limped along at five knots. The main vents would not hold air, and the crew had to close emergency vents. Bilge pumps had to be kept going constantly to pump out the leaky hull. Torpedo tubes and deck guns were ruined, so *Perch* was defenseless. In this condition, Skipper Hurt made for cover; his goal was to cross the Java Sea to the southern coast of Borneo, where they could lie on the bottom in shallow water to make repairs.

It was in this state—and worse, with the stern down underwater after an aborted attempt to dive—that the next set of Japanese destroyers and a cruiser came upon *Perch* just before dawn the next day. They started shelling the sub. *Perch* tried to dive, but the trim wasn't working, and thus there was no way to maintain control and no way to effect a watertight seal on the main engine room and control room hatches. Water poured in. There was nothing *Perch* could do; she couldn't dive, outrun, or even fire on her pursuers. Captain Hurt gave the order that devastates any skipper: to abandon ship and sink the boat (to hide its technology and other secrets).

Skipper Hurt went up on deck and helped his men get overboard safely in life jackets; two of the men stayed down in the engine room to open the vents. "So we brought her back up and leveled her off and we went down and opened all the flood vents and let her go to the bottom," recalled Turk Turner. When the ship started sinking, the last two men dashed to the conning tower, then fought their way off the ship through a wall of water to the surface. Hurt's son says of his father: "I later learned from one of his crew that he and a second man had taken my dad over the side with them after my dad had told them that he would not leave the control room. He told them to leave the ship immediately as it was settling rapidly." Crewman Turk Turner confirms this when he recalls Hurt's recalcitrance once they were in the water. One of the Japanese destroyers was gathering the *Perch*'s men up and taking them on board as prisoners. "I was the last man out of the water," Turner recalls. "I got his [Skipper Hurt's] feet on the ladder and he come on out. If I'd a went on up the ladder [before him], he would have stayed there, yeah, I'm sure. Yeah, he would have stayed in the water if I'd a let him." Whether this was an act of will or exhaustion is hard to say.

I asked David Hurt, Jr., what the expectations were for skippers at that point in naval history. "Without being present at the pre-patrol briefings," he said, "it's hard to say what counsel may have been given. However, I can't—by the wildest stretch of my imagination—believe that any skipper was advised to go down with his ship." This is because good, aggressive submarine captains were in short supply and extremely expensive (in terms of training) to replace.

Skipper Hurt had been without sleep for three days, however, so he may have been harking back to the tradition he was steeped in at the Naval Academy, where the loss of one's ship is unthinkable. David Hurt, Jr., himself a product of the academy, reports a proud tradition of going down with one's ship that's "embedded in one's soul. I'm certain this was a strong influence on my dad."

The public seems to have assumed this notion of sacrifice as well. Long after the war, a survivor of the *Perch* was invited as guest speaker to a meeting of submarine veterans in New England, submarine veteran Bill Tebo told me in an interview. The survivor had never told his story and was reluctant to do so, fearing that he would break down in tears at the memory of losing the ship and spending the rest of the war in a Japanese prison camp. But his wife persuaded him to get his feelings out and accompanied him to the meeting. Hesitantly, the veteran told his story. At the end, as he and his wife were passing through the meeting hall on the way out, someone from the audience called out: "You should have gone down with your ship!"

Such is the staying power of this long-held belief. I suppose it springs from our democratic ideal—that a skipper should not ask anything more of his crew than he would be willing to do himself. So if the crew goes down, it would be an affront to equality if the captain saved himself. However, no one died when the *Perch* went down, so I would think people would cut her survivors some slack.

But Skipper Hurt seemed to be his own harshest critic. "The loss of his ship preyed heavily on his mind," his son recalls. "Those who know the whole story of *Perch*'s ordeal have had nothing but the highest regard for my dad's fight against insurmountable odds, but he had trouble accepting that. He felt very badly about the loss of his ship."

There was more that he felt bad about, too. After the Japanese destroyer picked up the entire crew of *Perch,* the men were allowed to sleep for about a day, during which they received only one cup each of yellowish warm water. They were then transferred to the *Optenoort,* a Dutch hospital ship commandeered by the Japanese. They were kept in a hole on the third deck for three days. "Once a day a Jap soldier would throw a paper bag down with hardtack cracker crumbs and pieces, nothing larger than one inch big," Sam Simpson remembers. "We elected Victor S. Pedersen our leader and he divided the crumbs into equal size little piles. . . . We each took a pile, thankful. Someone had found the morgue and several formaldehyde bottles, which we caught water in from a slow-running spigot. After several days in the hole, the ship came alongside a pier. It was Makassar, Netherlands East Indies, on the Island of Celebes."[11]

The crew spent the rest of the war—three and one-half hellish years—in the prison camp of Makassar-Celebes. Skipper Hurt and the officers, plus the radiomen, spent only the first month there and then were transferred to Japan for interrogation. "My dad spent his first eighteen months in solitary confinement at Ofuna Naval Interrogation Camp," says David Hurt, Jr. "All that time he was listed as 'missing in action.' Next, he went to the Headquarters P.O.W. camp at Aomori. Finally, he was sent to the copper mines at Ashio. A dreaded P.O.W. Camp, unregistered with the Red Cross, and noted for its death rate—at 135 a week when the prisoners were finally liberated in late August 1945."

Nine *Perch* crewmen died in prison camp, and fifty-three, including Skipper Hurt, made it home. However, reentry was hard, and there were no mental health or counseling services to ease the transition. And, cruelly enough, there seems to be a stigma attached to having been captured, especially in a war that we won. "There's no glory in being a prisoner of war," affirmed John Cowan, historian for the New Hampshire chapter of the U.S. Subvets of WWII, when I talked with him in the fall of 1999. The story of the *Perch* survivor's reception as guest speaker reflects this. And sadly, men who were forced to spend most of the war in prison seemed to internalize this attitude. It didn't help that our government virtually silenced them, not wanting them to publicize the bad treatment they had endured at the hands of the Japanese, for fear of alienating our new allies.

Even though Skipper Hurt was promoted to the rank of captain on his return to the United States in September 1945, he felt keenly responsible for his men's fate. "It is hard to see your friends walking around with Navy Crosses, etc.," says David Hurt, Jr. "And you have just returned from prison camp, where you spent most of the war. It made my dad feel as though he had done nothing."

My mother—on that rainy school day in the fifties—told me about a dinner she had for Captain Hurt and his wife in those early months after his return to the States. "I had set the table with candles," Mother said. "And he asked me to take them off. 'The Japanese burned my feet with them,' he said." She stared into the middle distance as she said this, her face ashen with some awful picture, and when she turned back to me, she said, "I'll always be thankful that your father didn't have to go through that."

"And what happened to Captain Hurt?" I asked.

Her hazel eyes turned almost black with pain, like an animal with its paw clamped in a metal trap. "He died," she said.

Ned Beach confirmed in a letter the details I vaguely recall my mother telling me: while Captain Hurt was on "POW leave" from the navy shortly after his return to the States, he went hunting. He propped his loaded rifle against a fence post, climbed over the fence, and when he picked up the gun on the other side, it discharged. "A tragic ending," Beach said, adding: "There's nothing wrong or dishonorable with having been a POW." And reiterating that Hurt had done the best by his men, Beach said: "The *Perch* was in extremis, they couldn't do anything to move their ship, and the general consensus as I heard it was that her skipper did right to abandon ship and give his crew a chance for their lives, even at the expense of nearly four years as POWs."

This story is the most tragic of all I've come across in my research on World War II. And yet I'm afraid it's only the tip of the iceberg. We have very little idea of the suffering that these men and their families endured in World War II, especially in the Pacific war, which gets less coverage than the war in Europe. Negative experiences just weren't talked about or reported on in any depth. Paul Fussell rails against the silence around the grim reality of war: "The letterpress correspondents, radio broadcasters, and film people who perceived these horrors kept quiet about them on behalf of the War Effort. As [war correspondent] John Steinbeck finally confessed in 1958, 'We were all part of the war effort. We went along with it, and not only that, we abetted it. . . . I don't mean that the correspondents were liars. . . . It is in the things not mentioned that the untruth lies.'"[12]

14

Jim keenly felt the "untruth" cited by correspondent Steinbeck by the time he reached Australia in March of 1942. He and his crew had noticed that the World War I–vintage Mark X torpedoes on the *S-39* tended to run deeper than they were set for, so when they got to Fremantle and heard similar stories from other boats, they suspected that they had a fleetwide problem. Skippers on the newer fleet boats were complaining about deep-running torpedoes, torpedoes that wouldn't explode, premature explosions, and—most chilling (as we saw on *Perch*)—circling torpedoes.

These complaints were all met with a version of Steinbeck's "untruth." Administrators in the navy's Bureau of Ordnance (BuOrd) simply ignored the complaints, or—when forced to respond—attacked the submarine command with the charge that their skippers weren't properly preparing and setting the torpedoes by BuOrd specifications. Ned Beach wrote me, still impassioned more than sixty years later, summing up the characteristic denial around this issue: "For my money, the torpedo fiasco was an unmitigated disgrace. How as high-minded an outfit as the U.S. Navy could have been so careless with its weaponry is totally beyond everyone who was a victim, and indeed, this may be part of the problem. It's one of the things we are willing to sweep under the rug. After all, we won the war, didn't we?"

Looking into torpedo history, I found that the navy had endorsed and distributed a new torpedo in the first months of war. The Mark XIV had never been tested in live waters. Building on an idea first created by the Germans in the early twenties, submariner and engineer Ralph Christie and his colleagues worked on a proximity detonator, which fired the warhead without the torpedo's even touching the target itself. The detonator was triggered by the magnetic field around the metal hull of the target battleship; the torpedo was directed to pass beneath the ship, and as it did, the torpedo exploded, tearing out the ship's bottom. The bottom of the battleship, being thinner than the sides, was a more vulnerable target, and so the proximity detonator was seen as a significant improvement over the old contact exploder, which had to bump up against the thickest part of a ship to detonate. But the Mark XIV had both kinds of exploder, and as the supply of torpedoes was compromised at the start of the war, submariners were directed to use the magnetic exploder feature of the Mark XIV exclusively. Theoretically at least, only one torpedo would be needed to inflict fatal damage against a ship's bottom, whereas it usually took several torpedoes to tear through the heavily armored sides.

In the one live test of the proximity detonator that the navy's BuOrd allowed to Christie and his men, in May 1926 off Newport, Rhode Island, a first torpedo ran too deep underneath the target (an old, obsolete submarine) to trigger the exploder. But a second torpedo demolished the target so thoroughly that the navy thought there was no further need for live testing. "Nor were there tests of variables of storage conditions, handling, target types, or odd magnetic conditions that might be encountered in the field," writes torpedo historian Robert Gannon.[1] One of these odd conditions was the fact that the magnetic field generated by a metal hull varies with latitude. Close to the equator, the field spreads out, making the sub's own field more of a risk factor and extending the influence of the target ship to a perimeter of fifty feet—resulting in the danger of early detonations.

But the navy wanted to believe that they had a potent new weapon in the proximity- or magnetic-exploder. In the years just before we got into the war, Britain warned our navy that its navy's experiments with magnetic exploders had failed and recommended that torpedoes be equipped only with the more reliable, old-fashioned contact exploders. But BuOrd ignored the advice, and once World War II started, submariners experienced problems with the new torpedo almost immediately. In addition to torpedoes that exploded prematurely, skippers were seeing torpedoes pass too deep beneath enemy ships to trigger the magnetic detonator. And every one of these dud torpedoes gave away the position of the firing submarine to the Japanese.

The navy yard at Newport had run a limited torpedo test in October of 1941 and found that the Mark XIV tended to run about four feet deeper than set. But bureaucrats at BuOrd turned a deaf ear to this news, never alerting the skippers in the Pacific, who saw their torpedoes run harmlessly underneath their target ships and out the other side. These men desperately needed the data and permission to modify their settings. Instead, they were left to fail repeatedly in the dangerous waters of Manila Bay and the Java Sea. In 136 submarine attacks against the Japanese by March 1942, only 36 Japanese ships had been sunk. (Japanese postwar records reduced this number to ten.) An example of probable torpedo failure was encountered by Commander David Hurt in *Perch,* who fired a total of six torpedoes at a convoy on Christmas 1941, just two weeks into the war. None of them exploded.[2] And then there was the four-torpedo spread, mentioned earlier, in which only one exploded, right over the *Perch's* own deck!

Skippers risked their careers to complain repeatedly about defective torpedoes, proffering constructive solutions, but to no avail. BuOrd continued to stonewall or to blame skippers themselves. When skippers tried such alternatives as deactivating the magnetic exploders, they were chastised and threatened with court-martial. Clay Blair says that by the spring of 1942, submariners in both the Pearl Harbor and Asiatic fleets thought their torpedoes and exploders were duds: "Turkey Neck Crawford [G. C. Crawford, Pacific sub division commander] had brought word from Europe that the British and Germans had abandoned the magnetic exploder. That Withers, McCann, English, Styer [heads of Pacific submarines], and the other deskbound staffers refused to listen to suggestions and criticisms from those they had sent into combat with this weapon seems, in retrospect, incomprehensibly stubborn and stupid. At the very least, Withers could have expended a few days conducting live tests against an expendable target—shortage [of torpedoes] or no shortage."[3]

Of those who managed to survive these defective weapons, some were haunted for years afterward. Skipper Roland Pryce, who was relieved of command of his *Spearfish* after missing several targets in the Java Sea, wrote later: "I have lived with the complete frustration of those three months for over thirty years, and even the knowledge we all now have that defective torpedoes were my critical problem doesn't alter the anguish I felt at the end of February 1942."[4]

Pryce's anguish was shared. Bad torpedoes took a terrible toll on skippers' morale. Years later, Lieutenant Commander Ignatius J. Galantin, skipper of the *Halibut,* spoke for all submariners when he wrote that after watching six of his torpedoes do nothing against an enemy destroyer in the first attack of his command, he never again felt confident on setting up an attack.[5] Some skippers quietly disconnected the unreliable magnetic exploders, sending their torpedoes to explode on contact. However, even these wouldn't always detonate, sometimes hitting the hull of the enemy ship and bouncing off in full view of the attacking submarine.

Yet the skippers' superiors were merciless, weeding out the captains who hadn't damaged enemy ships by their second patrol. This forced retirement may have seemed necessary to prevent cheating, which was only possible on a submarine. On surface ships, there was little opportunity to slink away from battle, traveling as they did in formation with other ships. But a sub commander was alone and thus could fudge his patrol reports if he was so inclined. So perhaps Wilkes and Fife, supervisors of the southwest Pacific's subs, felt increased pressure to police their men.

After exploring torpedo history, I began to see Jim in a steadily closing vise. He was far from the gung-ho military man, or even the reluctant hero following orders, whom I'd imagined when I came into this project. He was now a man trying to do his duty, forced to fight not only the Japanese but also the "untruth" of his superiors as well. I saw no way out for him but disgrace, a path he would not—by all I'd seen so far—take.

One of the skippers "saved" by the newly designated "disgrace" of cautious adherence to prewar training was *Skipjack*'s Larry Freeman. Having missed several targets on his first two patrols, Freeman was relieved of command as soon as he reached Australia. The *Skipjack* was then turned over to Jim, who was seen as an aggressive skipper because of his reportedly sinking two ships in the decrepit *S-39.* (Japanese postwar records confirmed only one of these, but surviving *S-39* vets remember a hit that at least did damage: "The war was only about a week old when we hit an enemy ship," Guy Gugliotta affirms. "She was badly damaged; we don't know whether she was sunk or not.")

Poor Skipper Freeman—like David Hurt before him—was baptized by fire. On December 10 in the Philippines, the first day of her patrol, the submerged *Skipjack* began taking on water, and the men had to pump bilges frantically. The spent water surfacing revealed the sub's position to some Japanese destroyers that happened by, and the *Skipjack* received a severe depth charging. The men then knew that they could no longer rid the boat of water; as it took on water again, they had to simply watch the engine room bilge flood up to waist level and pray. To keep her from sinking, they had to run the boat at an angle with her bow up, all the while being hammered with depth charges. They finally had to risk surfacing before the battery gave out. Miraculously, the enemy had gone. *Skipjack* had almost become the first submarine lost in World War II. "Without the hand of the Lord on us, we would not have survived that day," *Skipjack* officer Frank Bennett wrote me.

One can hardly blame Skipper Freeman, then, for being overly cautious. But his officers and men soon complained of boredom. "The idea of going out on a war patrol [to Freeman]," *Skipjack* torpedo officer Paul Loustaunau later remembered, "was going down to 100 feet and staying there. And make as little fuss as possible."

"Mr. Freeman was a dud as a fighting submarine skipper," *Skipjack* electrician Tom Davis agreed.

"He was smart and intelligent and all that," Loustaunau recalled, "but the idea of going to war and fighting the Japs was just, well, 'How can we do this?' 'What are we doing this for?' He just didn't have the guts or something, I don't know."

But Skipper Freeman was not afraid to face his poor results. "Although I was told that I was being relieved in order to give me a physical and mental rest after exhaustive patrols," he wrote later, "I'm sure that the fact that the *Skipjack* had not inflicted any damage on the enemy had a great deal to do with this decision—in fact, I think it was the primary reason."[6]

At least in hindsight, some submariners saw the injustice of this. *S-39*'s Tom Parks wrote about deskbound administrators who knew nothing of combat: "They instilled in the submarine force an adherence to tactics which were totally ineffective, and then cashiered skippers for following them. . . . The majority [of skippers] should have been given another chance. One thing comes through loud and clear and that is that war is an exercise in stupidity and it gives too many idiots the opportunity to apply their stupidity."

As Skipper Freeman went off for what he was told was an extended rest, his replacement, Jim Coe, could have used a rest, too, but his service record shows that he was transferred from *S-39* to *Skipjack* only a week after he limped into Fremantle on one engine. Jim must have been exhausted. Submarine skippers had little time for unbroken sleep, with constant interruptions from the bridge, radio, and periscope watches, in addition to being responsible for the safety and morale of all men on board. Then there's the primary duty of hunting Japanese ships and monitoring their whereabouts at all times, plus keeping accurate deck logs and patrol reports and repairing all the boat's breakdowns.

On top of all this, Jim had been two-and-one-half years in service without leave when the war broke out and fifteen months without seeing his family. Phoebe noted in a letter to Peg years later that Jim's letters of this period pined for Rachel and the kids. Families during wartime just had to accept that they could not know when or if they would ever see each other again. They had to depend on the luck of assignments and on letters in the meantime. Jim and Ray numbered their letters so they knew what order to read them in and whether any went missing. They tailored their lines to the censors, Jim describing his leaving on patrol as "I'm about to be off, Darling, on a business trip. Keep your fingers crossed."

While Jim oversaw the refitting of *Skipjack,* the navy chiefs were reassessing Fremantle/Perth as the new base of operations for the old Asiatic Fleet's subs. After the fleet's forced retreat from Java, Captain John Wilkes, submarine task force commander for the southwest Pacific, received word, through U.S. code breakers, of a possible Japanese invasion of Australia. Wilkes and his assistant, Captain James Fife, ordered five boats to guard the approaches to Darwin. It seemed then that the fleet's withdrawal to Australia had been strategically advantageous.

However, it soon turned out that the Japanese command was just dithering among themselves, divided as their forces already were among China, Indochina, Burma, and the Philippines, where MacArthur's troops were still holding out on Corregidor and Bataan. From there, MacArthur called on the Fremantle submarines for special missions to the Philippines. Wilkes and Fife dispatched various subs to support the relief effort on Corregidor and finally to evacuate personnel from there, while the defense boats remained in place at Darwin in case of attack.

Eventually, the threat of invasion of Australia dissolved, Corregidor fell, and Admiral King—commander in chief of the U.S. fleet—had to decide whether to leave the former Asiatic Fleet in place in Australia or bring it back to Pearl Harbor to consolidate with the Pacific Fleet. After much deliberation, King decided to keep the old Asiatic Fleet—now the Southwest Pacific Force—where it was. Clay Blair thinks this was the wrong move, forcing the nineteen fleet subs—the only ones properly equipped to cover the vast, three-million-square-mile stretch of the southwest Pacific assigned them—through days of extra travel among islands where Japanese vessels could easily hide. The distance the subs had to travel from Fremantle to get to their patrol waters took huge amounts of fuel, severely limiting their time on patrol. Furthermore, Blair pinpoints the Luzon Strait as the optimum hunting ground, the strategic bottleneck through which all Japanese shipping had to pass as it steamed between Luzon, at the northern tip of the Philippines, and Formosa. But it took Fremantle subs two weeks to get there. Skippers had to thread their way slowly and carefully through shallow waters close to Japanese air bases. Once in the strait, they had only a few days' fuel left before they had to start the long trek home.

The Luzon Strait was the ideal hunting ground because its deep waters were perfect for submarines to submerge and lie in wait for a wealth of passing targets. In hindsight, one can see that concentrating subs in these waters would have made perfect sense, rather than dispersing them over three million square miles of poorly defended islands. If Admiral King had zeroed in on this area and consolidated all his forces at Pearl Harbor to get there, subs could have reached the straits by traveling a straight shot across the open Pacific. Because these deep waters were safer than those northwest of Australia, the subs could have traveled on the surface at high speeds. Refueling at Midway or Johnston Island, the fleets could have shared staff and material. As it was, the two widely dispersed fleets vied with each other over targets as well as resources. The Southwest Pacific Force was last on the pipeline of scarce material, costing the Fremantle boats spare parts, modern upgrades such as radar and sonar, fresh torpedoes, and relief crews to spell the exhausted sailors just in from patrol.[7]

Despite the hardships the navy was experiencing with the Fremantle/Perth problem, Jim's career surged forward with his transfer from *S-39* to *Skipjack*. Phoebe's letter to her daughter about Jim's letters indicates that, besides missing his family, Jim expressed another chief theme at this time. He voiced a constant faith in aggressive fighting, holding it as the ultimate key to getting home sooner. In this he was like many men of that period. As a skipper, however, he had to voice his belief more as a conviction than a hope, and he received more recognition for it. Frank Bennett, a young ensign on *Skipjack* when Jim took over, remembered: "The thing that pleased us the most was his aggressive way of pursuing the purpose for which we were there, namely to sink Japanese ships."

And the *Skipjack* would help him do it. Unlike the decrepit *S-39, Skipjack* was a modern "fleet boat," built in 1936 and equipped with all the improvements of her class of boats, the *Salmon* class. She had four torpedo tubes aft and four forward; could dive within sixty seconds; and had new lightweight, supposedly high-performance diesel engines. She had a new system of power supply (called "diesel-electric" drive) that allowed her to cruise on the surface and charge batteries at the same time. This was a great improvement over the S-boat, which had to lay to in some hidden cove or lee of an island or—as a last resort—the open sea, where it floated like a sitting duck for hours while its engines recharged the batteries. The *Skipjack* could travel farther and faster than the coastal S-boats, and it could dive deeper. And, finally, *Skipjack* was air-conditioned, which kept the men more comfortable and reduced the condensation on the inner hull that could cause electrical short circuits.

She also had a new device—the Torpedo Data Computer (TDC)—that used information from the periscope or sonar on an enemy ship's course to set the path for her own torpedoes—already in their tubes—to intercept the ship. This was a welcome improvement over the S-boat's torpedo officer having to set the course by hand, load the torpedoes into the tubes, then maneuver the whole submarine in the direction of the torpedo run.

Skipjack torpedo officer Paul Loustaunau recalled the step up from the S-boats as "the difference between a rowboat and a battleship. On these [fleet] boats, ninety percent of your operations are pushing buttons."

Jim took this step up gladly, and on the long trek north up the west coast of Australia from Fremantle to their patrol waters, he got to know his men, a crew of fifty-five as compared to the *S-39*'s forty-two. "There is plenty of time during a patrol," Ensign Frank Bennett remembered, "for the officers and Captain to become very well acquainted." Jim put this time to good use with crew as well as officers. "Captain Coe knew what he and his crew were out there for," electrician Tom Davis wrote me. "He didn't just stay up in officers' quarters; he mingled with the men on watch in every compartment. Sometimes he would even eat in the crew's mess."

Frank Bennett concurred with another memory regarding mealtime. "Captain Coe was careful to consider the needs of the enlisted men at all times. He insisted that they get to eat the same meals as the officers."

As with the *S-39*, this egalitarianism paid off. But it also seems the only sensible way to lead on a submarine, where every man had to—in a pinch—be able to take over any other man's job. There was no corner on knowledge, no fixed hierarchy of skill. Everyone had equal power to affect outcomes. This policy made egalitarian rather than top-down leadership the only sensible way to manage one's ship (although there were many officers who led in an authoritarian style). Egalitarian leadership took flexibility, common sense, humor, a "pleasing personality," and vision, or an ongoing sense of purpose. Jim Coe quickly showed *Skipjack*'s crew all of these.

15

On our March 1999 research trip to Washington, D.C., my brother Henry and I met Jeanine Allen, a fellow war orphan whose father— Lloyd McKenzie —had been lost on the submarine *Triton* in March of 1943. Jeanine opened her door to us with her arms full of flowers she was repotting, and I felt an instant bond. She was fresh-faced, without makeup, and beautiful with wide-set brown eyes full of curiosity. She welcomed Henry and me in, and we soon felt like we were in our own living room sharing our lifelong hope that a mistake had been made, that our dads were really alive and well somewhere— maybe on some Pacific island. Jeanine made her postwar schooldays come alive with the image of herself in her first-grade classroom, her round face pressed against the window as fathers just home from war hurried up the walk for their kids. Their wives were with them, giddy with excitement as their kids raced from the school into their daddies' arms. Even though Jeanine's mother had told her that her father had been lost, Jeanine never stopped believing that he'd be the next soldier striding up the walk in front of all her classmates.

It was one of the rare times that I wasn't restrained or censoring myself in front of a stranger; as soon as Jeanine got us settled in the living room with cups of tea, the three of us talked straight from the heart. We quickly found that in addition to fantasies, we also shared many of the same realities of missing fathers. Jeanine's mother had remarried, just as ours had, and there was a silent but palpable conflict between the living husband and the dead hero. Silence about the lost fathers seemed to be the only way the widows could cope.

The next day Jeanine drove us to the National Archives in College Park, Maryland, where she steered Henry and me to relevant World War II sections and files, saving us time. She's been researching the fate of *Triton* for years.

We sat at a table in a cavernous research room looking at deck logs, the monthly documents of ships in which each four-hour watch is recorded. The *Skipjack*'s logs show that Jim took over her command on March 28, 1942. From this day on, every officer recording his watch begins his entry with a statement new to *Skipjack*'s deck logs: "At war with Japan." I showed Jeanine, asking her whether she'd ever seen this in the many deck logs she's perused. She shook her head; then Henry suggested that it might be something Jim thought up as a way of keeping their purpose uppermost in his officers' minds. I could feel my eyes widening over the table. If this were true, if this was a signature part of Jim's leadership, it brought together other testimonies: his mother's talk of his letters, plus his men's memories of his faith in aggressive tactics to bring them home sooner. His reputation for aggression, then, his difference from the cautious skippers who got bilged out of the fleet, had not been a fluke or just an adherence to external training. It was an internal discipline that Jim deliberately cultivated, a focus he taught his men from the first day he came aboard. I was filled with the sudden realization of Jim as a strong and purposeful leader, a person who thought he could make a real difference in something as huge and chaotic as war.

Later, I wrote to other World War II sub skippers, asking them whether they'd ever seen this phrase or used it themselves. Slade Cutter, decorated skipper of the high-scoring *Seahorse,* echoed what they all told me: "The 'At war with Japan' was your father's idea and a good one. We never used the phrase in the ship's log. Nor, do I believe, did anyone else."

Even when the boat was safely moored, as *Skipjack* was in Fremantle for two weeks after Jim took over, a similar entry appears with each change of watch: "Conditions Normal. At war with Japan" or "At war with Japan. Moored as before."

These *Skipjack* logs are in pencil, on yellowish, thick, fuzzy-textured pages like the school drawing paper we were issued as children in art class. The pencil marks are embedded in the deep nap of the page, inviting touch. I ran my fingers back and forth over the bottom of each page, feeling Jim's signature. The minute paper hairs plumped around his marks and worked magic: I could see Jim staring at this same page some fifty-seven years ago. He's in his wardroom on *Skipjack,* sitting on the edge of his bunk with the logbook open on his knees. His hair is a damp mahogany, and his khaki shirt has sweat stains under the arms and across his back. Behind him on the wall is a photo of my brother Henry as a toddler. (In an earlier interview, *Skipjack* torpedo officer Paul Loustaunau told me that that picture had been on Jim's wall.) Now, I picture Jim's knuckles curl around a pencil, and I note that he's left-handed.

Yellowish pages blot Jim out, and I'm suddenly back in the archives. I look up and see Henry across the table, taking notes in a crabbed left hand.

The deck log's April 11, 1942, entry marks the beginning of *Skipjack*'s drills: "1700: Underway in accordance with orders of higher authority. At war with Japan." They practice exercises for "Depth Charge Attack, Collision, Lighting Power Failure, Forward Engine Room: Chlorine after battle" (caused by seawater seeping into the battery well). Then, on April 13, they're back in port: "Moored as before. At war with Japan."

On April 14, they steam north for their patrol area in the South China Sea. This is when the war-patrol report—the skipper's detailed day-to-day narrative—takes over. Whereas the deck log is simply a series of abbreviated notes by the officers in charge of each successive four-hour watch and signed at the end of each day by the skipper, the patrol report is written or closely edited by the skipper himself. It provides detailed coverage of patrol routes—with uncensored place names and specific latitude and longitude—and it gives Japanese shipping and maneuvers and reports on boat efficiency and handling, mechanical breakdowns and repairs, crew effectiveness, approaches and attacks, and recommendations for the future. The report is thus the essential teaching document of submarine warfare for task-force commanders and other navy brass on shore, and skippers knew as they wrote that it would get plenty of scrutiny. Jim took full advantage of this by writing his heart out for needed improvements. Some of these recommendations were ignored, but at least in the vital matter of defective torpedoes, he was able to fight and write his way through the entrenched smugness of the navy's Bureau of Ordnance to effect change.

But even before coming across his torpedo analyses, I was thrilled to discover this additional source of Jim's own words. Reading his patrol reports

Skipjack's path of third patrol (her first under Jim Coe as skipper).

showed me how he strategized, and because he seemed to be very clearly and methodically thinking his way down the page, I could imaginatively hear a voice saying the words. It was slow and a bit worried, as if articulating opened up a whole new passel of problems that vaguely distracted him.

On April 15 and 16, 1942, *Skipjack* steamed up the west coast of Australia. She made for Ombai Strait, on the north side of the island of Timor. On April 17, the men transferred a sick crewman to *Skipjack*'s motor boat, which then met a small seaplane for evacuation. After summarizing this operation, Jim made his first pitch for a fleet improvement: "0840— . . . Had we had a small collapsible rubber boat aboard, the one-hour period of getting M.B. (motor boat) in and out of water and restowed could have been eliminated. All this time we had about ten men on deck, various gear about, and were in no condition to dive. . . . All submarines should be provided with a collapsible rubber boat for a rush job such as this one."[1]

After eleven more days steaming north, the *Skipjack* reached the Manipa Straits (between the islands of Buru and Seram). Jim made another suggestion: "2100–2400—Passing through Manipa Straits. No ships sighted. Several blinking lights sighted on the hills of Booroo. This passage is so narrow that by moonlight as existed this night it is impossible to pass through on surface undetected. If the primary object is to gain some station to North undetected, then I believe the route should be off West Coast of Booroo and well clear of beach."

The last sentence's conditionals, "If the primary object" and "I believe," show an evolving attention to audience over the first entry. Jim would need this more diplomatic tone in future entries with more at stake.

On day eighteen, they reached the Balabac Strait at the north end of Borneo: "0254–1731—Submerged patrol passing through Balabac Straits. This is a narrow bottle-neck easily stopped by mines. The enemy could plug this opening and still use the shallow and narrow passages between the reefs to the South which would not be feasible for our submarines. I was glad to get through this."

From the strait, they headed northwest across the South China Sea, making for Camranh Bay off French Indochina (Vietnam). On the twenty-third day, May 6, they sighted their first ship along the Indochina coast. Jim wrote: "The moon was behind us and to approach on surface would end in our certain sighting. Therefore we changed course to South and ran at full speed on four main engines (16.4 knots) in order to gain a position ahead of target prior to dawn. We kept easing over ahead as range increased." (This maneuver is known as an end-around and was increasingly used as the war progressed.) An hour and a half later (at 4:36 in the morning), he reported: "Submerged, being about 18,000 yards ahead and about 20 degrees on port bow of target. Commenced approach. Fired three torpedoes at 0527 to 0527-20, range 500 yards. One hit at 0527-34, target sinking and completely out of sight at 0529-44. She was a 6000 ton heavily loaded freighter.

For further details see 'Attacks' and 'Ships sighted.'" The section on "Attacks" shows that Jim was able to take what was essentially a mistake and innovate a correction: "I misgauged our approach speed in an effort to fire at a low range, and got in too close to wait for a favorable track and gyro angle. Let go when range was 650 yards and distance off track was about 300 with around 50 degrees right gyro angle indicated and 20 degree track." In plain English, after submerging to periscope depth at 18,000 yards ahead of his target, Jim starts an approach. Both boats steam toward each other. Jim miscalculates the closing speed and finds himself too close to the target to wait for it to zig or zag sideways and thus present a wider target for him to shoot at, as he'd been trained to do. Instead, he faces a narrow target: bow first. But under threat of the ship spotting his periscope in the moonlight and attacking first, Jim quickly resets his torpedoes to this narrower angle and shoots.

> Fired three torpedoes with periscope and TDC, using as points of aim, 1-foremast, 2-amidships, 3-mainmast. A single loud explosion occurred 34 seconds after firing first shot or 25 seconds after the firing of the second, and 14 seconds after firing third. Immediately upon hearing explosion raised periscope and observed target to be heeled badly to port, down by bow and breaking in two just under stack amidships. Fuel oil was pouring out port side at main deck evidently from full tanks. Her bow slid under, stern came out of water showing a big red single screw [propeller] which never stopped turning over and she slipped on down completely in just two minutes after being hit. . . . We crept off to the East at 150 feet fully expecting retaliatory measures, which did not materialize.

Jim and his crew were lucky; at least one torpedo in their spread worked perfectly: "Although torpedo depth setting was 10 feet, it is believed that during 500–600 yard run, fish [torpedo] was not up to that depth and magnetic exploder took charge, blowing entire bottom out of target and thus accounting for fast sinking." This sinking converted Jim to the new piece of equipment on board (the Torpedo Data Computer): "As I came to the *Skipjack* just prior to this patrol and had become only slightly acquainted with the TDC since then, my intention on this first approach was to fire straight bow shots using Mark VI angle solver for periscope bearing. I felt very sheepish in discovering I had overshot the correct firing point with insufficient time and range for an adjustment. I was therefore profoundly impressed in discovering that ignoring my error in position, the TDC had kept grinding away and all was not yet lost; I give all credit to that magic box for the resultant hit and am now 'convinced.'"

The above account, which Jim saw as a lucky accommodation to error, the official naval chronicler Theodore Roscoe recasts as pioneering a bold new strategy called "down-the-throat":

> The first successful down-the-throat shot on official record was fired by Lieutenant Commander Coe, early in *Skipjack's* third patrol. . . .
>
> Here was a situation that demanded instantaneous adjustment. The Jap freighter might be armed, and the submarine, almost dead ahead, was in that tactical position deplored by pre-war doctrine. According to current theory, Coe should have gone deep and prayed. He did neither.[2]
>
> [Skipper Lew Parks in *Pompano* had made the first attempt at a down-the-throat shot, on January 17, 1942. But the torpedo malfunctioned.]

Another trick of the moon that night—and perhaps bad periscope optics— showed *Skipjack's* target much bigger than it really was. Postwar records identify it as *Kanan Maru,* a cargoman of only twenty-five hundred tons, significantly smaller than the six thousand tonner of Jim's original estimate.

Torpedo officer Paul Loustaunau remembered another incident in this attack that doesn't show up in the patrol report. Referring to the TDC, he said, "The skipper didn't understand the system too well, but the executive officer knew it real well, so he told me what to do, to come down and get the torpedoes. I kept matching it up, and the second torpedo hit, and the ship went down real fast. The skipper called, 'Tell the torpedoman in the forward room to come up here right away.' He wanted me to see the ship. Oh, you know, nobody else would do that! Talk about a morale-builder!"

Later that same day, in the afternoon, *Skipjack* sighted another ship. Jim approached the other boat, carefully and patiently closing the distance from fifteen thousand to twenty-five hundred yards, and fired three torpedoes. At only one thousand yards after leaving the ship, there were two loud explosions, and columns of water shot up against the target in the background, but no hits. Jim conjectures the two torpedoes were premature.

This day, then, although yielding first blood for the *Skipjack* and undoubtedly thrilling its crew, also gave them their first exposure to the unreliable Mark XIV torpedo. Although it saved them in the first instance, the second encounter must have eroded the crew's confidence. With the price of firing being certain detection by the enemy, every defective torpedo created a residue of hesitation, doubt, and distrust for future attacks. And, of course, torpedoes were in short supply. Skipjack had used up six on this day alone, only one of which damaged the enemy.

The next day, May 7, *Skipjack* chased and fired at two ships in a column, but got no hits. On the morning of May 8, she gave chase to another ship, with no results. Late in the afternoon, she sighted three "beef boats," or cargo carriers, in a column, escorted by one destroyer. Jim decided to try for them "in order of size."

> 1513—Fired two torpedoes at the 10,000 ton AK, the third in column, range 700 yards. One and possibly two hits 25–30 seconds later, broke him in two aft of bridge and he started down, commencing to man life boats and rafts at once.
>
> 1514—Fired four stern torpedoes at second vessel, the 7,000 ton AK, using a wide spread which included Maru and the DD [destroyer]. Mean range about 1500 yards. Heard a dull thud one minute later and observed second vessel to be definitely down by stern about 15 degrees. It appeared she had been "pooped" [shot in the stern] by one torpedo. DD now coming in fast for depth charge attack so we went to 300 feet and ran silently on 090 degrees to clear area. Sound reported three explosions at short intervals commencing one minute after firing first stern tube shot.

Jim may have gone this deep—300 feet, a defensive luxury compared to the 150-foot limit of the old S-boats—because submariners were by this time catching on to the Japanese navy's only flaw, its depth charge. As Clay Blair notes: "It was not a powerful charge—perhaps no more than 200 or 300 pounds—and it apparently could not be detonated below 150 feet. . . . To escape its full force, the submarines had merely to go deeper than 150 feet."[3]

And so *Skipjack* escaped: "1520–1644—Counted 39 depth charges dropped in pairs in groups of about 10. Closest estimated range 300 yards . . . ; no damage."

Two hours and forty-five minutes later, *Skipjack* came up to periscope depth. Enemy ships were still in sight, but the sub's battery was too low to make another attack. Jim reported watching the ships for an hour. The first ship they'd hit was missing, now completely sunk. The second was slowly sinking, with the water level now even with the main deck in the stern. The third and smallest ship sat close by, as survivors and cargo were transferred to her from the second ship. And around all of these ran the destroyer, continually circling the two ships.

There was a dark side to this observation. Some of it was required in order to verify outcomes of attacks. But even with hanging around a sinking long enough to snap photographs through the periscope or from the deck, many reported sinkings didn't hold up in postwar matches with Japanese reports. And this observation was dangerous, of course, when target ships were in convoy. Those ships that didn't have destroyer escorts stuck together. Robert Casey describes the strategy: "All [Japanese merchant ships] had depth charges and deck guns fore and aft. Whenever he [Jim] attacked one, the other was certain to close in and drop a load of bombs."[4]

But beyond this danger, there were other, more personal costs of watching targets go down, and they involve the instinctive empathy all seamen, regardless of nationality, have for each other. This identification seems more intense for submariners, with their greater exposure to the sea's dangers. The sub vets I talked with didn't readily volunteer this feeling. But when questioned closely, they admitted to qualms on their first experience of another ship's destruction. Jim Ward, veteran of *Tuna* and *Rasher*, and in 1999 a guide on the USS *Lionfish*, the World War II memorial submarine in Fall River, Massachusetts, told me that early in his career he heard one of his sub's targets implode under water pressure as it went down. He reported hearing a crying sound that was almost human as the hull broke up. "You felt sorry for the Japanese at that moment," he said.

Ned Beach writes of another sinking ship: "We could all hear the grim cascade, the torrent of suddenly released black water smashing through thin bulkheads, filling compartments with shocking speed, compressing the air with the frenzied pressure of the sea. Then another noise, crunching, rending [as the ship hits bottom]."[5] And George Grider even admits to empathic imagery:

> Now we pictured the men themselves, trapped in tiny compartments like our own as the torpedo hit. In the moment of the explosion, we looked at one another with stiff faces.
>
> About two and a half minutes later came an unexpected climax. Plainly through our hull we could hear a crunching noise, the sound of metal collapsing inwardly. It was easy enough to interpret that. Some of the poor devils had got a compartment sealed off in the first seconds after she had been torpedoed, and they had lived a pitiful fraction of time longer in the sealed compartment until the submarine sank deep enough for the water-pressure to collapse the compartment.[6]

Watching the process had to be as bad as listening to it. Paul Fussell suggests this in his example of what German U-boat sub crews kept on hand: "[They had] plenty of animal intestines to shoot to the surface to deceive those imagining that their depth-charges have done the job. Some U-boats, it was said, carried (in cold storage) severed legs and arms to add verisimilitude."[7]

But these details—even if included by some candid skipper in his war patrol report—would not make it to light in wartime. Such gruesome truths were bad for morale. In the celebrated third patrol of the sub *Wahoo,* Mush Morton, although a very descriptive writer about torpedo attacks, leaves out the consequences of the up-close shooting by *Wahoo's* deck guns of the many Japanese in the water: "Fired 4" gun at largest scow loaded with troops. Although all troops in this boat apparently jumped in the water our fire was returned by small caliber machine guns. We then opened fire with everything we had. Then set course 085 degrees at flank speed to overtake the cripple and tanker."[8] And although the *Wahoo* crew obtained ample photographic evidence of torpedoed targets on this patrol, a selection of which were splashed across newspapers on her triumphant homecoming, there were no photos of this shooting incident. Newspapers were sanitized this way for morale purposes. "Among the thousands of published photographs of sailors and submariners being rescued after torpedoings and sinkings," says Paul Fussell, "no evidence of severed limbs, intestines, or floating parts."[9]

But surely such sights had to be part of naval warfare. And Jim had ample opportunity to see it all. When he surfaced in *S-39* after sinking the freighter, Robert Casey reports: "The ocean was littered with floating stuff. Apparently the ship had been carrying something in bales. . . . It looked as if there might be several acres of this stuff and to Captain Coe it seemed that there were at least fifty Japs hanging onto every bale."[10]

Even if there weren't blood and guts among those bales, it must have been disturbing—if not wrenching—to turn one's back on these seamen. In the movie *Das Boot,* there is a similar scene, where the conflicted submariners reluctantly turn the boat away from the drowning enemy, ignoring their cries for help. On wartime submarines, which had little room for prisoners, the suppression of the natural bond between humans at peril on the sea must be frequent and devastating.

Did it take a toll? To look at pictures of Jim by the time he takes command of the *Cisco* a year later, it does. As mentioned earlier, in Jim's two short years of war, he appears to age decades, looking middle-aged in his final photographs when he was just thirty-three.

But back on May 8, 1942, epitomizing the "Silent Service"—the name the submarine service had gotten for forbidding its men to talk about what they did—Jim showed nothing as he watched the two sinkings from the enemy convoy through the periscope. Then he moved *Skipjack* off the scene and resumed the patrol. It was the evening of the twenty-fifth day, and he had the full confidence of the crew. "He was a likeable guy and a good captain," said crewman John Rutkofske. "He wasn't scared to take it on!"

Torpedo officer Paul Loustaunau told Henry and me: "When your dad came on, he was the best thing that ever happened. . . . When I think of him I have to start giggling. He was such a happy-go-lucky person. But God, he was very serious when he had to be."

These opposite traits are intensified by the nature of the skipper's job. Historian Norman Friedman explains: "Unlike the surface commander, the sub captain is forced to work face to face with his entire crew. But even with that closeness, the captain is alone. He can't look out the window like a surface commander and see friendly ships everywhere or communicate quickly with the fleet commanders."[11]

The report of *Skipjack*'s third patrol reflects this paradox, as Jim narrated long days of boredom punctuated by short bursts of tension and terror. He tied these extremes together by teaching, couching his lessons as personal learning so that he wouldn't come across as preachy: "0332—Surfaced. There was now insufficient time before dawn to run to position ahead of target. This experience convinces me that the surest system of attack on a target picked up at night is to run on surface to a position ahead of him on horizon and wait for dawn submerged approach."

This was the night of May 11, with a ship silhouetted against the moon. *Skipjack* submerged and began an approach, but the men soon found that they had underestimated the angle on the bow (so they didn't go far enough left or right of dead center to catch the ship).

On May 13 near Camranh Bay, *Skipjack* failed another attempt to attack two military auxiliary ships after a careful two-hour approach. Here we see the first evidence of Jim's frustration with defective torpedoes: "1759—Fired two torpedoes at second target at range of 800 yards. Actually saw smoke wake of 1st pass under poop of target. No hits! These fish set at 10 feet but must be running mighty deep below 1000 yards. Target fired at us with forward deck gun for about 15 minutes. . . . This was a bitter dose and I now have little confidence in these torpedoes."

On the afternoon of May 15 at periscope depth, the bow planes, which keep the boat at its assigned level when submerged, jammed in the up position. To prevent a quick, uncontrolled lunge to the surface (a broach), the crew had to flood ballast tanks with seawater to hold the sub down. They were able to hold her this way at about one hundred feet below the surface for two hours while they repaired the jammed motor. Jim, in an appendix to the patrol report, describes how the repair crew instigated a manual option that would break the electrical circuit to the driving motors in case of future jams, letting the bow and stern planesmen operate the trim gear by hand. This is a good example of how self-contained and innovative submarines were; they required the best of American ingenuity. Flexibility, adaptability, quick decision making, and hands-on engineering determined their survival; if the solution didn't work, and they broached in the face of the enemy, death or capture was almost a certainty. So keeping the sub seaworthy at every moment was as vitally important as attack and defense tactics.

Later on that same day, *Skipjack* received a dispatch from headquarters that a Japanese aircraft transport had been spotted heading for *Skipjack's* patrol waters, and she was told to intercept it. Jim set a course for the reported rendezvous point, but never saw anything. His report on this incident contains more teaching for the brass at base, although couched—as before—as a personal lesson softened by "in my opinion," and "I feel." This language would ease the lesson on up the chain of command. "The depth of the water in the vicinity of the rendezvous point was from 29–33 fathoms which, in my opinion, is definitely too shallow for this type submarine to take effective evasive steps in case of a DD or air anti-submarine attack. I feel that when possible, the depth of water should be at least 60 fathoms and the attack point along enemy track selected accordingly."

Jim could have been speaking here for the *Perch's* David Hurt, who now fought for survival in a Japanese prison camp because he'd been similarly ordered to water that was too shallow. This order, along with the navy's denial of torpedo defects, underscores the impracticality of a system where deskbound brass—many of whom had never even been in a submarine—gave orders to men on the front lines.

On May 17, 1942, after setting a course toward Balabac Strait to start the long route back to base as scheduled, Jim sighted two more ships. It was night, and he commenced the strategy that night approaches earlier in this patrol had taught him: to steam on the surface to a point well ahead of the ships, then submerge by dawn and lie in wait.

He did this until the ships, both armed military auxiliaries, got close enough that he could pick out the bigger of them. He made an approach, working his way to a dead-ringer range of seven hundred yards, then fired.

Was so sure of a hit that I held up firing second fish to save it. Watched smoke from wake pass directly under stern counter of target; no explosion.

[One minute later] Fired a second torpedo which exploded with a terrific bang at 0556-45. This fish struck at point of aim under bridge. Target heeled about 15 degrees to port at once and started to settle by bow. Life boats were being manned at once. . . . Ship sank at about 0643.

Jim then fired two torpedoes at the second ship, which was steering "a snake-like course." Whether this zigzagging was effective or the torpedoes were duds is not known, but they missed—from a dead-ringer range of one thousand yards and then again at two thousand. The second ship circled the sinking ship's lifeboats and fired her deck guns continually at *Skipjack,* still at periscope depth. Jim decided to go deep and wait until the target, thinking the sub was gone, stopped to pick up her survivors from the lifeboats. However, on resurfacing later, he found that the target had already scooped up all survivors and was steaming off to the north at high speed, well out of range. He recorded the lesson: "This was a golden opportunity which I feel I botched by firing before having better data. In such a case it would probably be best to sit tight undetected until rescue vessel was stopped in the act of picking up boats before firing. Our consolation was in having at least eliminated the big one after an 'approach' of 42 miles."

Although the patrol report doesn't show it, the sinking of "the big one" may well have been when Jim let the crew line up at the periscope to have a look at their work. "On one sinking, he let everyone in the control room take a look," electrician Tom Davis remembers. Because the remaining ship in the above account was firing wildly while glued to its lifeboats, and the first ship took more than an hour to sink, Jim may have thought he had the margin to let everyone line up.

This is just what Jim did on the *S-39* (and what he told reporter Casey he wouldn't do again). But perhaps he couldn't help celebrating this long-awaited success. By May 17, when they turned toward Fremantle and the two-week return trip, they had sunk four ships. This was a hefty change in fortune for the beleaguered Southwest Pacific Force.

16

When *Skipjack* got back to base, her men found themselves minor celebrities, with the best record of sinkings for a single patrol of any Asiatic (now Southwest Pacific Force) submarine.[1] Their performance greatly boosted the morale of the Fremantle-based fleet, which was frustrated and despondent. None of the southwest Pacific subs patrolling that spring had had any results. *Skipjack* gave them hope that they were not out of the fight.

But the boat paid a price for her success. In his patrol report Jim describes her condition on docking:

> Broken rings, cracked blocks, wiped connecting rod and main bearings, cylinder water jackets corroding through, excessive fresh water leakage and a host of lesser casualties spared no engine. Luckily at least one main generator engine was kept running until we reached the Malay Barrier during the return to Fremantle. The passage of Lombok Strait however, seemed to indicate to the generator engines that they had completed their jobs and upon surfacing that night, neither would run. The charge was put in on the two auxiliary engines.
>
> During the trip South from Lombok, as fast as one engine could be gotten in running condition, another one would break down, and our engineering plant is in a deplorable condition on completing this patrol.[2]

After defending his crew's care of the engines, Jim pulls out all the stops, but still inserts "in my opinion" to make his plea palatable to the brass: "It has been a constant hard but losing battle to keep this plant running, and in my opinion the trouble is solely due to poor design and general weakness of these engines, which was recognized by the trial board and Board of Inspection and Survey as long ago as 1938 when the engines were not recommended for acceptance."

A few months earlier, Lewis Parks, skipper of *Pompano* (Pacific Fleet, Pearl Harbor), had recommended that his sub's engines be replaced as outmoded. The *Pompano* and *Skipjack,* along with many other fleet submarines, had Hooven-Owens-Rentschler (HOR) engines, a model flawed by the necessary speedup in diesel-engine production for the war. But Skipper Parks was dressed down by his superior, Admiral Withers. In the face of all contrary evidence, Withers stubbornly declared that HOR engine performance had vastly improved over the past year. This was a bald-faced cover-up of a deficiency the navy had neither the time nor the money to correct. HOR engines were so unreliable that the company's chief engineer suffered a fatal stroke trying desperately to fix design flaws that proved uncorrectable.[3] Finally, a whole year after Jim wrote his complaint, Admiral King ordered all boats in Pearl Harbor's Squadron 12 returned to Mare Island to have their HORs replaced with Winton engines. Years later, a veteran submariner said that "the HOR engines saved the Japanese thirty or forty ships."[4]

Skipjack's engineering officer, W. Frank Bennett, wrote that the ship's men gave 1.8 hours of maintenance labor on the HOR engines for every hour of operation.[5] To fix these execrable "rock crushers" or "whores," as the men called them, the *Skipjack* needed an overhaul period of six weeks, which could have given her exhausted crew a well-earned rest. But that was not to be. Because repair services in the Southwest Pacific Force were in short supply, the boat would have to travel down the coast and around the southwestern tip of Australia to Albany, where she could tie up for band-aid repairs at the overworked sub tender, *USS Holland.* But before setting out, *Skipjack*'s crew had to fix her enough even for this abbreviated run. "There were no relief crews at that time to take over," Machinist Mate Charles "Slip" Haislip wrote me. "Before moving to Albany, W.A., we overhauled our own engines in Fremantle."

Haislip remembers Jim looking in on the overhaul: "One night while we were working [on the engines], your dad came aboard with a quart of whiskey and proceeded to the engine room. 'Let's take a break, fellas,' he said, and we had a few rounds."

Electrician's Mate Tom Davis said, "Captain Coe was just like the men he was commanding; he liked a little nip now and then."

This overhaul marks more than a year and a half that Jim had been separated from his wife and children, much of this time under great pressure to prove his aggressiveness. (By the end of this first year of war, one-third of all submarine skippers would be replaced for failure to sink ships.[6]) And now, although he'd just turned in the Southwest Pacific Force's top performance, he'd followed it up with a scathing war patrol report calling for HOR engines to be replaced and—as we shall soon see—torpedoes to be overhauled.

Jobs and reputations were ruined for less. In March, well before Jim set out on patrol, Admiral Withers sent out word that anyone who complained about the Mark VI magnetic exploder would be kicked out of the submarine force. His assistant, Captain Robert English, was squarely behind him.[7] They adhered to the claims of the Newport torpedo factory and the navy's Bureau of Ordnance that the torpedoes were fine and that all error lay with skippers and crew. When challenged to test the torpedoes, these bureaucrats said torpedoes were too scarce to "waste" in tests. A notable exception to this party line was Captain John Wilkes, who, as noted earlier, was commander of Fremantle/Albany–based submarines. He believed his skippers' accounts of deep-running and premature or nonexploding torpedoes. But Wilkes, as a captain, did not have the "flag rank" of Withers, so the admiral's policies prevailed, quashing all criticism. (Two results of this destructive policy show it stubbornly persisting far into the war: in the spring of 1943, Skippers W. J. Millican and L. P. Ramage complained of torpedoes after returning to Fremantle from their patrols, and Admiral Ralph Christie—then in charge of that station—relieved them of command.[8])

So Jim must have been pushed to desperation to complain in the patrol report, an irrevocable forum. Submarine chronicler William R. McCants says: "Career naval officers knew that 50 copies of the patrol report would be disseminated throughout the service. It was common for early war patrols during World War II to be the subject of unfounded criticisms and second-guessing by desk-bound commanders, captains, and admirals."[9]

To challenge the bureaucracy in any form went against all Jim's training up to that point. As one submariner told Clay Blair: "You have to remember that the Bureau of Ordnance was a mighty bureaucracy. A naval officer, conditioned to believe the Bureau's word was infallible in matters of ordnance, did not lightly challenge it."[10]

Before I started getting to know Jim Coe, I might have asked—given my Quaker and Vietnam-era disdain for military authority—what did Jim have to lose? If relieved of command, he'd get to at last return to Rachel and his kids and the safety of a desk job. But now that I know the keen sense of duty ingrained in him by naval training, the years of study and determination to master submarine technology and strategy, plus the pride most submarine officers took in being appointed to an operational command position, I no longer question his choices and motivation. And cementing all this background into a fiery mission was his firsthand experience of war. Australian submarine author David Jones wrote me: "The war would have been a struggle for survival for him as the Japanese quickly overran the Philippines, Singapore, and Java. He would have seen Japanese power at its peak and he would have known many people who were left behind to fall into the hands of the enemy. For him the war would have been a clear-cut struggle to control a cruel and aggressive foe."

W. J. Holmes takes note of the two fronts Jim had to fight on: "Coe, an outstanding submarine commander in action, was also articulate and forthright in his patrol reports."[11] But this candor demanded exhaustive effort. Using hand-drawn charts, graphs, and pictures illustrating attack positions, Jim had to support and elaborate every statement he made, while couching all lessons and suggestions as personal opinions so that they would travel up the chain of command. "Coe," says Clay Blair, "a methodical as well as a courageous officer, submitted a careful analysis of Mark XIV torpedo performance for his patrol."[12]

Jim placed this analysis at the end of the report, where it had the best chance of reverberating in commanders' heads after reading. To make his analysis impartial, he eliminates three of the torpedoes fired at low speed and excessive ranges. Of the eighteen left in the running—those fired at high speed and reasonable ranges—he constructs a chart of each torpedo's performance, showing its gyro angle, range, target track, and speed, along with the result. He then calls the four that hit—at 22.2 percent effectiveness—a dangerously poor outcome, concluding: "It therefore appears that these torpedoes, when fired at ranges of 500 to 800 yards, run considerably deeper than set depth and can only be depended upon to explode about 40% of the time even though they pass below target. This makes me wonder if there is any advantage in trying to gain that attack position between 500 and 1000 yards where 'you can't miss,' which has been a premise I have always tried to follow. Evidently it is only as true as torpedo performance is good." All of this diplomatic wording—"It appears that," "This makes me wonder," and "Evidently"—has now bought him the good faith to make some requests: the Bureau of Ordnance needs to give skippers the means to program its table of lead and lag angles for curved shots into the Torpedo Data Computer for attacks requiring fast action. And the anticounter mining device that renders a torpedo ineffective for five seconds after a previous torpedo has exploded should be reduced to a one-second lag time. After constructing scenarios that support this, he concludes with the biggest, most politically charged request:

> To sum up, I take full responsibility for all misses fired at ranges of over 1000 yards except the two prematures, and for one miss fired at 550 yards on an undesirable track and with a large gyro angle, although a second torpedo hit; however, the other short range misses were due, in my opinion, to torpedo defects which should be corrected.
>
> To make round trips of 8500 miles into enemy waters to gain attack positions undetected within 800 yards of enemy ships, only to find that the torpedoes run deep and over half the time will fail to explode, seems to me to be an undesirable manner of gaining information which might be determined any morning within a few miles of a torpedo station in the presence of comparatively few hazards.
>
> The above statements may seem extreme and rabid; they represent my honest opinion and explain why "sure hits" resulted in misses on this patrol. I believe that many of the wartime misses of the other submarines of this squadron are also explained by the same discussion. If it can be shown that this explanation is wrong, I shall be the first to acknowledge it.
>
> What we on the submarine firing line need is a dependable torpedo; and at least the knowledge of what the fish will or will not do. When we have this, some of those Jap ships which "got away" will start going to the bottom.

I was proud to find part of this passage and other sentences from the patrol report reproduced in Samuel Eliot Morrison's *History of Naval Opera-*

tions in World War II.[13] Having come to this project thinking that Jim was a hero in our family solely because of his fighting and dying, and being slow—from my pacifist perspective—to honor him for that reason, I was surprised and gratified to find that he was cited in an inclusive history of World War II naval operations (not just submarines) for standing up for his convictions. This was in keeping with the Quaker ideals I grew up with.

——✺——

Although it was more than he ever could have hoped for, Jim had inadvertently hit on the most favorable time to fight and write his way to a hearing on defective torpedoes. Commander Charles Lockwood, a fiery, no-nonsense, hands-on submariner, had just replaced John Wilkes as submarine task force commander for the Southwest Pacific Force. This was in April of 1942, right before Jim came off his successful maiden patrol in *Skipjack*. Lockwood had also just been promoted to rear admiral, as well as to the command of all Allied naval forces based in western Australia. This gave him the flag rank to challenge the status quo.

A feisty, independent optimist, Lockwood was disturbed by the low morale he found on his new post, and he determined to find out why the Asiatic Fleet had not slowed the Japanese onslaught in the Philippines and Java. As a newcomer who had to bring himself up to speed in order to turn the threatening Japanese tide, Lockwood read Jim's report with an open mind. And the *Skipjack's* recent sinking of four ships was added persuasion.

Paving the way, too, for this reading were many brave skippers who came before Jim in raising their voices against poor torpedoes; Tyrell Jacobs, David Hurt, Fred Warder, Lucius Chappell, Hamilton Stone, William Ferrall, Roland Pryce, and Eugene McKinney were just a few of these men. Their earlier complaints—at great risk to their careers—helped Jim's resonate up the chain of command.

After reading Jim's report, Admiral Lockwood asked the Bureau of Ordnance whether there was any evidence of deep-running or exploder defects in the Mark XIV torpedo. BuOrd fired back that there were no defects and that this was just an excuse the skippers trumped up for their own poor marksmanship.[14]

Now furious, Lockwood took matters into his own hands, giving Jim permission to conduct the tests he had lobbied for in his patrol report. Jim tested the *Skipjack*'s remaining torpedoes off Albany, Australia ("any morning within a few miles of a torpedo station") on June 20, 1942. Torpedo officer Paul Loustaunau recalled Admiral Lockwood ordering them to fire their last three torpedoes from their recent patrol through a fishnet, with an officer from BuOrd watching:

> We fired the first two torpedoes through the net and both ran about eight to ten feet deeper than set. The Bureau of Ordnance man said that we were at fault. A Chief Petty Officer, Sid Kelf, who had been on *Skipjack* but was now running the torpedo shop on the *Holland,* our tender, and I cornered Captain Coe and asked him to delay firing the last torpedo until the next day. In the meantime, Kelf took the torpedo over to the tender, unbeknownst to the BuOrd man, and overhauled it [to make sure that it conformed to bureau standards, precluding any further BuOrd criticisms]. We fired it through the net the next day and it ran fifteen feet deeper than set. Apparently this pretty well convinced the Bureau that their torpedoes were faulty because they got official word out so skippers could adjust.

The tests—showing that torpedoes set to run at a depth of ten feet burst the fishnet at eighteen to twenty-five feet down, too deep below the target hull to activate the magnetic exploder—convinced a powerful ally in Captain Bob English. But under English's questioning, BuOrd charged that Lockwood's tests were not "scientific." The tests led to "no reliable conclusions . . . because of improper torpedo trim conditions introduced," BuOrd wrote.[15] Lockwood—again furious—followed up with a second series of tests in July. The results duplicated those of June, forcing Newport to run its own tests. In August, BuOrd finally conceded that the Mark XIV ran ten feet deeper than set, and word officially went out so that skippers throughout the Pacific could adjust their torpedo settings accordingly and thus have a better chance of hitting targets.

The testing did something else as well. It showed submariners who didn't have a voice in all this wrangling, and didn't have access to the patrol reports, that Jim would speak up for them. Former *Skipjack* crewman John Rutkofske told me how the men felt after the tests: "The torpedoes were going against us. He [Jim] was a godsend because he was doing something about it. All the men give him his credit for that. He must have not been on the best of terms with the higher-ups, because they didn't want to hear about bad torpedoes."

The BuOrd's belated acknowledgment of torpedo malfunctions that finally let skippers adjust their settings, although a ray of hope to the beleaguered southwestern Pacific sub fleet, would have to last the men for longer than anyone cared to think. It was only the first in a long series of political skirmishes that forestalled the improvement of torpedoes until late in the war—1944, in fact. *Skipjack's* depth tests had addressed only the problem of torpedoes running deep. There were additional dangers of torpedoes exploding prematurely, estimated at 10 percent of the torpedo supply, and torpedoes that simply hit target hulls without exploding, estimated at an astounding 50 percent.[16] And finally, there were the deadly circling torpedoes, *Perch's* nemesis, which took out the subs *Tang* and *Tullibee*. Their incidence, although small, was well enough known in the tight-knit submarine community to inspire doubt and contribute to the sagging morale throughout 1942, as bureaucrats in BuOrd kept their heads firmly in the sand.

In addition to these ostriches, there were a few submarine administrators standing firmly in the way of progress. Admiral Ralph Christie, who inherited Lockwood's command of the southwest Pacific submarine force after Lockwood was sent to Pearl Harbor to command the central Pacific subs, retained full faith—in the face of all contrary evidence—in the magnetic exploder. This was Christie's "baby"; he'd developed it in the twenties and dug in his heels behind it after that.

In June of 1943, a full year after the *Skipjack* tests, Admiral Chester Nimitz, commander of the Pacific Fleet, finally let Lockwood order all submarines under his command to deactivate the defective magnetic exploder. This deactivation allowed torpedoes to explode on contact. But Christie, still claiming the proximity device as "a marvelous automatic engine of war," made his Fremantle skippers sail with their magnetic exploders intact.[17] This split between Lockwood and Christie further complicated operations for the already overburdened submarine commanders. "A boat going from Pearl Harbor to Australia on the exchange program," says Clay Blair, "departed with the magnetic feature deactivated. On the way down, when the boat fell under the operational control of Fife or Christie, the skippers had to reactivate the magnetic feature. Boats returning from Australia followed the opposite procedure."[18]

I shivered when I heard how obsessively entrenched Christie was. Jim was stuck until the end under Christie's command, and in the fall of 1943, he must have believed he had brought his new boat, *Cisco*—supposedly his reward for outstanding performance—in a nightmarish circle back to his bureaucratic battle of more than a year earlier. Being under the command of Christie seems a viable reason for the marked aging and worry I see in Jim's photographs of that time. When Lockwood was reassigned to the Pearl Harbor command, the Fremantle submariners lost an empathic, sensible leader.

But Lockwood went on from that first test in Jim's *Skipjack* to make the torpedo debacle his mission. Deactivating the magnetic exploder had revealed the deficiencies of the contact exploder. This was amply demonstrated by Skipper Dan Daspit in *Tinosa*, who had an enormous Japanese tanker—a nineteen-ton whale factory—dead in the water west of Truk in July of 1943. *Tinosa* fired fifteen torpedoes from a dead-ringer 875 yards off the tanker's beam, straight at the broadside of *Tonan Maru*. Not one of them exploded! *Tinosa*'s crew actually saw a torpedo bounce off the ship's hull.[19] Daspit's heroically detailed patrol report, plus his saving the last torpedo for examination back at Pearl Harbor, lit a fire under Lockwood. The admiral took two Mark XIV torpedoes out on the sub *Muskallunge* and tested them against a submerged cliff on the Hawaiian island of Kahoolawe. He discovered that in torpedoes fired head-on, hitting the target at a 90-degree track, the impact jammed the firing pin so that it didn't reach the fuse to ignite the explosive. Lockwood immediately sent this information out to all skippers, urging them to fire torpedoes at oblique angles to the target, rather than at 90 degrees.[20]

With the bureaucratic wrangling that erupted in the wake of this discovery, it wasn't until October of 1943—too late for Jim—that some submarines received torpedoes equipped with modified firing pins that worked at all angles. But this happened only on Pearl Harbor–based subs. The Southwest Pacific Force labored on with old (and scarce) torpedoes.

Nevertheless, change had begun: Lockwood had given skippers a voice at last, and their spirits rose as improvements slowly followed.

17

In June of 1942, at odds with an entrenched naval bureaucracy and knowing that the sub command might be bristling over his patrol report, Jim needed some good news. It came on June 7, 1942, with the rumor that he'd been nominated for a Navy Cross as a result of the *Skipjack*'s outstanding patrol. This must have given him the fresh confidence needed to once more sit down at his writing desk in the docked *Skipjack* and try to nudge the bureaucracy. This time, it was the labyrinthine office of Navy Supply.

After receiving a letter from the Mare Island supply office rejecting *Skipjack*'s year-old request for badly needed toilet paper, Jim fired back a response in perfect bureaucratese, complete with a square of toilet paper enclosed as a "sample of material requested":

USS SKIPJACK

June 11, 1942

From: Commanding Officer
To: Supply Officer, Navy Yard, Mare Island, California
Via: Commander Submarines, Southwest Pacific
Subject: Toilet Paper
Reference: (a) (4608) USS HOLLAND (5148) USS SKIPJACK req. 70-42 of 30 July 1941.

(b) SO NYMI Canceled invoice No. 272836

Enclosure: (1) Copy of cancelled invoice.

(2) Sample of material requested.

1. This vessel submitted a requisition for 150 rolls of toilet paper on July 30, 1941, to USS HOLLAND. The material was ordered by HOLLAND from the Supply Officer, Navy Yard, Mare Island, for delivery to USS SKIPJACK.

2. The Supply Officer, Navy Yard, Mare Island, on November 26, 1941, cancelled Mare Island Invoice No. 272836 with the stamped notation "Cancelled—-cannot identify." This cancelled invoice was received by SKIPJACK on June 10, 1942.

3. During the 11 and three-fourths months elapsing from the time of ordering the toilet paper and the present date, the SKIPJACK personnel, despite their best efforts to await delivery of subject material, have been unable to wait on numerous occasions, and the situation is now quite acute, especially during depth charge attack by the "back-stabbers."

4. Enclosure (2) is a sample of the desired material provided for the information of the Supply Officer, Navy Yard, Mare Island. The Commanding Officer, USS SKIPJACK cannot help but wonder what is being used in Mare Island in place of this unidentifiable material, once well known to this command.

5. SKIPJACK personnel during this period have become accustomed to the use of "ersatz," i.e., the vast amount of incoming non-essential paper work, and in so doing feel that the wish of the Bureau of Ships for the reduction of paper work is being complied with, thus effectively killing two birds with one stone.

6. It is believed by this command that the stamped notation "cannot identify" was possible error, and that this is simply a case of shortage of strategic war material, the SKIPJACK probably being low on the priority list.

7. In order to cooperate in our war effort at a small local sacrifice, the SKIPJACK desires no further action be taken until the end of the current war, which has created a situation aptly described as "war is hell."

J. W. Coe[1]

Skipjack torpedo officer Paul Loustaunau remembered Jim giving a handwritten version of this letter to the yeoman, telling him to type it up. But once the words sank in, the yeoman went looking for help. Loustaunau remembers, "The yeoman brought it to the exec. and said, 'Mr. Clemenson, I think you better read this before he sends it out!' And Clemenson, he read the thing, and he showed it to me and said, 'Look! Look at what this guy's gonna *do!*'

"And I said, 'Okay. We gotta talk him outta this!' I had the letter, so we went back to the skipper's cabin and knocked on his door and said, 'Uh, sir, this letter.'"

"What about it?"

"You sure you want to send it?"

"I wrote it, didn't I?"

"Well . . . uh . . . Captain . . . it's up to you."

"He gave a wave of his hand, and we sent it out. Well, that letter created more consternation over the whole U.S. fleet!" [This wouldn't happen until—in good bureaucratic time—seven months later, which we'll take up in the next chapter.]

Meanwhile, the summer of 1942 continued to prove interesting for *Skipjack*. On June 19, Jim was promoted to lieutenant commander. On June 20, Admiral Lockwood stretched the historic fishnet across the harbor off Albany, and *Skipjack* tested its last three torpedoes, proving they ran deep. Then, two days later, Jim received confirmation of the news he'd heard bandied about back in Fremantle.

Skipjack crewman Charles Haislip wrote me, recalling the ceremony. On June 22, 1942, all hands were called to the deck of the *Skipjack*, and Vice Admiral Leary, commander of the navy forces in the southwest Pacific, came on board from the USS *Holland* and awarded Jim the Navy Cross. Then he pinned the submarine combat pin on the chests of all *Skipjack*'s men. Commander Leary returned to the tender, and Jim addressed the crew. He said that *they* were the ones who had really earned the cross. He told them to look down at the medal on their chests to always remind themselves of that, and he thanked them for their service.

So Jim's outspokenness about bad torpedoes hadn't led to career damage after all. Although it was probably true that the higher-ups weren't fond of him, they couldn't ignore his record of sinkings. That forced them to listen. Undoubtedly he knew this, and the passion in his patrol report was fueled by his success on the water. That—or pure anger, frustration, and exhaustion. But the care with which he framed his report suggests more than impulse; it's a voice seizing a newfound credibility while acknowledging its own limitations. And just as it did on the water, this strategic balance of aggression and humility paid off on the page.

Later in the summer, a Richmond, Indiana, newspaper reported excerpts from a letter Jim wrote his mother for her birthday. Dated July 16, almost a month after the Navy Cross ceremony, the blend of confidence and humility is there:

> I am well and fit, having just finished a good rest between business trips, another of which I am about to start on. . . . Just knock on wood now and then, Mother, for me and don't worry, for we are going to get this job over with soon.
>
> Please thank all of my Richmond friends who have asked about me and tell them we are doing our best out here to enable all of us to come home again soon. . . .
>
> I am finally a lieutenant commander, along with many others, but rank doesn't mean a thing to me now and that's no fooling. This war has changed all that—it's the job you're doing and how you're doing it that counts. The gold braid is superfluous. . . .
>
> They gave me the Navy Cross recently. My officers and crew and the two boats we served on really won it, but it is a good feeling to know that after all the training and time that my country has spent on me that I have at last been able to repay it to some extent, and hope to keep on doing it with interest. . . .
>
> Keep your spirits up and other people's, too. That helps most.[2]

The "business trip" Jim mentions to Phoebe started on July 18, 1942, patrolling the west and north coasts of Timor, an island northwest of Australia and then crossing the Ombai Straits to the south and east coasts of Alor, a smaller island north of Timor. This proved to be a frustrating patrol, with no hits and the severest depth charging to date. It showed me, more than the successful patrols ever could, how Jim salvaged good out of bad. His patrol report is full of lessons learned from each failed approach and bone-jarring counterattack.[3]

Monk Hendrix, an officer of *S-39,* summed it up: "I won't forget how he [Jim] always said to make the best of what you've got and try to keep it in fighting shape. I learned good submarine from him."[4]

I like to think of this precept—to make the best of what you have—as distinctly different from the unspoken ethic of positive thinking that I grew up with in the fifties. A key ingredient of that thinking was denial, the kind that prevented my family from admitting any problems as my stepfather lurched off drunk to do brain surgery.

Jim's positive thinking, in contrast, issues from a ready acknowledgment of failure. "This unsuccessful attack," he writes in his patrol report, "brought home several points." This is the order of every event, with failure listed first, then the lessons salvaged. This transformation of failure into something good is the point of Ariel's song ("Full fathom five") in Shakespeare's *Tempest,* which originally launched this search. It is fully embodied on this fourth *Skipjack* patrol.

After three weeks without targets, they finally sight a small ship (about twenty-five hundred tons) close to the shore of Ambon Island. Jim elaborates in the patrol report: "Any misses would put torpedoes on beach 3000 yards away, and since our position would be given away, it was questionable if firing would be wise. However, TDC solution was excellent, target looked like Q-ship reported by *Thresher* (silhouette 100) which needed eliminating, and we needed a hit to snap us out of a long period of lethargy."[5]

They set torpedo depth at six feet to compensate for running deep and then fired two torpedoes. They immediately dove to eighty feet. They waited for two and a half minutes, but hearing no explosions, they started to rise back up to have a look and *bang!* "Terrific explosion close aboard, our depth 75 feet. This damaged pit log, knocked needle off conning tower depth gauge, knocked paint off overhead in machinery spaces, and started slight leakage around studs of circulating water line flange on hull in forward engine room. This charge was evidently very close aboard, probably aft. It must have been dropped by a plane using origin of our torpedo wakes as a point of aim, since only screws heard were weak. Went to 250 feet and ran silently."

But ten minutes later, *Skipjack* was jarred by a series of six depth charges, all close aboard: "These shocks were all severe and the boat actually made a noticeable 'jerk' followed by a shudder, during which time water could be heard swooshing through superstructure or perhaps through ballast tanks and out opened vents. They were either much larger than all others previously felt by any of the personnel on this boat, or very much closer. Since they were dropped one at a time and at regular intervals of about three minutes, coupled with the fact that no A.S. [antisubmarine] vessels were sighted just previous to our firing, indicates that charges were dropped by planes."

Skipjack takes five hours to run silently away from the planes. That night, when they are finally clear and back up to periscope depth, Jim analyzes the situation: "It was, of course, a great disappointment to miss on this attack in view of excellent solution on TDC, and a careful 'rehash' showed that one of these fish must have run under the target without exploding. The fish were not heard to explode if and when they hit the beach. It was a rude shock to be counter-attacked so quickly and accurately with no A.S. forces in sight, and brings home the fact that such an attack must be expected after firing during daylight close to enemy air bases."

The long dearth of targets seems to have made Jim less cautious here. The shock of such a close answering depth charge is almost indescribable. Tom Parks tries:

> If the charge is close the click of the detonator pistol could be heard before the charge exploded. That was the time to be really nervous.
>
> The noise when a depth charge explodes is almost deafening. Water doesn't compress and the force of the charge hits the boat like a huge hammer.[6]

Add to this the chilling sense of being stalked with no outlet for your fear. You must hold yourself back from the natural fight-or-flight response and stifle cries of fear, surprise, or pain. The model is your skipper; he must appear calm, giving orders in a quiet, steady voice.

One of the best descriptions that suggests the sensory confusion and inarticulate nature of a close depth charging is provided by crewman

Frenchy Corneau of the submarine *Flasher:* "I could feel the pain all over my skin."[7]

Skipjack's men experienced much of this on August 17, 1942. Jim wrote about these men in his patrol report: "There was a marked difference in apparent effect of depth charging between old submariners and the new men aboard for their first cruise in subs. The depth charging on 17 August 1942, which was the most severe experienced to date by any one on the boat, put solemn faces on some of the old hands and caused them to pass off numerous uncomplimentary but apt remarks concerning the Japanese in general and those in the Ambon area in particular. The new men were more openly nervous."

Six days later, they made another failed attack. Shortly afterward, Jim sighted a sampan, a small local fishing boat, which he suspected might be an antisubmarine vessel in disguise. But not knowing, he didn't attack it, and Admiral Lockwood, in his endorsement of this patrol report, says that although the patrol was carried out well and aggressively, the sampan "should have been destroyed by gunfire."

By contrast, George Grider, skipper of *Flasher,* attacked two sampans by gunfire in February of 1945. This might show that submarine warfare grew more vicious over time, or it might show a difference in the two commanders' characters. As a pacifist it's tempting to read Jim as more humane than Grider, but—as I've now learned—any such judgment is too glib for wartime. Instead, Lockwood may have been trying to loosen the restrictions against attacking civilians that Naval Academy graduates had internalized in formative peacetime training. But in August of 1942, only seven months into the war, there wasn't the command, reason, or precedent to attack sampans, so Jim hesitated.

Long after the war, Grider himself sounds like a pacifist when he describes the man blown out of his sampan by a grenade the *Flasher's* men threw in to finish the little boat off. "Many a night I think of that poor man, who probably wasn't even Japanese, who perhaps wasn't a combatant at all, whose sampan was doubtless his only livelihood. He . . . had given me my deepest scar of the entire war, in that one flashing glance."[8] This suggests that the two skippers—both Naval Academy graduates—probably had the same values around peace, war, and human life and that the difference in their behavior came down to a few moments' hesitation or confusion. In Jim's case, these were moments in which the target slipped away.

—

During this frustrating patrol, Admiral Lockwood was trying to reorganize the southwest Pacific sub fleet, which he considered "a bastard organization." He tried to restructure it according to the one at Pearl Harbor. But because submarines made up the only real naval fighting force on the west coast of Australia, the fleet had become a sort of fiefdom that various administrators fought over. "Chips" Carpender, Lockwood's replacement as commander of the overall naval forces on the west coast of Australia, and Lockwood, who remained solely in charge of submarines, squabbled over the restructuring. They also fought over everything else—from the use of slang in the skippers' patrol reports, for example "fish" for torpedoes, to whether skippers were being aggressive enough.[9] These turf wars made the commanders' reviews of the patrol reports—in the form of endorsement letters attached to them and circulated among the fleet—excessively picky and combative, with none of the squabbles contributing anything to beating the Japanese.

As Jim had with the toilet-paper letter, another submarine commander, pushed to the limit by the pettiness of his superiors, fired off a poem. Here are excerpts:

Squat Div. One
by A. H. Taylor

They're on their duff from morn till nite;
They're never wrong, they're always right;
To hear them talk they're in the fight.
. . . .

A boat comes in off a patrol,
The skipper tallies up his toll
And writes it up for all concerned.
He feels right proud of the job he's done,

But the staffies say he shoulda used his gun!
Three fish for a ship of two score ton?
Outrageous! He should have used but one!

. . . .

The freighter he sunk settled by the stern—
With depth set right she'd split in two!
So tell me, what is the skipper to do?
He's on the spot and doing his best,
But that's not enough by the acid test.
The staff must analyze his case
And pick it apart to save their face.

. . . . [10]

Robert English, now head of the Pearl Harbor submarines, railed against this poem as "subversive literature" and tried to punish its author. That, of course, just gave the poem faster and wider circulation throughout the sub fleet.

And in Fremantle, the situation of picky, carping commanders deteriorated to the point that Carpender and Lockwood refused to speak to one another. Lockwood devised missions that would take him away from the sub base altogether for long periods. Needless to say, this absence didn't help the Fremantle skippers.

In addition to overly critical assessment of patrol reports in which deskbound commanders seemed to be one-upping each other in the unfettered use of hindsight, these leaders—according to Clay Blair—showed no imagination or skill in deployment of their sub force. As mentioned earlier, Blair saw the division of submarines between Pearl Harbor and Fremantle as spreading the fleet dangerously thin over too big an area; he cites the deepwater, strategic bottleneck of Luzon Strait through which the majority of Japanese shipping passed as a focal point around which a single fleet should have been deployed. But this strategic geography was ignored as administrators hunched over patrol reports, looking for weaknesses in skippers' courage, firing skills, or diction.[11]

18

Besides carping, myopic administrators, skippers of the shorthanded Fremantle fleet had to contend with battle fatigue. The strain of command was fierce and ongoing. In addition to the constant threat of enemy (and even friendly) air, surface, and submarine attack throughout the patrol, there was always the danger of mechanical failure preventing the boat from surfacing, setting it afire, or generating deadly gas. Submarine duty was hazardous even without the enemy. The strain of these ever-present dangers was compounded by the constant breakdown of equipment. And in port, while skippers' patrol reports were closely scrutinized for error, skippers had to supervise overhauls of their boats by relief crews, if they were lucky, or—for the Fremantle fleet—by their own exhausted men.

Although I was not able to find naval policy giving skippers any respite from all this work, there is at least one item of correspondence showing that the navy—but not till late in the war—was aware of the need for such a policy. On May 11, 1945, U.S. senator C. Wayland Brooks of the Committee on Naval Affairs writes Admiral Randall Jacobs, chief of the Bureau of Naval Personnel, that skippers are under a severe mental strain because of the demands on them. He suggests "a system in the submarine command whereby men who have had a given number of missions be put on the same basis as aviators are after completion of fifty missions."[1]

In a reply of May 14, 1945, Captain H. Crommelin of the Bureau of Personnel mandates a policy for enlisted men: (1) that complete relief crews be available at bases and aboard tenders; (2) that after patrols, the entire crew get two weeks of rest and recuperation; (3) that a relief crew refits the submarine and prepares it for its next patrol; and (4) that one-third of the regular crew be replaced by relief crew after each patrol to allow crewmen longer periods in port.[2]

We have seen, however, that southwest Pacific submarines were not even provided with spare parts and submarine tenders to repair their boats, much less relief crews. Fremantle-based Walter Lundgren, crewman of *Cisco,* Jim's next command, remembers: "After three war patrols you were supposed to be transferred into a relief crew and replaced from the relief crew, as I understood the rule. But I made seven [patrols] in a row on the *Bowfin,* and was starting my eighth when the war was over."

So Jim's men were stretched thin, and Jim himself—heading into his sixth successive patrol after thirty-nine months of continual service—was undoubtedly exhausted. Although there appears to be no documented policy of relief for commanders, there is anecdotal evidence of a limit on successive patrols for skippers instituted by Admiral Lockwood after he was sent from the Fremantle command in January of 1943 to the Pearl Harbor command. Clay Blair says that Lockwood, even though short of qualified sub skippers, was concerned for their welfare and wanted to reduce submarine losses. He therefore sent his skippers for a rest after five consecutive patrols.[3] Submarine author James DeRose explains: "The five patrol-in-command limit was created in Pearl Harbor and rigidly enforced by Lockwood. He sometimes relieved men after 3–4 patrols, without prejudice, if he thought they were burned out. Christie and the Australian command were not quite as good at this policy."

Lockwood was more humane and concerned with his skippers' welfare than Christie. Clay Blair reports that Lockwood and Christie locked horns over this issue after the outstanding skipper Sam Dealey, of *Harder,* was lost in August of 1944: "Lockwood and his staff took the view that Christie had pushed Dealey too hard with the luckless Patrol Number 5B and had made an error in judgment in permitting him to take *Harder* on Patrol Number 6."[4]

Battle fatigue was an omnipresent danger to the fleet, where well-trained, aggressive skippers were in short supply. The skipper of the hard-hitting *Flasher* felt the effects in the fall of 1944: "Both Reuben Whitaker and his exec, Ray DuBois, returned from *Flasher*'s third patrol physically and mentally drained. . . . He had reached the point, he said later, where he hated to make contact with the enemy," Clay Blair writes. After racking up one of the leading scores for ships sunk, Whitaker stepped down as skipper after five successive patrols.[5]

George Grider gives an idea of the unremitting strain of command when he first took over *Flasher* in 1944: "In every other wartime situation in which I had found myself, no matter how much reliance might have been placed on me, I had known there was someone nearby who had to make the final decision and assume the final responsibility. I had become conditioned to the idea of calling the captain in any emergency. Now, suddenly, there was no one to call but me. It was a glorious feeling to stand on the bridge and look at the *Flasher* and know she was all mine, but it was also a lonely feeling, and a disquieting one."[6]

In the World War II novel *The Caine Mutiny*, the new captain of the minesweeper USS *Caine* elaborates the tortuous nature of this loneliness: "You can't understand command till you've had it. It's the loneliest, most oppressive job in the whole world. It's a nightmare, unless you're an ox. You're forever teetering along a tiny path of correct decisions and good luck that meanders through an infinite gloom of possible mistakes. At any moment you can commit a hundred manslaughters."[7]

Lockwood, as a former submarine skipper himself, was well aware of this oppressive balancing act. His five-patrol limit, despite its inadherence by the southwest Pacific command, still appears to have had effects. The seventy-seven top skippers of World War II listed by Clay Blair, although ranging from two to ten in number of patrols commanded, averaged five apiece. Jim, rated seventy-second on this list in terms of ships/tonnage sunk, commanded seven patrols.[8]

So he must have been buoyed by the orders he received in the fall of 1942. *Skipjack* was to leave Fremantle and sail to Pearl Harbor, patrolling en route. This meant that Jim might get to see his family after two full years away. In a letter to his mother, he hedges his bets: "I think it would be best if no one mails gifts over for the holidays. We can have a family reunion later and celebrate all the anniversaries and holidays at that time."[9]

The *Skipjack* set out on September 27, short—as was the rest of the southwest Pacific fleet—of good torpedoes. The Fremantle squadron averaged about seventy-five torpedo shots a month, but Lockwood (still in command there at the time) was sent only eighteen torpedoes a month. He dealt with this shortage by emphasizing the offensive use of deck guns and assigning some of his submarines to mine-laying operations.[10] But the aggressive skippers received torpedoes, albeit some of them well under par. *Skipjack* set off with twelve Mark XIVs and four Mark IXs, an ancient model that hadn't been test fired for twenty-three years.[11] Jim loaded these in the stern tubes.

Meanwhile, Admiral Nimitz had ordered Robert English, still commander of Pearl Harbor–based submarines, to send a contingent of boats to Truk in the Caroline Islands to intercept Japanese ships en route to the Solomon Islands. The submarines were also to report enemy ship movements. This intelligence would advise Admiral Ghormley in his fight for Guadalcanal. English sent eleven of his submarines to Truk in July through September. Targets were scarce for these boats, and antisubmarine measures were fierce near the island, all of which didn't bode well for *Skipjack,* arriving at the end of this operation. Clay Blair concludes that this strategy was a bad move, interrupting the sub war against Japanese merchant shipping.[12]

En route to Truk, *Skipjack* mounted a forty-two-mile chase after a smudge on the horizon. By noon, after an end-around approach, *Skipjack* submerged ahead of what turned out to be two ships, a seven-thousand-ton AK (supply vessel) and an old, smoke-belching freighter of about four thousand tons, which Jim later identified as an AP (military auxiliary). *Skipjack* fired two torpedoes at the AK at 950 yards; both fish hit and exploded amidships. Then she fired one torpedo at the AP, which had turned away from its track. Both ships fired at the sub's periscope. The AP started zigzagging toward the eastern horizon, with *Skipjack* in pursuit. The AK sagged in the middle as it took on water; she appeared to be heavily loaded, with bomber fuselages on her bow deck. Lifeboats went over her side.

Jim followed the AP's smoke over the horizon. He spent the rest of the night and part of the next day chasing her, then unsuccessfully attacked her. She escaped his torpedoes by a last-minute zig, setting the tone for the rest of the patrol. In the next two weeks, *Skipjack* was called to various targets from Truk to New Ireland Island, northwest of the Solomons. None of these targets materialized. On November 10, they received a last order to a new location to intercept "big stuff." *Skipjack* cracked on the speed and on November 11 sighted a large tanker. Jim started an end around on her at night, planning a dawn attack.

At dawn *Skipjack* submerged twenty thousand yards ahead of the target and began her approach. As she got within shooting distance, the target made a sharp zig, revealing a destroyer escort behind her. The escort made straight for *Skipjack,* and Jim was afraid she'd spotted *Skipjack's* periscope. The escort, however, ran right over them, leaving the tanker abeam of *Skipjack* at a good firing range of twelve hundred yards. Jim ordered four torpedoes fired in a spread from the target's stem to stern.

The men then waited for the explosions, hardly breathing. But there was nothing, no sound but that of the escort's propeller as it wheeled around and came on fast, riding *Skipjack's* torpedo tracks right down on her waiting men. The sub dove to 250 feet, and her men heard echoes bouncing off her hull from the escort's sonar.

The destroyer dropped three depth charges, which exploded about two hundred yards from *Skipjack* as she tried to creep away. Then the escort pinged the waters again, finding the sub with its sonar. It dropped a depth charge right on top of *Skipjack,* which exploded above the men at about 150 feet, breaking lightbulbs and causing air leaks. The *Skipjack* crept away. In the eerie red lights of the control room, the officers whispered orders. Sweat slid down the men's sides into their shoes as they strained after the pinging, now fainter. The destroyer's propeller noises gradually faded.

An hour later the sub rose to periscope depth, and Jim took stock: "Nothing in sight. It was a bitter dose to miss such a valuable target, especially after shadowing him all night during a 135 mile run. Believe our error was in using 10.5 knots which was speed we had determined him as making good during night, while he actually was making about 13 along zigzag track. Periscope ranges during short submerged approach in dim twilight not accurate enough to show this speed error. An expensive lesson."[13]

Although I'm proud of Jim's willingness to admit failure, I also wonder whether he was being strategic here. If one's superiors are going to pick over one's performance, why not beat them to the punch?

Still, even with Jim handing his superiors ready criticisms, Commander

English in Pearl Harbor, who refers to himself in a lofty six-word third person in his endorsement letter (attached to the patrol report for all to see), has to quibble:

> The Commander Submarine Force, Pacific Fleet, does not agree with the commanding officer's analysis of the attack on the tanker on November 12th. Considering the range and the estimated target length, the spread employed would have permitted at least one hit, even with an error in target speed as great as 4 knots. With a known speed of advance of 10.5 knots as determined by all night tracking, it is not conceivable that the enemy would employ a zigzag plan, particularly at night, which would so materially reduce the speed made good. There is a possibility that the enemy, in order to conserve fuel and still obtain maximum protection against submarine attack, is employing high speeds during daylight and economical speeds at night.

English here is presupposing that all torpedoes fired were functioning as they should, a large assumption given the problem of defective torpedoes. And his differing about enemy behavior, whether they zigzag or slow down at night, serves no conceivable purpose except the appearance of keeping him in the fray.

After the "expensive lesson" of the November 12 miss of the large tanker, the *Skipjack* proceeded to Jaluit in the Marshall Islands, en route to Pearl Harbor. By this time, three-quarters of the crew were sick to their stomachs. Although Clay Blair attributes this to bad drinking water, Jim thought they were simply burned out and used this exhaustion in his patrol report to advocate for an authentic relief policy: "Since most of the men unaffected [by the sickness] had just come aboard from relief crews, while the majority of those sick have made all patrols since the war started, it may be that the latter group is simply a bit run down. If this is the case, it is believed that efficiency would be increased by leaving one section in as relief crew every third patrol, to be replaced by a section of the relief crew."[14]

On November 19 *Skipjack* surfaced about twenty-six miles northwest of Jaluit and was spotted by a destroyer. The sub was in the process of recharging batteries; she cranked on the steam and then dove. The destroyer dropped eleven depth charges, but they landed far enough astern that *Skip-jack* escaped.

On November 26, after sixty days of patrolling, *Skipjack* reached Pearl Harbor. Her results were meager, and her men were weak and run down. Out of five vessels attacked and two more chased but unable to close, *Skip-jack* sank only one seven-thousand-ton freighter, a disappointing result for a long and aggressive patrol. And all during this time, the men had to make constant repairs to keep the boat running.

Eroded copper piping caused salting of 3,900 gallons of the crew's fresh water and allowed sixty gallons of dirty water from a waste tank to flood into a dry food storage compartment. Leaky engine exhaust valves required the men to wipe them constantly, to little avail. Resistors failed, causing the boat to lose all propulsion for one twenty-five-minute period until they could deenergize the trip circuits and replace the failed resistor. Luckily, they were submerged when this happened.

The batteries leaked excessive amounts of hydrogen gas, which built up during all-day dives. Jim had ordered new batteries back in July, but to no avail. At moderate speeds the port propeller shaft made loud squeaks, which were detectable to the enemy. And a submerged antenna leaked so that there was no use of the radio on dives.

Through all this, plus ten days of nausea that was probably caused by the copper piping eroding into their water, the crew jerry-rigged repairs, aggressively pursued targets, and kept up their morale. Jim commended them in his report, saying he was especially gratified by the lookouts, who spotted Japanese planes on seven occasions, all early enough for *Skipjack* to submerge and avoid detection. One of these lookouts, Petty Officer Joseph McGrievy, known for his outstanding night vision, even remembers some fun: "Gifford Clemenson was the exec. [executive officer]. And Giff was a real gung-ho guy. He wanted to fight the Japs face to face, so he says to Barger [another petty officer] and I, 'Make me a Jap man-o-war flag out of canvas, and sew an American ensign on the other side of it, and when we surface on Jap ships, we'll fly the Jap flag till we get up close, then turn the American flag on 'em and start shooting.' Well, Captain Coe didn't agree with that, so we didn't do anything with it. But we brought that two-sided flag back to Pearl Harbor and Mare Island."

More antics ensued when they reached Pearl Harbor. Jim's toilet-paper letter of the past summer had finally reached the naval supply depot in Mare Island; Quartermaster McGrievy remembers rumors that all the officers in the navy's Supply Corps "had to stand at attention for three days because of that toilet-paper letter." The letter had then apparently been mimeographed and slipped to various submariners coming in for overhaul, where it spread like wildfire throughout the fleet.

Now, as *Skipjack* made her way into the harbor and readied her mooring lines, Jim and the crew saw toilet-paper streamers blowing from the lights along the wharf and noticed pyramids of toilet paper stacked up seven feet high on the dock. Two men balanced a long dowel on their shoulders with rolls of toilet paper spooled along it; they marched down the wharf to greet the *Skipjack* as a band played behind them. Band members wore toilet-paper neckties in place of navy neckerchiefs. The wind section had toilet paper rolled up inside their instruments; when the players blew, white streamers unfurled from trumpets and horns. Admirals and staff came on board, grinning at Jim and his officers as Jim ordered his quartermasters to load the badly needed toilet paper on board. After all the frustration of bad torpedoes, equipment breakdowns, defeat and dissolution of the Asiatic Fleet, nausea, overwork, and carping commanders, Jim and his men were finally getting some recognition—if not exactly for their fighting, at least for their wit.

But this notice, according to Ned Beach, was double edged. After the admirals instituted a policy of meeting homecoming submarines with all the foodstuffs the men had missed while out on patrol, Beach reports that "whenever *Skipjack* returned from patrol, no matter where she happened to put in, she received no fruit, no vegetables, and no ice cream. Instead, she invariably received her own outstandingly distinctive tribute—cartons and cartons of toilet paper."[15]

This first toilet-paper reception, in December of 1942, was the only evidence Jim had seen of his letter's effect. He had no way of knowing how far it had already traveled or how long it would last in navy annals. Paul Fussell, in his book *Wartime,* suggests a reason for all this attention. Fussell traces the recurrent theme of soldiers sacrificing their individuality to the mindless military machine in both world wars. This sacrifice could involve one's mortal safety, as in the case of the navy's refusal to acknowledge problems with their torpedoes. So for submariners, the military's mindless protocol that cements the status quo (what Fussell terms "chickenshit") is doubly despised because it endangers entire crews of seventy or more men whenever they go out on patrol. Jim was thus like Fussell's infantry soldiers, who "defend themselves against the grosser kinds of chickenshit by devising compensatory brief narratives—rumor-jokes, they might be called. If good enough, these will fly on their own wings all over the army."[16]

Jim's letter flew all over the navy, winging back to the States where it landed on President Roosevelt's desk, finding its way into submarine histories and even a Hollywood movie, and eventually coming to rest at the Navy Supply Corps School in Pensacola, Florida. There, it still hangs on the wall under a banner that reads, "Don't let this happen to you!"[17] Nancy Richards, collections manager of the Bowfin Submarine Museum in Honolulu, tells me the letter, titled "Paperwork," is their most requested piece of submarine history.

Tom Parks of *S-39* wrote me that the letter had a dual effect: "It was one of the best pieces of humor to come out of WWII but it also had serious intent. Captain Coe's crew was being inconvenienced and he didn't like that. The letter became famous throughout the Navy and did much to boost morale."

Skipjack torpedo officer Paul Loustaunau recalled its aftereffects:

About the time the letter reached Pearl Harbor, the Navy was sending some submarines off together with some troops to go down to some little islands there the Japanese held. And among them was a Roosevelt boy. I think it was John Roosevelt, one of the older boys. And he happened to see the letter, and he got a big kick out of it, and before he went off to this mission, he mailed a copy to his dad. And the President knew the officer who was in charge of the Mare Island Supply Depot, and he sent him a copy of the letter and said "Boy, you're really doing a good job!"

And we came in there about eight or nine months later. I went into the Depot to get something; the officer in charge happened to come in. He saw I was in submarines, and he had two sons who were in submarines. He said, "Oh, so you're a submariner." I said "Yes sir."

"You know my two boys?"

"Oh yes sir."

"Fine. Well, it's good to see you. By the way, what ship you off of?"

"The *Skipjack*," I said.

"The *Skipjack*! Get outta here!"

My mother told me about the letter when I was in fifth or sixth grade. It was a safe memory for her, because she laughed while she told it. But I knew, although I was too young to put it into words, that just under her chuckling about the *Skipjack* men having to use pages of navy regulations in place of toilet paper, there was grief. So although I didn't think it was very funny—what's funny, anyway, to a kid about a letter?—I laughed with her.

She never told us kids that the letter got into the 1959 movie *Operation Petticoat.* Cary Grant, playing captain of the World War II fictional sub *Sea Tiger,* issues a stinging memo asking what the heck supply officers are using in place of toilet paper, that "unidentifiable material once so well known to this command?" My mother loved Cary Grant, and she surely would have told us if she had seen the movie. But even her favorite actor couldn't entice her to sit through a war-related movie. This was also the year before she finally divorced our stepfather, and their marriage was so bad that she would not have added to her misery by renewing any reminders of Jim.

It strikes me that although my mother didn't have words for it, she disdained the dishonest way World War II was purveyed to the public. She vetoed not only war movies but also group memorial services (for instance, those held in memory of the lost men from Jim's Naval Academy class of 1930), Memorial Day commemorations, and musicals such as *South Pacific.* The satire with which Jim handled "chickenshit" had hardened into a silent contempt in Mother, something I mistook most of my life for alienation or disloyalty toward Jim. I now realize it might have been plain good taste on her part to turn away from the way World War II was—in the words of Paul

Fussell—"systematically sanitized and Norman Rockwellized, not to mention Disneyfied." Fussell could as well be talking here about Mother when he says of the World War II vets that "optimistic publicity and euphemism had rendered their experience so falsely that it would never be readily communicable."[18]

No one wanted to hear the war's real effects—on traumatized vets or troubled widows. Our friends and neighbors of the fifties would rather have Mother humming songs from *South Pacific* or sighing over Cary Grant in *Operation Petticoat*. All the grown children of lost World War II men in the American WWII Orphans Network have the same story: their mothers' heartache was systematically ignored by the postwar culture.

And so Jim worked a miracle sixty years after disappearing. In a way that is indeed "rich and strange"—his satirizing a lack of *toilet paper*(!)—he led me to a complete turnaround about Mother's silence. Rather than withholding anything, our mother might well have thought she was giving us kids something, preserving Jim from caricatures of the World War II hero she heard all around her. This way, we could think of him—or discover him later—as he really was. To have given us the view of World War II as a duet between Mary Martin and Cary Grant to the accompaniment of Glenn Miller would have diminished Jim. And not wanting to err on the other side—showing us such a particular individual that she would unleash an avalanche of pent-up grief on us—she could only keep quiet about him. Yes, it would have been nice for her to have saved his letters to pass on to us some day. But they were hers, their shared, private language of love—probably intensified by war. I think about the few love letters my husband and I have written each other, and I doubt if I'd want our daughter reading them—and not because of any prurient material but because of the banalities lovers feel confident in expressing to each other. They can have a diminishing effect on the page.

And yes, it would have been nice for Mother to tell us anecdotes that would reveal Jim's character without making us sad at what we lost. But that is a narrative balancing act far beyond most of us; it was unfair and unthinking of me to ever expect it.

And finally, it would have been great if Mother had been able to come clean with us about her own grief, openly mourn Jim in a way that would provide a healthy catharsis for us all. But that would have been impossible without inflaming Frank, and it is asking her to go beyond her own historical context, to perform a feat of independence and candor way out of keeping with the values and standards of her day.

So all of my judgments of Mother's silence about Jim as shallow or unloving were most likely wrong. They were certainly unfair. Again I'm amazed at the universality and power of Shakespeare's image of the submerged father that put me on this journey and resonates throughout it. A search for the lost father has led me to a new understanding of my mother. In death, she's grown beyond the frustrated victim of Frank I grew up with; she's now a strong guardian of Jim's memory.

19

In January of 1943, Jim received a new assignment, his reward for more than two years of continuous command. He was ordered to new construction back east, out of danger, and would reunite with his family for a precious six months. The fleet boat *Cisco,* now under construction at Portsmouth Naval Shipyard, was his new command.

After the toilet-paper reception in Pearl Harbor, then four days' rest, Jim sailed *Skipjack* back to Mare Island, California, for overhaul. Although I don't know this, it's likely that Mother traveled to Honolulu and/or California to meet him. On January 17 he said goodbye to his men and caught a train back east. It would be his first visit with family in more than three years, and I imagine him coming home a changed man. The depth chargings, near-suffocation of prolonged submergence, and the horrors of seeing Manila, Java, and other ports fall must have made him more serious and appreciative of life than he had ever been. Danger and deprivation could have made all the things that passed by his train window—orderly towns and peaceful, green countryside—doubly precious and lovely because they had all been nearly lost to him.

Jim stopped in Richmond, Indiana, to visit his mother. While there, he gave a speech to one of the city's service clubs. Jim did nothing to aggravate the censors, but he clearly tried to stress to his audience that the war in the Pacific wasn't a simple series of heroic feats against an inferior or subhuman enemy, as had been painted in the press. The Richmond newspaper summarized his message: "Even though we have had reports of men who have shot down a dozen or more Japs or some member of the armed forces taking on a number of the enemy single-handed, that doesn't mean we have them conquered by any means, Coe warned. . . . 'Those Japs are excellent seamen and they have good ships. They are hard nuts to crack.' . . . He said the people of this nation have not taken the Japs as seriously as they should and believes that the sooner Americans recognize the fact these Japs are doing an efficient job of fighting the sooner we will win the war."[1]

Again, Jim's words brought home, as nothing else could, what our family lost in him. Here was a man who would have taught his kids to look squarely at problems and acknowledge them, rather than deny or cover them up as Frank had led us to do.

I also noticed how general Jim kept his comments, with no mention of specific incidents, locations, or names of ships. The submarine service warned all skippers: "Officers and crew will at all times be security conscious. It is of vital importance that every officer and man prior to going ashore has impressed upon his mind the fact that he must refrain from talking to *anyone* on the subject of where the ship has been, what was accomplished, how long it has been gone, and that the ship's name should never be mentioned ashore. They must further realize that the subjects of submarine construction and submarine equipment are also taboo. POUND THIS IDEA INTO YOUR PERSONNEL."[2]

The submarine service was more invested in censorship than other branches of the service for two reasons. Subs had been ordered, shortly after the attack on Pearl Harbor, to conduct unrestricted warfare, contrary to international convention. And a U.S. congressman, Andrew Jackson May, in a fall 1942 newspaper interview, unwittingly disclosed submariners' greatest secret protection up till then: that the Japanese weren't setting their depth charges deep enough to destroy our boats.[3] The newspaper published the story, and the Japanese soon reset their depth charges to inflict real damage on our subs. From then on, the submarine force became the "Silent Service," with its men sworn to secrecy about their activities.

Unfortunately, this silence kept the American public from knowing— even to this day—how crucial submarines were to our victory. Although they made up only 1.6 percent of our navy, submarines sank 30 percent of the Japanese navy and 60 percent of the Japanese merchant marine— imposing a virtual stranglehold on Japan.[4] And this was with defective torpedoes, a leadership in disarray, boats that needed constant fixing, and shortages of equipment and manpower.

This remarkable initiative and persistence have gone unheralded. Nor does the public know submariners' great sacrifice: they suffered the worst losses of any military branch, with 22 percent of their men killed or missing in action.[5]

The secrecy cultivated by the "Silent Service" kept its feats—like its boats—submerged. While newspapers and movies reported the air, ground, and surface fleet battles daily, submarine warfare went largely unnoted. "Even now," says one submarine aficionado, "it is common for books on World War II to address the American submarine role with only a passing reference or a footnote, while emphasizing surface fleet confrontations, island fighting, and the air war."[6] Tom Brokaw's *Greatest Generation* books epitomize this: no submariners.

After his visit to Richmond, Indiana, Jim continued east to Wilmington, Delaware, and finally Portsmouth, New Hampshire, where he and Ray rented a small house near the shipyard for his next assignment. My sister, Jean, remembers switching from Wilmington's Tower Hill School to a parochial school in Portsmouth, where she was in the first grade. She recalls ducking under her desk in air-raid drills and vigorous war games against "Japs and Germans" out on the playground. In one of the coldest winters on record, Jean remembers walking to school through snowbanks, and Mother once told me about Jim sledding down a hill with two-and-one-half-year old Henry on his back.

Jim started work at Portsmouth Naval Shipyard on January 30. His new submarine, *Cisco,* had just been launched, and Jim had to fit her out and take on crew and officers. *Cisco* was among the first of a new class of thicker-skinned submarines; her hull was 7/8-inch thick as opposed to the previous 9/16-inch steel. This and an updated trim pump allowed diving to four hundred feet instead of the three hundred feet of earlier fleet boats, such as *Skipjack.* In a feverish competition with other boatyards to put out the most ships fastest, Portsmouth Naval Shipyard had military and civilian relief crews working day and night on *Cisco.* She set a record for fastest construction. The *Portsmouth Herald* reported proudly on December 24, 1942: "The USS Cisco was on the ways a few hours more than 56 days, as her keel was laid Oct. 28. . . . As near as can be determined, this is the best time that has ever been made in any one of the United States yards where underseas craft are built."[7]

One can get an idea of just how fast this was by comparing other boats in *Cisco*'s class (*Balao* class) of submarines coming off the ways in Portsmouth in the same year. The number of days from keel laying to launching for each ship was as follows:

Archerfish	126 days
Balao	123
Batfish	129
Bowfin	137
Cabrilla	128
Capelin	128
Cisco	56
Crevalle	100

Cisco's record time—doubly amazing in a winter so cold that the Piscataqua River froze solid—inspired a new pugilistic fervor and competition in sub crews: "Until recently," the local paper reported, "the keel-laying to sinking time [of the first enemy ship] was 492 days, but a short time ago one of our ships, built in Portsmouth, reported that it had chopped nearly 100 days from that record. The goal these men are aiming at now is to register their first victory over an Axis warship or merchantman in less than a year."[8]

In less than a year, *Cisco* will indeed have attacked her first convoy, but no one would ever know the results. Her story remains forever unfinished. Many veterans I interviewed think that this is a direct result of *Cisco* being rushed off the ways and into battle in virtually half the time other subs were built. She was a new model, and her workforce had to learn how to fashion her new thicker skin plus her increased carrying capacity (an eighty-five-man crew as compared to *Skipjack*'s fifty-five men), all at breakneck speed. Submarine historian Stefan Terzibaschitsch claims, however: "Worker morale was very high. And teams competed with one another to clear slipways as quickly as possible. Three shifts were worked, often with voluntary over-time and extra-shift working."[9]

But two crewmen who got off *Cisco* before her first patrol wrote me sto-ries of workers cutting corners: "They took some parts from other boats under construction to save time," says *Cisco* apprentice seaman Walter Lund-gren. And Machinist's Mate Second Class Slip Haislip elaborates: "When I had the below-deck watch one night I noticed a motor with another boat's name on the name plate. I started looking at other motors and pumps. A lot of other boats' names showed up, so I started asking questions. Why? That is when I found out they were trying to build the Cisco in record time by using parts and gear that were assigned to other boats that they hadn't even laid the keels for."

I received this letter in August 1999 at the Submarine Veterans of World War II convention that I attended in Fort Worth. While there, I met crew-men on the submarine *Balao,* which was docked next to *Cisco* in the spring and summer of 1943. These men reported being spooked by *Cisco. Balao's* Marcus Klein remembered scuttlebutt that the *Cisco's* welds were brittle and breaking because of the bitter cold. "Yes, *Cisco* was welded in below-zero temperatures," *Balao* crewman Bill Hart concurred. "Several of us assigned to *Balao* were requested to volunteer to become crew on *Cisco.* Joe Barrett, our COB [chief of boat] quietly advised us against it." Fellow crewman Sid Wellikson remembered a friend on the *Cisco,* once she started training runs in the spring, telling him that "she leaked like a sieve!"

Men's memories, of course, are tinged by hindsight. Knowing that *Cisco* never made it home makes some sub vets look on her now with a jaundiced eye, so it's valuable to turn to sources who balance this tendency: "As a graduate student at MIT, I spent the summer of 1942 on the waterfront of Portsmouth Naval Shipyard overseeing construction of submarines," says retired navy captain Edward Arentzen. "An excellent inspection system, headed by H. C. Preble—a survivor of the *Squalus*—was in effect. I can as-sure you that welds were properly checked particularly any involving the pressure hull. In cold temperatures appropriate pre-heat was used before starting welds. I am reasonably certain that the *Cisco's* loss was not due to its expedited construction. . . . Scuttlebutt from sailors is true only occasionally."

Another voice against the scuttlebutt I heard at the convention was retired admiral Jack Lee, one of Jim's classmates at the Naval Academy. "It seems that you made many contacts at the convention and that some of them left you with the impression that your father took the Cisco to war in a dangerous condition. It is very difficult for me to accept that as a fact. Your father was not a timid man and I feel certain that he insisted that the Cisco be in top notch condition when she left the building yard."

Support for this view lies in the fact that despite the *Balao* crewmen's memories of *Cisco* as a boat to avoid, others remember her as a sought-after berth. Bob Norton writes: "The last time I saw your father was in New London. I was in the lower base when I saw him walking along one of the piers with some other officers. I went over to see him and during our conversation I asked him if he had room for me on his new boat. He replied that he had been told that he could not take any more of his old crews. This shows that many more people had the same idea that I did."

I was relieved to get Mr. Norton's letter and blessed him in my mind. I couldn't bear thinking of Jim's boat as a pariah in his last days. He had enough to contend with by leaving his family, negotiating the politics of his superiors, and leading his men into enemy waters.

Some men who bore out Norton's view had more capricious reasons than Norton did for wanting to be on *Cisco*. A sub vet named Robert C. Asin, from the *Skipjack*, wrote me that he had been originally assigned to *Cisco*. One Fred Coe and he had joined the navy in San Francisco in early 1942, Asin remembered. After training on the West Coast, they both volunteered for the submarine service and were sent to New London for six weeks of radar school. Asin was then assigned to *Cisco* and Fred Coe to *Skipjack*. "Fred Coe had the same name as the new skipper of the new USS Cisco, and he also had a girl friend there in New London. So we decided to trade our papers; we were allowed to do that at the time. I agreed as I could go through San Francisco where my wife lived and could spend a few days before going to Pearl Harbor and USS Skipjack."

Former *S-39* radioman Howie Rice also wanted a berth on the new boat.

He adds a third reason why Fred Coe got on *Cisco:* "I got a call from the base personnel officer stating that Coe wanted me as his lead radioman, and to pick one of the technicians in my class to be assigned to the Cisco. I asked several men, and what I thought was the best of the technicians, whose name was also Coe, said he would like to go."

Stories such as this bolster my feeling that submarine vets' memory of *Cisco* as a pariah is a product of hindsight. Jack Lee, who skippered an unprecedented ten war patrols, supports this opinion: "In my experience, I never heard of an officer or an enlisted man requesting transfer from a newly completed submarine because he thought it to be defective. Transfers usually occurred at the request of the individual for personal reasons or because the Commanding Officer did not believe he fitted in with the crew." *Cisco's* coming months would bear out this observation.

As I said above, Jim had enough to contend with without being a pariah. He was undoubtedly overworked during his months in Portsmouth. *Wahoo's* executive officer, George Grider, gives us an idea of what was involved:

> I never worked harder in my life than I did during the building, commissioning, and testing of the Wahoo. We had a little shack of an office . . . in the Navy Yard. It smelled of diesel oil and tired sailors, and—with its few desks and a typewriter and telephone, it was the nerve center from which the building of the boat was controlled.
>
> As the crew came aboard, a few men at a time, we added to our building job the task of training the crew. Besides that, of course, we had to read the patrol reports, which were now coming in regularly, get our papers, codes, and charts in order, and test every piece of machinery.[10]

Seeing from the patrol reports how methodical my father was, plus his tendency not to ask his men to do anything he wouldn't do himself, I'm sure he checked every detail of the boat's construction. I picture him up to his elbows in the bilge or ballast tanks. A compelling reason for such thoroughness is again voiced by Grider: "The builders were responsible, but they weren't the ones who were going out to fight in it. We were, and we wanted to make certain it was properly constructed. What's more, we wanted to know how it was constructed, every inch of it, so that when something went wrong, we would know what it was and where it was."[11]

This urgent standard makes me wonder when Jim had time for his family. There are few records from this time. "It was just too sad," my mother said of the pictures she'd jettisoned of Jim with Jean, age six, and Henry, two-and-one-half years of age, during these months.

But Jean and Henry remember Jim bringing home lobsters one night for dinner and letting them scuttle across the kitchen floor. Henry was scared of them. He also remembers Jim spanking him for being mean to Jack, one of the two cocker spaniel pups Jim had been given on a recent CBS radio show by his *Skipjack* crew.

These, sadly, are Henry's only two memories of his father, and perhaps because they're not happy ones, he—of the three of us—has seemed the most troubled by Jim's loss. "Do you think we'll ever get over it?" he said through tears recently. Henry has a remarkably sunny disposition, has carved out a comfortable life for himself with a milk-delivery business in rural Vermont, and has friends from high school who still come to see him. He has a loving family, with one of his grown sons—Jamie, an architect—born on his namesake Jim Coe's birthday. But Henry still feels his father's loss every day.

Jean remembers being read to by Jim. He was a hands-on father, making a game of small tasks, such as keeping her clothes neat and the living room rugs clean, that made Jean feel proud.

Mother remembered Jim playing the flute and taking her out dancing. But undoubtedly there was less of this during wartime in the frigid northeast than there had been in Hawaii and Manila. After the ample domestic help they had in the Pacific, Jim and Ray were probably faced with housework and child care for the first time together in their marriage.

With their minds on domestic matters, Mother and Jim started to put down roots during these precious months. They gave notice to the renters of the house they had built in Annapolis during 1938 and 1939, and Ray planned to move there in August, when Jim was due to ship out again. And they planned to visit their piece of land on the Eastern Shore of Maryland to do some crabbing in the coming spring. When Jim was an instructor at the Naval Academy, they'd visit the Eastern Shore, and they had grown fond of the softshell crabs that you could catch off the docks there. Mother once told me that she had used a year's clothing allowance from her father to buy the land. (She must have associated it strictly with Jim's and her dreams, because she sold it shortly after she remarried in 1945, even though she knew it was destined to increase greatly in value.)

Meanwhile, at the shipyard Jim forged a team with his *Cisco* officers. Five of them reported for duty in January and February, with Clarence Petersen, who had served under Jim on *S-39*, the last to arrive, on March 10, 1943. Jim's executive officer, Gus Weinel, was a brilliant man who graduated first in his class of 1936 at the Naval Academy. He had proved himself (with his friend George Grider) on the outmoded sub *Pollock*, and Jim must have been grateful to have him aboard.

In addition to Lieutenant Weinel, *Cisco*'s other officers were top-notch. "They were the best I ever served under," Howie Rice told me. By contrast, however, Rice despaired of the enlisted men. Many of them were unruly and green, and Rice didn't know how Jim and the other officers could train them in time to handle the sophisticated new sub.

Judging from *Cisco*'s administrative log kept during this time by Gus Weinel, one can surmise that Rice's memory was correct; Jim had to discipline crewmen almost constantly for infractions such as "chicanery," "creating a disturbance ashore," and being away without leave (AWOL). He did this through captain's mast, during which he meted out such punishments as "10 days deprivation of liberty" or "3 days' solitary confinement on bread and water."[12] These sentences were served in the brig on the grounds of Portsmouth Naval Shipyard, a building ironically beautiful enough to have been spared the wrecker's ball in subsequent years.

Either this trouble in gathering and training crew or the enormous demands of fitting out, inspecting, and testing every part of the new *Cisco* got to Jim, according to photographs of this period. Then again, perhaps it was the cumulative fatigue of his six previous war patrols, or the knowledge of war and the truth of what he was preparing to again face, or the renewed realization of what he would have to leave in his family—the formative years of his children he'd have to miss. Whatever the cause, there is a new anguish in Jim Coe's face as he sits on the rock between his kids, with two live Easter rabbits in his hands, that May of 1943 in Portsmouth. This is the picture that made me need to know who he was. Compared to other photos of him from just a few years earlier, there is real pain behind his eyes. His brow is no longer clear, and all the playfulness, the look of sharing a private joke with the viewer, is gone from his half smile. This is the photo that friends thought showed a grandfather with his two grandchildren.

Since the discovery of this photo, submarine veterans have sent me other photos of Jim's last days in Portsmouth—most of them in conjunction with *Cisco*'s commissioning. All of them, even those at a party and dance for *Cisco*'s men and their wives, show a dour and troubled Jim, a man looking middle-aged. In this last big social occasion for the *Cisco,* my mother is infected by Jim's worry. She stands beside him like a ghost: pale, stick thin, and unsmiling. In contrast to the animated couples around them, Jim and Ray look frozen by the camera's flash, startled and distrustful. It's one of the few photos where my mother, in particular, isn't posed and poised. Jim's and Ray's lips are thin and tight; they look like they've just had a fight.

Photos of *Cisco*'s commissioning show Jim glaring at the camera, his jaw tight, feet planted slightly ahead of his torso, like a mule who's decided he won't go any farther. When Guy Gugliotta saw these pictures a few years ago, he said, "That's a man who's angry at having to leave his family!"

These Portsmouth photos make me think again of what Uncle James once told me: that Jim *knew* he was going down. As I mentioned earlier, Uncle James remembered Jim in the middle of another party during these months, uncharacteristically just staring into space as if reading his future.

But perhaps he was just worried about the day-to-day problems *Cisco* presented. After her launching, while *Cisco* was still in dry dock, there was a fire on board. "Not too much damage," reports Slip Haislip. Then, he writes, a serious accident breached *Cisco*'s ballast tanks:

> One morning we went down to muster, and there was a gathering of Navy Yard personnel on the boat and on the dock. Everyone was talking and pointing at the starboard side of the boat. We looked down there and saw three plates that made up some of the ballast tanks on the starboard side. These plates looked like they were ready to blow out at the seams.

Officers of *USS Cisco. Left to right:* Lieutenant W. H. Louney, Lieutenant
J. D. Milier, Lieutenant Commander A. F. Weinel, Commander J. W. Coe,
Lieutenant H. B. Berry, Jr., Ensign C. R. Cummings, Jr., and Ensign C. I.
Petersen.

They had to be replaced. I have no idea of the dimensions of these plates;
a guess is 5 feet wide and 12 feet long. Later I found out there were two
plates on the port side that were damaged in the same manner. I heard
that someone must have shut off the pressure gauges to those tanks. Negligence or sabotage is my guess.

Howie Rice is more technical and remembers the repairs this entailed:
"During the night, the kingstons [flood valves that let fuel out of tanks] on
the bottom of one of the fuel tanks was closed; the vents and the equalizing
valve that allows salt water to enter the fuel tanks to equalize with sea pressure was also closed. Somehow a high pressure air bank was bled into this

fuel tank. Well, this stretched the tank till it bulged out and finally ruptured. Who did this was never found out. The tank had to be cut out, new steel installed and rewelded. Now the welding had to be done from the outside, not like when under construction."

Rice thinks that the reweld, done in patchwork fashion from the outside, didn't hold up under depth charging or perhaps even the long mileage of normal sea pressure. He speculates that this caused an oil leak that eventually led the Japanese to *Cisco*.

This possibility makes Haislip's conjecture of negligence or sabotage not farfetched. Tom Parks remembered the hasty workmanship of those days:

> Industrial concerns were in fierce competition with each other over workers. Many of the people performing sensitive labor in jobs which required great skills had very little training. They came to the mills and shipyards and received some on-the-job training and were put right to work. As a result many errors were made. In Boston Navy Yard, a submarine under construction even sank because someone disconnected the interlock which prevented both doors, inner and outer, on a torpedo tube to open at the same time. Although the Cisco event could have been investigated as an act of sabotage, I doubt that it was deliberate. It was probably just a bad mistake.

Despite this mistake, repairs to the ruptured tanks by the same civilian workforce were okayed by the navy. Months later, in the official investigation of the *Cisco's* loss by T. C. Kinkaid, commander of the Seventh Fleet, only scant mention of this accident is made: "Prior to commissioning and while water-borne, the Cisco was damaged by someone turning on high pressure air, at least 250 pounds, to her fuel ballast tanks which dimpled the hull of fuel ballast and ballast of after groups only, necessitating docking and cutting out dimpled plating plus some framing, which was replaced. Subsequent inspection showed repairs had been properly made."[13]

The board of investigation leaves it at that, making no follow-up queries or testimony about the possibility of this welding job not holding up under seagoing conditions. Instead, the investigation centered mainly on repairs to *Cisco's* hydraulic system, which we shall look at in the next chapter. These repairs were made the night before *Cisco* went out on patrol. The fact that these were the last repairs made seemed to take investigators' attention, and the more serious fracture to the fuel ballast tanks was virtually ignored. But Howie Rice does ask the question that should have been obvious to the board: "So the Cisco passed her 15-lb. [water-pressure per square inch] test after the fuel tank repair, but how many dives and how deep would it take to cause a rupture that a poor welding job could not take?"

This accident surely added to the worry I see on Jim's face in photos of these last months in the States. *Cisco* was commissioned on May 10, 1943, and from the tension and tentativeness on Jim's face in the commissioning photos, the accident with the ruptured fuel tank could have occurred just before the ceremony. After she was repaired, the sub was examined on June 7, and the Portsmouth Board of Inspection and Survey gave her a clean bill of health.

But more trouble followed. On June 23, according to the *Cisco's* only deck log, the communications officer, an ensign in the Naval Reserve, is relieved of duties and replaced. Although Jim gives no reason for this in the official record, scuttlebutt assigns it to adultery. The married ensign was supposedly having an affair with another officer's wife. He wasn't given a captain's mast or otherwise disciplined; he was just discreetly transferred. When I looked up his service record, I found that he went on to other submarines and was finally washed overboard (not by enemy action) off a submarine and lost somewhere in the Pacific in February of 1945.

The first thought I had on reading this was that this officer may have been haunted enough by the *Cisco's* demise to have done himself in. It is indeed strange for a seasoned submarine officer to be simply "washed overboard" from an unembattled boat. When I told my husband the story, his first thought was that perhaps this guy was caught with yet another shipmate's wife and that the cuckold exacted his revenge. This man's record was like a black hole pulling in the storytelling imagination that I had otherwise tried to discipline against embellishment and hindsight.

Whatever the truth about this young ensign, I suspect that although Jim was discreet with the guy's record, he was firm in not wanting this officer on his boat. Tom Parks remembers a code of conduct: "Aboard any ship in which I served, profanity was not tolerated. This was especially true on your father's ship. He was a sailor and I'm sure that he could swear loudly and profanely when the occasion demanded, but I never heard more than a mild 'hell' or 'damn.' This was true of all the officers on the boat. They were all gentlemen."

With the ensign's replacement in early July, *Cisco* started her sea trials off Portsmouth. The first problem that showed up was excessive noise made by her blowers (Roots-Connersville blowers to blow ballast tanks dry to surface or change trim levels); also Jim reported oil slicks caused by lubricating oil discharging with exhaust at all speeds and loads. Both these defects are serious because they can betray the submarine to the enemy.

Jim discovered these glitches in the course of *Cisco*'s first dives. But there was a more immediate problem; on the first dive, *Cisco*'s main induction and after-engine valves were not closed all the way, even though the valve indicator (a board of red and green lights called a "Christmas tree") showed that all valves were safely closed. On the dive, *Cisco*'s after-engine room started to flood, but the men were able to level the boat off in time and gradually take her back up. When Jim wrote up the report of *Cisco*'s trials, he was casual: "We took in about 12,000 lbs. during which time a depth of 473 feet was reached. [Cisco's official test depth is listed at four hundred feet.] The boat handled well in this condition and was brought back to 412 feet by merely speeding up."[14]

Slip Haislip remembers the aftermath of this dive: "One of our firemen (a real small fellow) crawled through the main induction and found there was a lot of debris that was not removed. Evidently no one checked it out beforehand. The crew had to clean out all the debris."

Haislip goes on to report hitting something on the next deep test dive for leaks. "I believe the depth was around 500 feet when we hit something under the boat. Sonar had reported all clear below." Later, when the boat finally left Portsmouth on the first leg of her journey to Australia via the Panama Canal, she stopped in New London to fuel up; there the men noticed that *Cisco* was leaking oil from No. 5A fuel ballast tank. They had to get a diver to go down and inspect the tank; he found that the forward flood valve was partially open. The men weren't able to close it with the operating gear. They then defueled the boat and entered the Marine Railway at the Electric Boat Company in Groton for emergency repairs. Apparently, another ballast tank had sustained damage when the boat's hull hit bottom or a rock on the deep dive. The repairs took three days.

At this point, Jim ran into his former torpedo officer on *Skipjack,* Paul Loustaunau. Paul was able to tell me that Rachel was with Jim for at least some of those last few days before the boat left the States. Paul and his wife had them over for lunch at their rented house in Groton. Although Jim was his usual gregarious self—cheerful enough to charm the socks off Paul's mother-in-law at lunch—he told Paul in private that he hoped the *Cisco* hadn't been built too fast, that there was a recurring oil leak that they couldn't seem to staunch.

When I probed Paul about Jim and Ray's relationship at this time, Paul seemed surprised that I would ask and indicated that they seemed genuinely happy together, showing it by joking back and forth, teasing each other. Paul and his wife, Ronnie, had extra gas rationing coupons; Paul would soon be stationed to Australia, and his wife and mother-in-law would be traveling by train back to Seattle, where Ronnie's mother lived. On hearing this, Jim raised his eyebrows at Ray, who was about to drive down to Annapolis to move into their newly vacated house. It's easy to see how Ray, an avid driver and disorganized housekeeper, would be low on gas coupons. "I know how you're getting to Annapolis!" Jim said.

I was glad to hear confirmation that Jim and Ray were together in these last days of Jim's in the States. It provides a clear window of when I was conceived: sometime in July up until the twenty-fourth, when the *Cisco* left the States for Coco Solo, Panama. (I was born the following year, on April 6.) Soon after hearing Paul Loustaunau's story of the lunch in Groton, I found evidence (which I'll share later) that my mother was experienced enough about pregnancy to recognize her condition within the first two months.

Someone else who saw Jim in these last days stateside was the wife of fellow submarine commander Bill Nelson, who, as mentioned earlier, was Jim's Naval Academy classmate and the best man at his wedding. Lil Nelson remembers seeing Jim in Groton just before he left. Ray had already started driving to Annapolis, and Jim had been invited to dinner by the Moseleys, a navy couple. Lil was also invited because her husband was off on patrol. Lil said she will always remember saying goodbye to Jim, that they hugged and cried. She hadn't heard from Bill for a while, and in wartime, that could mean the worst. And Jim was leaving for the war zone. In other words, this was a normal goodbye in wartime, with uncertainty ruling the day. I asked Lil if Jim acted differently, if she had any sense that he might have known he wasn't coming back. Lil said no, he was just like he always was: outgoing, funny, caring. But if he had known, she added, he would never have let on. This was in keeping with what Mary McGregor told me: that Jim never acted as if he wouldn't come back. I thought of something Guy Gugliotta had told me when I interviewed him down in Washington: "None of us on Asian duty thought we'd make it home alive," echoing Skipper Eugene McKinney's report that they were trained to think of their lives as "already forfeit." But as if reading my mind, Lil ended our phone conversation by telling me to let it go, that I was reading too much into their tears at this last goodbye. It's "pau," she said, Hawaiian for "finished."

Once *Cisco* left New London on July 24, she headed for Panama en route to Fremantle, Australia, where she would join the Southwest Pacific Force. Slip Haislip reports the boat making an emergency dive down around Cuba. "We found out later that we had three torpedoes cross our bow from a German U-boat. We stayed submerged for quite awhile before we surfaced."

By the time they reached Coco Solo, Panama, to go through the canal, Haislip had had enough. He was transferred off the boat. He remembers six other men feeling the same way: that *Cisco* must be jinxed or star crossed because she'd been built in only fifty-six days, and they got off with him. The administrative log indeed shows six—not seven—men transferred off the boat and were replaced by six new men, on August 4 and 5, 1943. Of the six getting off, two had been disciplined at captain's mast earlier in the summer. I called Haislip and, thinking that this disembarkment might just be sour grapes, asked how men got off: could they just request transfer at any time, or did they need something like a medical excuse?

Haislip said that the only way you could get off was to misbehave and be

asked to leave. And it sounded as if he and Sam McCurdy, another crewman, started misbehaving long before they left the boat. He told me that at
their stop at Coco Solo to refuel, the *Cisco* men had a softball game against
the crew of the *Cabrilla, Cisco*'s sister ship. Haislip said he and Sam drank a
lot of rum and got rowdy, then smuggled more rum on board *Cisco* after the
game. McCurdy had already been sentenced at a captain's mast on July 5
to ten hours' extra duty for being AWOL, and now McCurdy and Haislip
had a decision to make. Should they drink the rest of the rum and risk being kicked off the boat, or should they start casing the boat for a safe place
to hide the rum and try to sober up enough to get under way?

They decided to keep drinking. These fifty-some years later, Haislip sees
a pattern of mishaps stemming from *Cisco*'s fifty-six-day construction time
and sees that pattern as cause for McCurdy and him to decide to leave the
boat. A symbol of *Cisco*'s star-crossed condition, Haislip added, were some
little bird figurines he remembers, which the crew attached to each governor
of the engines in the forward engine room. The men called them "worry-
birds," and they were supposed to worry in the crew's stead if anything went
wrong with the engines. This, as Haislip told it, was more premonitory evidence that *Cisco* was jinxed. I asked Haislip if my father himself kicked the
men off. He said no, their immediate superior did.

This story, to me, is an example of hindsight embellishing memory. All
through World War II literature, there are men who are given a choice, and
the ones who choose to stay in a dangerous situation are seen as heroes. On
the famous submarine *Wahoo,* skipper Mush Morton announced that they
were going into dangerous waters and gave the crew the option of getting off,
no one stepped forward.[15] The men who got off *Cisco*
must have heard plenty of accounts such as these in what was then the fifty-
odd years since World War II; what, then, do these stories and other such
views of heroism say about those who got off when the going got rough? Isn't
it easier to see oneself as prescient, endowed with some kind of sixth sense,
rather than unruly or unable to fit in or bear up under pressure?

As with all the vets who gave me information, I am grateful to Mr. Haislip for his account, especially for his candor in how he and Mr. McCurdy

got off the boat. It helps me figure, as mentioned earlier, that Jim probably wasn't beset by a spooked crew. It also lets me know that Jim didn't have to kick these men off the boat himself. Both of these conclusions are reassuring; along with all else Jim was up against, it's good to know that in his last days, his personnel problems weren't as bad as the scuttlebutt from the submarine veterans' convention had led me to believe.

Cisco's only deck log shows her refueling in Coco Solo on Monday, August 2, 1943. She lay over there for a few days to stock up on supplies and to exchange crewmen. Jim also did some personal shopping, buying two beautiful small Sarouk rugs and having them shipped back to my mother in Annapolis for their new house. They sit in my living room today, the strong, natural dyes still holding their jewel-like colors. The fresh teal-blue leaves in them look like little bits of heaven, and I wonder whether Jim felt the same way when he first saw them. He also bought a big bottle of Chanel No. 5 and shipped it to my mother.

The log also shows that on Friday, August 6, one crewman was AWOL from the ship and that another was transferred to Coco Solo's naval dispensary for medical treatment. Then *Cisco* steams over to Balboa, where the men dock up overnight. The next day, August 7, they get under way for the Southwest Pacific Command in Brisbane, Australia. *Cisco* runs at thirteen and one-half knots on the surface, making about 340 miles a day, the crew keeping close watch for enemy activity. She reaches Norfolk Island, east of Australia, on August 30, where she drops off a crewman suffering from an advanced case of dermatitis. She then steams on to Brisbane, arriving on September 2.

Perusing the dispatch ordering *Cisco* from Balboa to Brisbane, I note again how the war has changed expectations of submarines from overly cautious to more aggressive behavior. Whereas prewar training taught skippers to submerge during daylight hours and travel on the surface only at night, the July 1943 orders call for *Cisco* to spend the first two days out of New London submerged, and then it says, "Dive at discretion."[1] This more-aggressive presence on the seas had its biggest leap forward in January 1943 with the third patrol of the *Wahoo,* when skipper Mush Morton kept the submarine on the surface most of the time for optimal speed. He did this in full daylight even when his lookouts sighted enemy planes in the distance. Morton was successful with this and other unprecedented aggression, sinking five ships on his third patrol (later corrected to three by Japanese records) and twelve ships on his fourth (nine by Japanese accounts).[2] These feats were highly publicized, with newspapers and magazines at last giving the submarine service some notice. So during his months in Portsmouth, New Hampshire, Jim surely heard of Morton's exploits. This news undoubtedly buoyed the submarine force and shaped subsequent tactics toward further innovation and aggression. It also upped the ante for all skippers, and Jim had a new boat to live up to as well.

In the first days of September 1943, *Cisco* conducted training exercises in Brisbane's Moreton Bay, then steamed up the coast toward Darwin, where she was scheduled to debark on her first patrol September 19. Howie Rice remembers:

> About three days before getting to Darwin, we got a message promoting your dad to commander upon completing a physical. I was in the washroom when a shipmate said, "Hell Rice, what's wrong with you; you look like a Chinaman." He was right; I was yellow all over my skin, my eyes. Well, we sent a message to Darwin for a doctor to meet us. Darwin has tides like the Bay of Fundy—forty feet. We arrived at low tide and docked. I got a call, "Rice topside," and went up on deck. The doctor was standing on the pier looking at me about twenty-five feet down. He cupped his hands around his mouth and shouted, "Get a mattress cover and put all your personal gear and come with me." This I did, and he took me to a hotel in Darwin that he had set up as sick bay.

I was sitting with Howie and his wife in their hotel room in Fort Worth when I first heard this. Howie, a springy, enthusiastic man, had one of his old World War II radios spread out on the hotel desk. He paused and played the message code for me. I leaned over the radio and urged him to go on with the *Cisco* account.

Jim showed up at the sick bay for his physical while Howie was there being treated for jaundice. Jim asked the doctor if Howie could be treated on the boat.

The doctor said no, that although it could be treated easily, it was very dangerous to me and to others, and he could not allow me to go. The navy doctors have the last word where a medical condition exists.

Your dad had his physical and was now a commander. I went down to the street with him to say goodbye. He had a jeep and a driver. As they drove away he turned and looked at me with a funny look on his face until they were out of sight. I was flown down to Perth, put in the hospital, given salts to flush me out, and in two weeks was discharged back to duty.

I said, "What do you mean by the 'funny look' he gave you?"

Howie stroked his chin, then said, "When we said goodbye and shook hands, he was very quiet, and when he got into the jeep and the driver took off, he turned around and just stared at me until they were out of sight. It was sort of a questioning look. I'm sure he was questioning why he was losing his lead experienced radioman."

This story made me wonder what Jim was heading off to. I found out that Admiral Nimitz was mounting an invasion of the Gilbert Islands, just south of the Marshalls. Admiral Koga of Japan, meanwhile, had gathered most of his fleet at Truk; when he heard of the Gilbert invasion, he steamed over to the Marshall Islands. Sub fleet commander Ralph Christie responded by deploying his Fremantle subs to target tankers bringing oil from Borneo and Sumatra to Admiral Koga's fleet. In addition to this route, there were the more-established shipping lanes to patrol, from Sumatra to Singapore and on up along the coast of Indochina, then up through the Formosa straits or Luzon Strait into the East China Sea. These would fuel Japan not only with oil but also with nickel and copper from the Celebes (now called Sulawesi); iron, copper, bauxite, cotton, hemp, sugar, and rice from the Philippines; oil, rubber, and tin from Malaya (Malaysia); and rice and lumber from Thailand and French Indochina (Vietnam). This list gives an idea of the territory that Japan now controlled. They had ports in Surabaya, Singapore, Balikpapan, Tarakan, Miri, Bangkok, Saigon, Davao, and Manila. These ports and their shipping were protected by air patrols, with airfields throughout the southwest Pacific. In addition to this, there were radar stations and mines throughout the area.[3]

To stop the heavily protected Japanese shipments of vital materials from getting back to Japan, American submarines in 1943 were deployed to the East China Sea and finally started exploiting the bottleneck of the Luzon Strait. This extended range, plus the adjustments to deep-running torpedoes, accounted for a twofold improvement in enemy ships sunk in 1943 over 1942: from 180 ships or 725,000 tons in 1942 to 335 ships or 1.5 million tons in 1943.[4]

Jim was directed to patrol the shipping lanes between the Gulf of Tonkin and Luzon Strait; his path was plotted from Darwin north through the Banda Sea, then Manipa Strait, Molucca Passage, Sibutu Passage, to the Sulu Sea, then on through Mindoro Strait into the South China Sea. He was to cross this to his patrol waters—a huge area extending along the northern curve of French Indochina in the west, along a northern border between China and the island of Hainan eastward to the north of Luzon in the Philippines, and then south through Luzon and on down to a point south of Mindoro. The southern border of the area lies just north of the quadrant in the South China Sea called "Dangerous Ground," an area of unsurveyed reefs. Jim's orders were to patrol these waters for about twenty-four days, paying particular attention to traffic lanes in Tonkin Gulf and the vicinity of Macclesfield Bank in the South China Sea.[5]

After leaving Howie Rice at sick bay, Jim and his crew got under way on September 18 to *Cisco*'s fueling area, doing exercises with aircraft and antisubmarine vessels en route. *Cisco* then returned to Darwin the next day because of trouble with the hydraulic system, which controls the diving planes, rudder, and other parts that move under load. An automatic bypass valve was sticking, bringing the oil in the system to a high temperature. In the shop overnight, an abrasion was found on the piston of the valve; it was stoned down, the valve was reinstalled, and about fifteen gallons of hydraulic oil were replaced in the system.[6]

Cisco left Darwin the next day. Ominously, a Japanese plane was reported over the harbor at twenty thousand feet as *Cisco* steamed out to sea; her departure may have thus been reported to enemy patrols up ahead in the Arafura, Banda, and Molucca seas.

And that becomes the first of many speculations about the fate of the *Cisco* because all facts end as of September 19, 1943, when she last steamed out of Darwin. She was never seen or heard from again.

I have asked every submarine veteran I interviewed what he thinks happened to the boat. Most men, to their credit, just shake their heads. But some ventured theories, which I then investigated, but I turned up nothing to substantiate them. One such theory came from a guide on the *Lionfish,* a submarine docked in Fall River, Massachusetts, as a World War II memorial and museum. I was kindly taken all through the submarine, with the head guide, Jim Ward, showing me the features of the boat that matched the *Cisco*'s. Another guide at the end of the tour urged me to feel the flywheel inside the head of a torpedo on display, then pointed out on a drawing how the firing pin, if hitting a target straight on, jammed and either missed the fulminate caps or hit them too weakly to explode. (This was the discovery of Admiral Lockwood after he tested torpedoes against a cliff in Kahoolawe, near Pearl Harbor in August of 1943.) The guide was passionate about what was obviously "his baby," the whole sorry torpedo-deficit history. He then stunned me by declaring, " *This* is what killed him!" tapping the torpedo. As I gaped at him, he explained that *Cisco* went down because her skipper broke radio silence (radio signals can reveal the location of one's ship to the enemy), calling headquarters in frustration to report that nineteen torpedoes he had fired turned out to be duds.

I stood there openmouthed, then asked for the guy's source. It was the first time he grew vague; he thought he'd read the story in an old *Polaris,* the magazine of the World War II sub vets.

Alarmed that my father may have brought on his own sub's demise, I spent the next several months trying to find the source. *Polaris* editors said there was no such thing. I then had researchers from the National Archives send me all radio traffic of the *Cisco*'s fleet during the fall of 1943. The main thing these dispatches showed was the resounding silence of the *Cisco* from

September 19 on. Paul Loustaunau, in the interview my brother and I had with him in Washington, explained this radio silence as a signature of Jim Coe's, causing doubts among the fleet of the initial reports of *Cisco's* presumed loss. When he heard via other submarines in the fleet that Jim hadn't acknowledged any dispatches from headquarters, Paul just thought that it was the usual Coe strict radio silence. Then, when headquarters sent dispatches demanding an answer, and Jim didn't respond, Paul knew. He told Henry and me that he was standing by the message board in Fremantle after coming off patrol. Men crowded around, and two former *Skipjack* sailors spotted Paul, called to him, and made their way over. "Have you heard?" they said. He shook his head, and they told him that the *Cisco* was overdue and presumed lost. Paul glanced sideways over the table where we sat in the Army Navy Club dining room. Then he looked down, shook his head, and said the three of them broke into tears.

Cisco had been due back in Fremantle on November 6. When she didn't show, the navy scheduled an official inquiry. The board of investigation, meeting in December of 1943, could find nothing, no possible reason for *Cisco's* disappearance. They did confirm what I had found from my investigation of message traffic: "The Cisco was expected back in Fremantle about the sixth or seventh of November. On 4 November, having heard nothing from her, we so phrased a part of a serial dispatch which would encourage her to open up on her radio, as follows: 'RED COE WHEN FEASIBLE GIVE US YOUR ETA EROSION OR PINAFORE.' No dispatch received on 5 November; we again sent a regular serial dispatch which was as follows: 'COE ACKNOWLEDGE THIS SERIAL 74 WITH YOUR POSITION CODE GROUP.' No reply was received."[7]

Other theories of *Cisco's* demise were not as easy to check out as the guide's on the *Lionfish* was about breaking radio silence. One that Ned Beach suggested to me was that she was hit by her own circling torpedo; another was that she had ventured into a mined area. This latter theory looked improbable because there was detailed intelligence on mined areas along her route, publicized in her operations orders.

Then there is Howie Rice's suggestion that the welding job on *Cisco's* hull to repair the ruptured ballast tank didn't hold up, allowing the boat to leak oil unbeknownst to Jim and the crew, thus marking her path for the enemy. The U.S. Navey's postwar investigation into submarine losses cites an oil slick that led Japanese planes to attack a submarine in Cisco's patrol waters on September 28, 1943.[8] I checked this report by locating a cousin of Mush Morton, my father's submarine colleague, in Tokyo. Bryan MacKinnon steered me, via the internet, to some researchers in the Military History Department of Tokyo's National Institute for Defense Studies. Two of these men, Captains Noritaka Kitazawa and Yasuhiro "Tommy" Tamagawa, were retired navy men from World War II. Tommy had even served in Japan's one-man midget subs. They were thus familiar with *Cisco*'s patrol waters and were willing to go above and beyond their usual duties to trace a fellow seaman. They also knew the more archaic Japanese that relevant World War II documents were written in and could translate them for me.

They studied the report from the Japanese air unit that bombed the submarine in *Cisco*'s patrol waters. No other American submarines but *Cisco* were in the area at the time of the bombing. The researchers translated the report for me and pinpointed the exact location of the attack on a nautical chart. They also sent me the surrounding context of Japanese naval operations in that time and place.

This is the researchers' story: someone was smuggling a continual supply of American materials to guerilla forces in the southern Philippines. The Japanese suspected American submarines. Vice Admiral Arata Oka, commander of Japan's Third Southern Expeditionary Fleet, headquartered in Manila, ordered his forces to patrol the islands in the southern Philippines for possible contacts between American submarines and guerilla forces.

Meanwhile, the Japanese oil tanker *Hayatomo* had loaded petroleum at Palembang, Sumatera, and was sailing north to Manila. The gunboat *Karatsu* was escorting her. On September 28, at about 9 a.m., *Karatsu* spotted telltale oil on the surface of the Sulu Sea forty-two nautical miles southwest of Naso Point, the southern tip of Panay Island in the mid-Philippines. *Karatsu,* interpreting the oil slick as an enemy submarine, dropped depth charges over the freshest part of the slick, the best indicator of the leaking sub's position below. She also radioed for backup forces. The nearest was an air squadron located on Cebu Island about ninety miles east. Two MK97

Kanko planes from the 954th Air Squadron rushed to the scene of the attack and began surveying the area. These planes were part of the forces trained to detect submarines supplying Philippine guerillas. The waters in this area, said my Japanese guides, were lined with coral, forming a bright background in daylight against which a submerged submarine would stand out.

However, thirty minutes after the *Karatsu* had dropped her first depth charges, she spotted the enemy submarine in shallow water but soon lost it in a rain squall. It wasn't until noon that one of the airplanes spied the submarine and dropped bombs on it. Forty-five minutes later, the aircraft dropped more bombs and saw black diesel oil gush up to the sea's surface. Both planes and *Karatsu* joined the attack, greatly increasing the stream of gushing oil. The planes circled over what they figured was a sure kill until five o'clock that afternoon. Ten days later, with oil still coming up, the Japanese sent two converted minesweepers to the location, and they depth charged again to assure the kill.[9]

The site of this attack is the Sultana Shoals, a relatively small, amoeba-shaped area of shallow water in a surrounding chasm of deep water. The shoals look to be about ten miles wide and ten to fifteen miles long. They are 53 meters, or about 175 feet deep at their deepest point, and this is the spot where the Tokyo researchers surmised—from the Japanese air unit's report—that *Cisco* was bombed.[10] The Sultana Shoals is surrounded by deep sea—from 731 to 1,236 meters (or about 3,600 feet), and a topographical map of the ocean floor shows that the shoals are really a summit in an underwater volcanic mountain chain bisecting the northern half of the Sulu Sea from west to east.[11] I wondered why Jim was caught atop this mountain when deeper, safer waters were all around, especially because there appeared to be about three hours between the first and second attacks. Why hadn't he crept off the shoals the way he had snuck away from all prior depth chargings in his patrol reports?

I contacted four veteran sub skippers, sending them the above information and asking them to weigh in on this question. There was general consensus with the view voiced by retired captain Guy Gugliotta: "Why did Cisco stay in shoal water after the first attack? Probably because the first bombing and depth charge attacks were so effective that she must have been

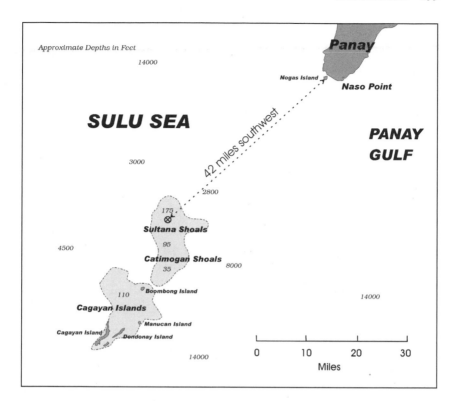

⊗ Probable location of attack on *Cisco*.

considerably crippled with little or no power to move from the initially-sighted oil slick position which had given Karatsu and bombers a precisely located target."

(Gugliotta seems here to be assuming planes bombed along with *Karatsu* in the initial attack, whereas I had understood the *Karatsu's* being alone at 9 a.m. when it first depth charged the sub.) But Captain Gugliotta is clear when he ventures a reason for Jim's being in such shallow water in the first place: "Red Coe was familiar with this area [he had hunted an enemy sub in precisely this spot on *S-39* on January 8, 1942] and followed a direct route crossing the shoals to regain some of the time lost thus far en route to his assigned patrol area. Cisco had no knowledge of her oil slick track, if it existed at this time, or she would have chosen to proceed in deeper water."

The Japanese report of an oil slick certainly supports Howie Rice's conjecture that *Cisco* had an oil leak from the patching of the ruptured fuel tank. (The hydraulic's repair she had in Darwin wouldn't account for such a leak.) Rice went on to say, after reviewing the Japanese report, that Jim may have been crossing Sultana Shoals in the direction of airplanes picked up by *Cisco*'s radar. These were probably aircraft protecting the oil tanker *Hayatomo* cited in the Japanese account. Rice says that the aircraft-detecting radar on *Cisco* could zero in on aircraft up to fifteen miles away. "So what is Coe going to do with this information? Head for it to see what gives, even if he had to pass over a shallow area. When the aircraft came near to him in their sweeps ahead of the convoy, he would dive and go slow. I'm sure he did not know of the oil leak, and was trying to get into position for an attack. But with the shallow water and the oil leak, the Japanese aircraft had the advantage."

Veteran skipper Slade Cutter suggested another way to look at Sultana Shoals—that it offered a last, desperate few hours of life: "They bombed the slick and damaged Cisco badly enough to cause oil gushing from the sub. Cisco was lucky to be near Sultana Shoals because with a bad oil leak she would soon lose positive buoyancy and sink to the bottom. And the area around Sultana Shoals was deep water that would have crushed the sub's hull."

As noted in the Japanese account of the attack, oil continued to surface at the attack site ten days later.

Captain Gugliotta picks up on this as a connection to Howie Rice's theory of the badly patched ballast tank: "The gushing of oil as late as 10 October would indicate rupture of the Cisco's main ballast tank that was carrying fuel oil. (This was general US sub. practice to provide additional fuel for extended and/or distant patrol areas.)"

—◁◇▷—

And where did all these findings leave me? I figured that the patched ballast tanks causing an oil leak was a viable theory of *Cisco*'s demise. My brother, sister, and I were frustrated when we considered this, looking for someone to blame. I had to struggle with this, thinking my way carefully through potential culprits, the navy's rushing out *Cisco* in fifty-six short days being first.

But there's no way to make a case, and no specific party responsible for rush in wartime, and thus no way this thinking can be constructive. Again, Jim comes to my rescue; he wouldn't waste time on negative emotion. He *acted*, writing a patrol report methodically laying out torpedo and equipment deficits, and then moved on. So the best I can do is lay out my theory here on the page and move on to *Cisco's* aftermath.

21

When *Cisco* was due back in Fremantle from patrol, November 6, 1943, Howie Rice, now cured of jaundice, climbed up on the submarine tender's bridge where he could see far out to sea. "I had no idea that radio messages to *Cisco* from headquarters had gone unanswered," Howie told me. He scanned the entrance buoys, where escorts waited to guide *Cisco* in. But there was no submarine. Rice waited, fighting off a growing feeling of shock.

Finally he came down and started making inquiries of the administration. He soon learned that *Cisco* hadn't answered direct radio calls and thus was presumed lost. "I was devastated!" he said. An officer handed him a sack of mail for *Cisco*'s men and told him to return it to senders, along with notice that the sub was missing. "Did your mother get her letters back?" Howie asked me. "I always wondered."

I shook my head, said I had no way of knowing, then pressed him for his feelings on learning *Cisco* was lost.

He ran a hand over his eyes, then stared at the table between us, struggling for words. Fingering his World War II radio, he said, "Well, I figured if I had been there as a sonar and radioman I could have done something that Cannon and Morressey [the other radiomen] may not have been able to do. Not until after the war when I heard the Japanese story [about the telltale oil slick] did I realize that I couldn't have done anything." He looked up, paused, a question in his eyes.

"What?" I said.

"Then I agonized over what your dad was trying to do to get away. I'm sure he didn't know of the oil leak and couldn't fathom how they kept after him." He shook his head. "In *my* mind, I blame the workers at the Portsmouth Navy Yard."

But I was gone on the phrase *what your dad was trying to do to get away.* I saw Jim racing through the boat shouting orders over the sound of water rushing in, men screaming, metal crumpling. As a wall of water knocks Jim to his knees, Rachel's name leaves his lips, and Mother sits bolt upright in bed halfway around the world, startled out of a sound sleep by Wordsworth's line: "A glory is gone from the earth."

I blinked, looked up at Howie. "Where was he?" I said.

"He would've been in the conning tower," Rice said, knowing what I needed to know. "He'd be trying to evade and also make repairs."

And then I knew that *I* was evading. Up in the conning tower, there's no escape from the present moment, no time to conjure up anything from the past. Jim hears only the cries of his men and curses himself. I've never been surer of anything in my life: it was his men and their dying that filled the end of Jim's mind.

I shook my head, telling Howie that what hurts most was finding out that there were three hours between the first and second attacks, giving Jim all kinds of time to beat himself up. Rice nodded and told me that he'd thought about the *Cisco*'s men every day for fifty years but couldn't figure it out. "Why me sitting here?" he gestured at the table. "And not them?"

The feeling was all around us that summer weekend in 1999. The official mission of the conference we were attending, the forty-fifth convention of U.S. Subvets of WWII, was to honor fallen comrades, those the veterans regard as the real heroes of the war. But there was no question of official mission at work in Howie. He seemed young amid the other submarine veterans, most of them white-haired or balding and in their seventies and eighties. Howie's hair was still steel-gray, and he was wiry, with a bouncy walk (a bit like Groucho Marx's). I was convinced that his daily swimming, his cutting-edge computer skills, his avid participation in radio and electronics clubs, and his writing his memoirs for his grandchildren was all because the gratitude for being spared was deep in his bones, pushing him to squeeze the most out of life.

And his story tells why. Not long after *Cisco*'s loss, Howie was assigned to another fleet submarine, the *Grenadier*. But he told *Grenadier*'s captain that he'd just come from *Cisco* and could not face going out on patrol so soon after her loss. The captain understood, and Howie stayed behind in Fremantle, working in the radar section for subs coming in for refit. In early

February of 1944, he was reassigned to *Rasher* and went on her third and fourth patrols. Meanwhile, *Grenadier* had gone down on the patrol Rice had been assigned to; most of *Grenadier*'s crew were picked up by the Japanese, becoming prisoners of war. So Howie was spared twice—an amazing stroke of providence for me and my siblings.

—◆◆◆—

After *Cisco*'s loss, there was no fanfare for her. Because she was lost on her first patrol, she didn't compile a record, no tonnage sunk to her credit in the history books. And so her men remain unsung, too, not only cut off before fulfilling their potential but also overlooked in memorials. In the hotel's ball-room during the convention, the submarine veterans met at tables under huge banners blazing the names of the subs they served on. To me, look-ing around the crowded room, there was a gaping hole: *Cisco* was not repre-sented. And at Bowfin Memorial Park at Pearl Harbor, where the fifty-two submarines lost in World War II are memorialized by plaques donated by their sponsoring states, *Cisco* was one of three subs that didn't have a sponsor come forward with funds to purchase a plaque. Her "gravestone" remained unmarked and forgotten for years until Howie Rice found out about it. He stormed into the Bowfin Memorial Park office with money to purchase a plaque. So now *Cisco*'s men's names are engraved for all to see.

When I found this out, a year before I met Howie at the convention, I contacted my siblings. My brother, sister, and I felt privileged when Howie allowed us to reimburse him for some of the cost of the beautiful engraved plaque. He said he knew it was important to us to feel part of it but that he'd let us pay only half, that he needed to remain part of it, too. The plaque is a true submariner's statement, where—free of hierarchy—our father's name comes alphabetically beneath his shipmate Fred Coe's. In perpetuity, Jim is one with his men, as he was in life.

Jim is also remembered by a peace memorial candelabra presented in his name in a memorial service at his hometown church, Richmond's St. Paul's Episcopal in May of 1947. Barbara Eastman, secretary of that church, kindly looked up the old church-service register book from that time and told me that Jim's memorial service had 148 people—both navy and hometown friends—in attendance, compared to 71 and 68 attending similar events the week before and after.

And at the submarine base in Pearl Harbor, there's a Coe Avenue in honor of Jim.[1] There's also a naval rest camp in Subic Bay named after him (from which World War II submarine veteran Jim Ward, when he guided me around *Lionfish*, kindly gave me his old membership card).

In the navy's record about the disappearance of *Cisco*, there is strikingly little regret. I had researchers comb the papers of Ralph Christie, Charles Lockwood, James Fife, and others in command at the time Jim went down. The only words that go deeper than bare facts about his loss are those of James Fife to Admiral Christie in a letter of November 12, 1943: "Please accept my sympathy regarding *Cisco*. From what I saw of Red he had a good ship and knew pretty well how to take care of himself. However, we can't throw bricks without getting some thrown at us and these things are a rub of the green."[2]

I took this "rub of the green" as Fife's invoking the Irish form of chance to dismiss the unexplainable, how the navy's newest ship under an outstanding commander could disappear without a trace. Clay Blair's write-up shows a greater sense of loss, where he refers to the lost *Cisco*'s skipper as "the much-loved and much-respected Jim Coe."[3]

I think of Mother at this time in Annapolis, getting the news that will blight every Christmas season thereafter. I imagine her with Jean, because at six years old, Jean knew her dad enough to miss him, grieve him. But she was never told.

Jean Coe sits on the front staircase between her mother's legs, her small fingers enmeshed in the black strands of her doll Mei-mei's yarn hair, pulling it tight to keep from fidgeting and whining under Mother's fingers. Because it's Monday, Mother is French-braiding Jean's hair, something the little girl hates because it has Mother poking her fingertips in a greasy jar of Suave to pull every strand from Jean's temples tight back against her head, stretching her eyes sideways.

Jean hears Skip and Jack, their cocker spaniels, through the front screen door snuffling the dead brown leaves that Mother has raked to the edges of the front walk. Jeannie can't see them, but she pictures their coats, the same copper color as the leaves, shining in the sun. "Me and Mei-mei brushed the doggies," she says, wanting to be sure that Mother knows how much better she is at Henry's job while her little brother is off in Washington visiting their cousins.

"Mei-mei and I," is all Mother says, tugging a strand up and away from her ears. But suddenly Mother's fingers stop as leaves crackle and the dogs bark. Jean cocks her head, listening for her friend Krinkle's trot down the walk. Instead, she hears heavy footfalls and the crackle and snuffle of the dogs following through dry leaves.

"Sit still!" Mother snaps, and Jean eases her head back. "I'm almost ready for the rubber band; just hold still and you can go with them."

There's a knock on the door.

"Hi, Fritzie," Mother says. "Almost ready."

"Uh, Ma'am?" comes a male voice, and Mother's hands stop. Jeannie rises with the pull on her hair as Mother gets up, and they come to the door together. Mother swings it open with her foot, her fingers still enmeshed in Jean's hair.

Jeannie sees two sets of black uniformed legs before she's yanked to the floor amid a long wail from her mother. She tries to raise her head from the hard floorboards, but Mother's clutching tight to her hair, whimpering, and Jeannie feels the cold floor under her cheek moisten with tears as a yellow telegram drifts down. A woman's voice suddenly sounds overhead; it's Krinkle's mother, Fritz, saying to someone, "C'mon, help me get her up; she's pregnant!" and she sees Mrs. Adkin's saddle shoes suddenly beside her, her knees coming into view as Mother's hands loosen from her hair and the stinging stops.

Thirty years later, Jean pushes her daughter in a stroller through Hampstead Heath in London. It's spring, and a catbird flies to a bush along the path up ahead, a strand of black yarn dangling from its beak. Jean inadvertently stops to cover her daughter's blonde head with her hand and gets a flash of Mei-mei, the beautiful doll that Daddy Jim brought her from Shanghai. "Whatever happened to Mei-mei?" she wonders, suddenly aware of her daughter's warm hair under her fingers. She looks at her hand, wondering what she's doing. Then back at the bird, straining to re-member. Did she ever leave Mei-mei outside, to be pecked by a bird look-ing for yarn for a nest? She tries to think back, but can't recall anything but the dry, sinewy feel of Mei-mei's yarn hair in her fingers, and now, a tightness in her scalp. She turns the stroller around and heads home, hoping it's not the beginning of a headache.

As befits the only child of Jim Coe to have any memory of that terrible day, my sister, Jean, inherited the fateful telegram below.

—◦⁄◦⁄◦—

Besides the grief that Howie Rice and I shared about Jim's last hours, there was something else in *Cisco*'s aftermath I struggled with. If the *Cisco* went down because of an inadequate patch job in Portsmouth, doesn't my father—as captain—bear some responsibility for not catching and correcting the re-sultant oil leak? His documented complaints of oil leaks in the records of *Cisco*'s sea trials and Paul Loustaunau's memory of Jim's talk of a recurrent oil leak showed that he knew something was wrong. Why, then, did he take a defective boat to sea?

At the submarine veterans' convention, after I interviewed Rice, an old submarine veteran inadvertently rubbed my face in this question (as if I wasn't doing a good enough job myself). This was an odd place for this to happen because, again, the submarine veterans' mission is to remember and honor lost shipmates, those whom the veterans regard as the real heroes of the war.

I was interviewing one of the few remaining *Skipjack* veterans who had sailed with Jim. He'd been on only one patrol with him—the last—and per-haps this short acquaintance plus the relative lack of distinction of this fifth war patrol accounted for the man's willingness to raise this dark subject. I listened, stunned and relieved I had a tape recorder to assure me later that

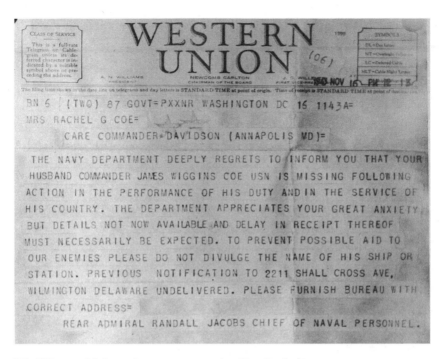

The Western Union telegram announcing Jim Coe's disappearance.

I'd heard accurately. Ironically, I'd come to value the few unflattering things I'd heard in the course of this project because I knew that these expressions were at least honest, compared to the more socially appropriate glowing reviews that filled my tape recorder and notebooks. Although I'd always try to assure people that I wanted to know *everything* they remembered about Jim, "warts and all," it's hard to imagine anyone—especially of this more formal and proper World War II generation—telling a daughter anything bad about her lost father.

So when I heard this rare candor in a Fort Worth motel room, I sat paralyzed, afraid that if I fidgeted or made a peep, this guy would realize how inappropriate he was and clam up. He was lying down, resting his heart and eyes as he talked. After an introduction about how every job on a submarine is vital, and if one person screws up his job the whole ship goes down, he said:

Well, you think about all the men who lost their lives on the boats, buried out there in the Pacific Ocean, you ask yourself, "Who are the lucky ones? Who are the heroes?" We [submarine veterans] all say, "Those are the heroes; we are the lucky ones." But you know, deep down in some of the lower filters of my brain, I think about "I am the hero. They are the unlucky ones. They did something wrong. We didn't do something wrong, so we are not lucky. We are the ones that are heroes." But that's a concept I have; those boats that were lost, were lost because of a mistake. And there had to be a certain amount of . . . [indecipherable] of that mistake because the Lord had already ordained that a long time ago. And those that made a mistake lost their lives, and those that didn't came back. So the skippers who brought their boats back are the heroes. Just a concept that I . . . I don't profess it or anything like that, but inside of me I think it. But for the grace of God go I.

At this point his wife, looking as shocked as I was, interrupted: "I've never heard you say that before."

"I've never said it before," he replied. "But who's the guy who gets in an accident? The guy who makes a mistake . . ."

"But what about the men who get bombed by Jap planes? What did they do wrong?" his wife asked.

"They didn't see that plane coming," he said. "The lookouts failed their job. The lookouts are up there, they sweep the horizon, then they sweep the sky."

This reminds the guy of more heroics, and he tells me that he had such good night vision that he was his captain's eyes for the remainder of the war. *It just happened to be something the good Lord gave me,* he said, while I gathered up my things and politely took my leave. For the next sixteen or so hours, the convention was spoiled for me as I excoriated myself for not calling him on his attitude, letting politeness win out against the question: "So what are you saying about my father?"

At the skippers' breakfast the next morning, I was riding a cascade of self-pity, the old submarine veteran's ramblings about the *real* heroes circling my mind. Did all the men around me secretly feel this way, that they are the real heroes, and the dead made the mistakes? As if in confirmation, the old admiral in charge of the breakfast had reacted with impatience when I'd asked him if children of lost skippers could attend the meal. He said I'd have to ask permission of the conference organizers because "we can't have children running around at the breakfast!" The conference director let me in—but I still wanted to stay out of the way of the old admiral. This wasn't hard, because he was wandering around the restaurant with a cash box in his hands, readying himself two hours beforehand to pay the breakfast bill.

It soon became clear that the old admiral didn't know what he was doing. There was no designated area for the skippers to meet, and the restaurant manager kept coming up to me as the youngest one there, asking me where I wanted people seated. I finally got it across that I wasn't in charge but that there should be a breakfast area set aside for the skippers, who were all waiting, puzzled, behind velvet ropes to be seated. The waiters scurried around and moved tables into a corner near the cafeteria line, turning the breakfast suddenly into a serve-yourself affair. I went through the line with the skippers, trying to introduce myself and tell them what I was there for. One old admiral's face actually fell when he met me, clearly pitying me. "I didn't know him well," he said of Jim Coe, looking over my shoulder for a familiar face to come to his rescue.

I went over to a group of older-looking men who had already filled their plates and seated themselves. Balancing my tray on the corner of their table, I asked them if anyone had known Jim Coe. I received some positive nods, but one of the men said—eyeing the table's one empty chair—"My wife's sitting there." I moved away to an empty two-person table, feeling like a leper.

Suddenly I saw the sleek personas of the old admirals as affronts: their distinguished white hair; the erect carriage; the beautiful sportcoats of silk, linen, or Harris Tweed; the well-heeled wives—many of them young things in their sixties and seventies—in elegant jacket dresses. These were now signs of complacency, even smugness, for making it home. I felt a giant conspiracy forming around me, everyone in league to raise their brows with fake interest or shake their heads sympathetically when I asked about Jim, all the while biting their tongues against the first word that leapt into their minds: "Mistake, mistake."

Meanwhile, the old admiral with the cash box who was in charge of picking up the tab had disappeared. The maitre d' again came over to me: "Do you want this all on one check?"

I explained again that the skipper with the cash box was somewhere around, that *he* was in charge of the breakfast. The maitre d' told me that no one had told him a thing and that he had to get paid. I offered to pay for my own breakfast, although it was cold by now, and he called all his waiters over and told them to write up everyone separate checks. Because the skippers were now up and on their way out, it was chaos as the waiters fanned out among them and tried to explain while writing up checks at the same time. I was getting a lump in my throat thinking of how all the world—even the guys gathered here supposedly to honor their lost colleagues—had forgotten Jim. I suddenly knew I needed help.

I went back to my motel and changed into my jogging clothes. Trotting the sweltering streets of Fort Worth soon dispelled my black feelings, and I praised endorphins. I realized that there's no way the submarine veteran I met with yesterday could know *what* went on on *Cisco* or any other downed ship and that he was probably just fishing for a reason to call himself a hero in the presence of an interviewer. It was pathetic that he forgot who I was when he did it, but his wife didn't, poor thing, and I'm glad I didn't take them to task for it. And the guys this morning—they were all in their eighties at the youngest. The only classmate of Jim's there from the Naval Academy was a frail ninety-one-year-old. And I'm asking them to go back sixty years, in the middle of a chaotic cafeteria line? What did I expect?

I ended the jog deciding that the submarine veterans and I shared the same purpose; we were just coming at it from two different ends. I was at the beginning of piecing together a father I hadn't known, trying to construct him out of others' memories. They were at the end of the story, looking back at shipmates lost sixty years ago to get their names, boats, and sacrifice out to the public. Our mission was the same: to honor these lost men. I just needed to meet these vets somewhere in the middle, to ask the questions that would put them back on the decks, docks, and harbor streets with my father.

In the years since that convention, I've actually come to be glad that the inappropriate submarine veteran called my attention to an attitude prevalent among the submarine veterans: pride in their skippers for bringing them home. It made me work through the issue, realizing that my prickly suspicion that the obverse was true was not fair. A skipper who says he's most proud for bringing his men home does not necessarily believe that those who didn't had made a mistake or don't deserve equal pride or the encomium of "hero." It was only that one submarine veteran in Fort Worth who equated pride in coming home with heroism and a judgment against the dead; I don't have to take that on.

And neither does Jim. For every complaint of the recurrent oil leak, there was a repair record and inspection pronouncing the *Cisco* seaworthy. Jim did all he could: submitted the boat for repairs and tested her out. He did this repeatedly, delaying his departure from the United States and arrival in Australia and—finally—his departure for patrol. All the time, he was under pressure to leave, to take *Cisco* to war and rack up the great record everyone expected of her. John Cowan of the New Hampshire chapter of the U.S. Subvets of WWII spoke for all the men I interviewed about this: "Well, you can only have your ship repaired so many times, then you've just gotta go."

"And make repairs yourself? En route?"

"Yes," he said.

I also found out that Jim would not have been able to know whether there was oil leaking from the fuel ballast tank once under way. "The wake would be boiling up with air as the ship moved forward," said Howie Rice, citing this "cavitation" as covering any sign of oil. "When submerged looking through the periscope, any oil leaking would not come to the surface until a long time had passed and would not be seen from the periscope."

Hindsight, of course, gives us access to patterns that Jim wasn't aware of. Bill Ruhe, an officer on *Cisco*'s sister ship *Crevalle,* wrote about his crew's response to the startling loss rate of two out of the four Portsmouth-built boats in *Cisco*'s division, both on their first patrol:

On December 31, [1943,] a large number of man-hours were spent checking all parts of the Crevalle for structural weaknesses that might have sunk the Capelin and Cisco. Quite by chance, I was able to identify what might be a fatal flaw in the Crevalle's construction. While running my hand over the flange in the vent-riser (the piping for venting the air from a ballast tank and which was under sea pressure when submerged) for the after main ballast tank in the after torpedo room, I felt a loose, jiggling, hold-down bolt. It was out of sight between the vent-riser and the hull. Sliding my finger further behind the riser I discovered an empty bolt hole. I tried the other side of the flange and found an empty bolt hole along with two bolts on that side not being tightly secured. Evidently, the yard workmen at Portsmouth had found it too difficult to screw down all bolts on the flanges because they were poorly designed and denied any use of leverage for tightening the bolts or even getting them into their bolt holes. As a result only about 200 degrees of the flanges' circumference was bolted tightly. Further investigation revealed that the flanges on the vent-risers in the forward torpedo room were similarly only partially bolted down. Since these vent-risers were exposed to sea pressure, the shock from a nearby depth charge might easily cause the flanges to open up and flood the room uncontrollably, particularly when the submarine was at deep submergence.

Two of the auxiliarymen went to work fashioning a ratchet wrench with a bent handle that could tighten bolts in the most constricted area of the flange. But even before the Crevalle's flanges were securely bolted, the captain sent a message to the Cabrilla alerting her skipper about the structural problem that had been uncovered.[4]

Because *Cisco* was hurried out so much faster than her sisters, she may well have suffered from these same loose flanges, if not other defects. There is no way we'll ever know—even if *Cisco* could someday be located and raised. And because no one can be held accountable after all these years, it is useless to cast blame—although I sure wanted to on first hearing of the oil leak.

One thing I do know for certain, however: Jim had a highly developed sense of duty. It took him out in a boat with problems, and it caused him to think carefully about his family in his last days in Fremantle and Darwin.

Three kids left behind.

After he went down, my mother received posthumous letters, three of which she blessedly kept for me to find with her effects. In the first, Jim talks about how much he enjoyed his long stay with her, "and was much luckier in the length of the stay than most." He makes light of "a few problems in the boat to iron out" and says they've gotten some good training in. In the next one, a V-mail, he gives news that he's boosting Mother's insurance allotment and that he's invested in more war bonds for her. "So you are making about $800 a year on this deal—take it easy, Pal, and we'll celebrate when I get back."

And then he drops a bombshell, giving the lie to my stepfather's claim that Jim never knew I was on the way. The "Fritz" whom he refers to in the excerpt below is Fritz Adkins, my mother's best friend, married to a fellow skipper who must have called her from Fremantle. Jim here refers to Mother's recent move to their new house in Annapolis: "Am glad all our things are finally in our own house and am proud of the way you have gotten it all arranged with practically no help. Hope you haven't hurt yourself

Darling—especially in view of the good news 'a la Fritz' which tickles me too and I'm squeezing for you Ray—also missing you like anything."

It's more than I ever could have hoped for, and as I set the V-mail down, my chest unlatched, as though a tight Ace bandage around my torso had finally broken. Tears poured out, a mix of gratitude and years of pent-up grief for Jim. He *knew* about me. For the brief moment it took him to write that single sentence, we connected.

The third letter, also a V-mail, is to his kids:

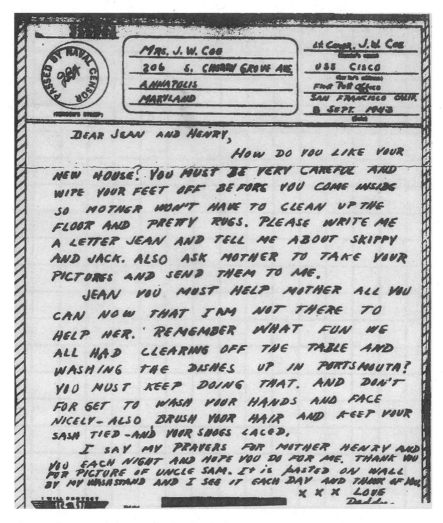

Copy of Jim Coe's last V-mail to his kids.

I flashed on all the times growing up when Jean was at the sink in Frank and Mother's battleground, the kitchen. She always had her hands in dish-water, as if the warm, sudsy water would protect her from the angry voices raging around her. And I see her now in London, where she lives with her family, never letting guests do the dishes. "I like it," she tells us, and now I know that this is one of the ways—indeed, as "rich and strange" as the "Full fathom five" song from *The Tempest* foretold—that Jim has lived on all these years.

III

Sea Change

22

At the beginning of each semester, I try to "sell" my creative writing course—a core requirement that students, particularly those going into accounting, computer science, and other nonwriting fields, wonder why they have to take. I tell them that imagination is the key to empathy, even compassion, and if they work their imaginations like a muscle, as we plan to do in this course, they will be better able to understand people. I give examples of crucial types such as future employers, customers, spouses, in-laws, and so on. By imagining themselves in others' (various characters') shoes, they will develop people skills that can serve them in all walks of life.

Now I can attest to this power of imagination with more conviction than ever before, because it's brought a new presence to my life: Jim Coe. In having to imagine this man's final moments, I was filled with his urgency and dashed hopes and—hardest to bear—his sense of failed duty as he heard the water crush his doomed ship. It was bad enough that he had to die; it was worse that he likely felt self-reproach with his last breath. I hope I'm wrong about it, but facing this worst possible state of mind not only made him vividly accessible but also taught me something I now bring to all my relationships: that this imagined psychic misery is harder to bear than any physical pain we can imagine our loved ones enduring. And so I better understand my daughter's silence during a recession some years ago, when she had a hard time finding a job. The times she felt like a failure were the times she didn't call. I'm grateful, now, for her sparing me and her dad.

Writing Jim to new life in my mind has also taught me what my cousin Fred Niles wrote me at the beginning of this search: "Be happy," he said, "as Jim would have wanted you to be." I'm trying now to uncover whatever of Jim's natural buoyancy he passed down to me, the happiness that the tension of my early years in a troubled household buried. I now try to reason my way out of negative emotions. If I can't, I no longer spread them around to family and friends. Talking about these feelings for the sake of openness, closeness, honesty, and so forth not only inflates the importance of what prove to be just passing states but also hurts my loved ones.

Jim didn't give much time to negative emotions. A vivid demonstration of this was the reaction of Tom Parks when I sent him a copy of a letter I wrote the Bowfin Submarine Museum in Pearl Harbor. I asked them to stop handing out a flier on Jim (that included his toilet-paper letter) because the writer referred to him as "pompous and belligerent." Although Tom Parks agreed with my protest enough to write the museum a letter of his own (and the museum stopped distributing the flier), Parks then said that he didn't mean any disrespect, but if Jim could know that he'd been tagged for all eternity as "pompous and belligerent," he'd laugh. Pomposity doesn't coexist with humor, Tom said, a fact that Jim was particularly aware of.

This letter from Parks showed me that if Jim, with his vast responsibilities during the time Tom Parks knew him, gave the impression that he could laugh at himself for the way he was depicted, then I could certainly afford to lighten up. Jim's good nature, plus the fact of his early death, made me realize that just being alive—let alone having peace and freedom—is a gift. Celebration, then, or at least a quick scan for the good, is a more fitting response than the cynicism and low tolerance for frustration that I grew up with. And so coming to know Jim Coe has offset the somber, inhibiting influence of the other father in my life.

I now realize that associating Jim for all those formative years in my mind with sadness and loss was seriously misreading (and underestimating) his nature. He loved life, people, pets, music, and the sea. Certainly the war made him cherish these things even more. In aspiring to do the same, I am drawing closer to who I might have been if I'd grown up under his influence. In this way, finding out who Jim was has completed my identity, made me the person I feel I was supposed to be.

A new respect for aging is part of this new persona. Knowing that Jim didn't get a chance to grow old makes me more tolerant of the physical changes that are commonly decried in our culture. New lines around my eyes and mouth are no longer disappointments; they're clues to how Jim would've looked if he'd lived. That makes looking in the mirror these days extremely interesting.

What first made me fully aware of this change was a remark about gray hair that Sara Shute, daughter of Jim's first love, Jane Rohe, made on one of our walks recently. She was looking at my hair—a cross between my mother's black and Jim's red that has aged over the years from blonde to a dull mouse-brown in which gray doesn't seem to show. Sara said she assumed that I dyed my hair. I grabbed a hank of it. "This?" I said in amazement. "This is all I have left of him."

A bit overdramatic, I admit, but the vehemence of my response showed me that I want to protect whatever I carry of Jim. And so he's transformed what society or my younger, more vain self considered flaws into traits I'm newly proud of. I used to be ashamed of my slow speech—something I feared might, at worst, be a sign of some slight brain damage from the time my mother found me at age three floating facedown in the neighbor's fish pond, my skin blue. But this changed recently when a tape of an old radio broadcast of a 1943 Vox Pop program that my father had been a guest on arrived in the mail. I'd started hunting for it five years ago.

When I heard Jim's voice for the first time, with a self-dismissive and drawn-out "Wellll . . ." beginning each answer, I was disappointed. This deep-voiced man who hesitated before each word, turning it over in his mind like some feeble old guy trying to make change at the checkout counter, couldn't be the lively, witty ham that my interviewees remembered, the eager extrovert I'd come to know.

And then I made the connection, one that my own shame had hidden. When I've had to replay a phone message I've left someone, I've always been amazed and chagrined to hear how slowly I talk, and I'm reminded of a long-ago burst of impatience from a friend after waiting for me to rephrase a convoluted thought: "Mary Lee, I've gotta be honest. I've never known anyone so smart who sounds so dumb!"

And I realize that it's because I judge my own slow talk with such harsh ears that I think Jim sounds doddering and klutzy at the mike. I listen again and realize he's not; he's simply someone who—yes, talks slow—but who's also tired, preoccupied with readying a new sub for war (it's May 24, 1943), and probably wants to cut through the glorification of submariners that the radio show's host tries to purvey to the audience by his questions.

"Tell us what it's like to be depth charged," urges the host, with the jauntiness of someone asking, "Hey kids, tell us about that ride on the merry-go-round you took the other day!" Jim seems stunned and buys time with a drawled "Welllll," then deftly sidesteps the unspeakable. The hardest thing about it, he says, is trying to avoid the feeling that everyone's looking at him, especially the new sailors, who snatch glances at the skipper's face to know whether they should be scared or not. "No matter what you feel, you gotta raise your eyebrows as high as the next guy's."

"What d'ya like best about submarines?" says the host, with hearty enthusiasm. And Jim, who by now is probably sick of submarines, sounds wary, reluctant, and bone tired of putting a happy face on war: "Welllll, when things get hot, every man knows what to do. They don't have to ask an officer."

And so I hear in Jim's voice this second time the hesitation of a man struggling to balance the ineffable terrors of undersea warfare, the audience's expectations of heroism and glory, and his pact with "the silent service." And I also hear the freeing message that no, my slow speech isn't because of my near-drowning as a child; it's probably genetic.

Jim has also made me newly interested in my brother Henry and my sister, who have the same slow, deliberate speech pattern and mole-colored hair that I do. My sister's fondness for water, from sinking her hands in warm dishwater to swimming in the ocean, reminds me of Jim's love of the sea. Her love of art makes me take new notice of the rugs Jim chose for Mother when he was in Panama. And my brother's natural leadership, athletic prowess, and intelligence that lifted him above the tyranny of his stepfather in his high school years are a new source of pride. The ongoing construction projects that Frank made Henry toil at when we were growing up robbed him of time for homework, sports, extracurricular activities, and a social life. Despite this, his high school classmates wrote Henry in for student-council president, a job he didn't seek, and without having the freedom from Frank to campaign or even create a platform, Henry won. He also—without being allowed to go out for sports in high school—got a tryout with the Philadelphia Phillies farm team after he graduated. (He took the geographical cure instead, going off to college in Providence, Rhode Island, rather than pursue an athletic career near home.) I didn't note any of this until a few years ago; it was learning Jim Coe that made me realize that Henry's early success, despite Frank's holding him back from the world of his peers, was extraordinary—and most likely a legacy from Jim.

I have a similar new appreciation of my mother. In seeing her as Jim's beloved, the woman he chose above all others, she has grown in stature from the victim of my childhood, "the moron," as she was denigrated by my stepfather. From the weak, childish woman who couldn't do anything right, she's grown in my mind into the life partner who fueled the fun, goodwill, and dreams of a remarkable man. She was the one Jim depended on to do business stateside, the one he entrusted his kids to, missed when he was away, and blizzarded with letters and gifts.

Looking at her this way, I now see all of her behavior through a softer lens. I had resented her in my teens and twenties for staying with Frank, and this blinded me to her strengths. It wasn't until my search for Jim Coe led me to stories of other World War II widows that I realized that we Coe kids were better off than many "war orphans," and this was largely due to Mother. She held herself together for our sake and stuck with us when—with her parents' resources and her intrepid desire for travel—she could have done otherwise. She could have parked us with her parents and run away or lost herself in drink. Plenty of World War II widows did.

But she remarried instead. I have no doubt that she thought we'd be better off with a stepfather. I now realize that she was trying, in her precipitate way, to take responsibility—to solve the dilemma of our fatherless state on her own.

Once I began, through the intervention of Jim Coe, to imagine myself in her shoes, I realized what had eluded me up until then. I had long been puzzled by a day we'd spent at the beach here in Maine in the late seventies, when Mother revealed herself to be the mother I'd always wanted. She opened up like she never had before, telling me that David—a man she had met in the Quaker Meeting she attended in Santa Barbara in her late middle age, a man she'd been playing bridge with and seeing on a friendly basis up until then—had just shown romantic feelings for her. She asked my advice about how to proceed, even mentioning thoughts about remarriage.

I made some innocuous suggestions, holding my breath against the fragile magic that suddenly let us talk together like a couple of teenaged girls. She rolled up her pant legs and rubbed suntan lotion into her calves. "What's that?" I said, pointing to a scar running down her left shin.

Her hazel eyes suddenly greened with moisture, and she looked away, saying that Frank had broken a beer bottle against it. It was the last night I was there in our old house. I was fifteen and had just come home from a school dance with a date, whom Frank insulted. The boy left, and then I yelled at Frank and started upstairs to my room; Frank lunged up the stairs after me, and suddenly Mother was there between us, letting me turn and run downstairs and out the door. I escaped to my grandmother's house a few blocks away. Mother came the next day and filed for divorce.

But there on the beach, she was angry as she told me about the scar, and I was glad, preferring it to tears. Anger you could do something with—go and make a new life for yourself, as she'd done. She was mad all right, but on this magical day, she didn't blame anyone else. When I said, "I'm glad we got out of it," she said in a wobbly voice, "Yeah, but it hurt you kids."

It was stunningly close to the apology I'd always wanted, and although I shrugged it off at the time, telling her she'd done just fine by us kids, I puzzled over it for years after the old silence closed down around us once more. What had opened her up that day, made her so intimate and unguarded?

It was only after I got to know Jim and started to sense how much Mother had lost in him that I suddenly remembered what else she had told me that day at the beach, the thing her scar had distracted me from. She'd told me about David, the only man she'd allowed herself to go out with since divorcing Frank in 1960. That day on the beach was the only time I'd ever seen her feeling lovely, desirable, *wanted*. I had always known her as the opposite (and I shrank to think that I was once party to making her feel that way). And so, to be chosen later in life, after she'd figured the time for such feelings was long gone, must have been doubly intense, doubly gratifying. This—call it love or the joy of being singled out, preferred—is what opened her up that day on the beach. It caused a temporary intimacy between us, and I realized that we kids would have seen more of this if Jim had lived. This was the different person, the concerned, expressive mother she would have been in Jim's love.

When I realized this, it was heartbreaking to think that I hadn't started the research into Jim before Mother died. Undoubtedly, I could have brought forth that more intimate, caring mother if *I* had given her more love. No wonder she never showed me her scars. I didn't have the compassion to understand them as such. So the circle of recrimination wound through my head.

However, now there was Jim in there to interrupt it. If I've learned nothing else from him, he's taught me to make the best of what you have—even if it's an old, worn-out S-boat. So, no longer having Mother, I'm learning to sit up and take notice of her memory. Things I glossed over before—like her delight in escaping Quaker Meeting by my coughs when I was little, shepherding me out of the building on a walk through Swarthmore College's lilacs; or her pointing out, in the Pocono Mountains, how much more beautiful ferns and orange salamanders look in wet than dry woods; or her ready agreement when I confessed that I didn't know if I really believed in God—these all pour back to me now with new significance. I remember the time she took me on a mystery trip—to see a litter of Dalmatian puppies. I was overwhelmed when she said I could pick one out for my eighth birthday. She must have known that I would need something to cuddle and teach, to care for and protect, in the coming years. And I remember her joy when I, as a grown-up mother myself, told her on the phone that my daughter and husband were on a sailing race together. I was bemoaning the fact, missing them, but Mother loved the thought of a father doing something like that with a daughter, and only after my learning about Jim did this memory resonate. Mother was finally seeing things put to rights; my daughter was getting the fatherly attention that Mother had always wanted for us. In rare moments of my adulthood, she'd told me she was saddest about the fact that I'd never known my father.

These memories now show me something I'd doubted before: my mother's love. And Jim's influence on her, his love for her, is the new lens that lets me see this. And so, a little more than sixty years after disappearing, Jim has caused a sea change in me, fulfilling the promise of Ariel's song.

Now, because of him, I drive down to Portsmouth, New Hampshire, each Memorial Day to stand beside the old submarine veterans as they lay wreaths and toll the bell at the submarine memorial. I'm honored to be among them, knowing now what their patriotism means. "I wake up in the middle of the night and think of them," said Charlie Witt, veteran of the *S-39,* about my father and the other *S-39*ers who went down on *Cisco.* "I wonder where they are." At the memorial service, especially during the tolling of the bells in which a submarine veteran calls out the name of every lost submarine, I can feel the minds of these old men go deep, wondering where their lost friends are and wondering why, oh God, why *them* rather than me?

The other day I came around the corner of a city building and almost mowed down a little kid who was straggling behind his mother. "Bang bang!" he said, pointing a toy gun at me.

"Wait!" I said, crouching in front of him, getting ready to tell him that shooting people isn't a game, isn't something to play at, but he'd already run past. I watched him cross the street with his mother, who smiled back at me with her head cocked, as if to say, "Isn't he cute?" I didn't smile back, wondering instead who the kid was pretending to kill. Osama bin Laden? Saddam Hussein? Other terrorists? I thought back to the funny-papers of my youth, where Japanese characters all looked like hyenas or jackals—with sickly, yellow skin, hair in topknots, and big buckteeth. What subhuman caricature was the kid picturing when he fired his toy gun?

I thought of what I'd say when I run into the next child like this. I'll tell him about the real cost of war, about the loss of my father—what it did to our family. About children robbed of fathers and about widows crazed with grief. This is what Jim was trying to do when he told the service club in Richmond that the real war wasn't all acts of glory and heroism.

Writing Jim to a second life has put a new presence in my consciousness. Occasionally, he takes me by surprise, as he did early one morning not long ago when I was awakened by the sound of the coffee grinder in the kitchen. In that haze between sleeping and waking, I thought it was Jim out there making coffee for his men! He was in my husband's bathrobe, his penny-colored hair a beautiful contrast to the Wedgwood blue flannel. I rolled over with the delicious feeling of being taken care of, watched over, *parented,* and fell back to sleep. When I woke up later and realized that it had been my husband, I was gratified that Jim is no longer a still life in old photographs. He's come into my life, our kitchen, moving among coffee grinders and microwaves in L.L. Bean flannel, scuffing his slippers across our tile floor.

The other day I wore his coat to a book-group meeting. On greeting me at the door, our hostess said, "Ahhh! There's nothing like a man's coat."

And suddenly he was there, welcoming us onto the deck of his boat. He's in his dark navy uniform, his coppery head hatless, his "dog ears" flanged out and reddened in the sun. He bends forward from the waist with his hands on his hips, cocking his head at me as if to say, "Hey, wayward sailor, where've you been?"

Feeling a smile heat up my face, I turn to the book-group lady. "There's nothing like *this* man's coat." And then I tell her about my dad.

Notes

Chapter 3

1. Susan J. Hadler and Ann B. Mix, *Lost in the Victory: Reflections of American War Orphans of WWII* (Denton: University of North Texas Press, 1998), xxiv; archives of orphans' accounts at American WWII Orphans Network (AWON), 5745 Lee Road, Indianapolis, Indiana 46216. The organization's Web site address is www.awon.org; their e-mail address is awon@aol.com

2. *Richmond (Indiana) Palladium Item,* June 14, 1960, 2.

3. U.S. Naval Academy Editors, *The Lucky Bag of 1930* (Annapolis, Md.: U.S. Naval Academy, 1930), 208.

4. *Richmond (Indiana) Palladium Item,* August 20, 1954, 4.

Chapter 4

1. U.S. Naval Academy Editors, *Lucky Bag,* 208.

2. Carl Lavo, *Slade Cutter, Submarine Warrior* (Annapolis, Md.: Naval Institute Press, 2003), 48.

3. U.S. Naval Academy Editors, *Lucky Bag,* 208.

4. *Big Shot* (newsletter of USS *Chicago*), July 4, 1932, 2.

5. Ibid., November 5, 1932, 1.

Chapter 5

1. W. J. Holmes, *Undersea Victory* (New York: Doubleday, 1966), 36.

2. Robert Casey, *Battle Below* (New York: Bobbs-Merrill, 1945), 15.

3. Herman Wouk, *The Winds of War* (New York: Pocket Books, 1971), 451.

4. Carl Lavo, *Back from the Deep* (Annapolis, Md.: Naval Institute Press, 1994), 22.

5. Charles A. Lockwood and Hans Christian Adamson, *Through Hell and Deep Water* (New York: Greenberg, 1956), 79.

6. John F. Davidson, *Reminiscences* (Annapolis, Md.: U.S. Naval Institute, 1986), 85–86.

7. Margaret Solenberger, "Don't Pull the Plug," *China Gunboatman* (newsletter of the South China Yangtze Patrol Asiatic Fleet), September 1999, 15.

8. H. C. Bruton, "The Far China Station II (1936–37)," *Shipmate,* April 1986, 25.

9. Holmes, *Undersea Victory,* 37.

Chapter 6

1. Samuel Eliot Morison, *History of United States Naval Operations in World War II* (Boston: Little Brown, 1950), 3:30.

2. Casey, *Battle Below,* 87, 85.

3. Ibid., 17.

4. Ibid., 86.

5. Ibid., 77.

Chapter 9

1. Bobette Gugliotta, *Pigboat 39* (Lexington: University Press of Kentucky, 1984), 27.

2. Morison, *History of United States Naval Operations,* 3:12.

3. Herbert Bix, *Hirohito and the Making of Modern Japan* (New York: Harper-Collins, 2000), 146–47.

4. C. R. Bartholomew, "What They Never Told," *Polaris,* June 1999, 15.

5 Gugliotta, *Pigboat 39,* 12.

6. Ibid., 57.

7. Ibid., 62.

8. Ibid., 2.

9. Ibid., 34.

10. Ibid., 41, 42.

Chapter 10

1. *Silver Dolphins* (newsletter of Three Rivers Chapter of U.S. Subvets of WWII), August 2001, 5.

2. Edward L. Beach, *Submarine!* (New York: Zebra Books, 1990), 144–45, 312.

3. Gugliotta, *Pigboat 39,* 86.

4. Clay Blair, *Silent Victory: The U.S. Submarine War against Japan* (Annapolis, Md.: Naval Institute Press), 60.

5. *Richmond (Indiana) Palladium Item,* December 8, 1941, 12.

Chapter 11

1. Gerald Astor, *The Greatest War* (Novato, Calif.: Presidio Press, 1999), 54.

2. Casey, *Battle Below,* 234–35.

3. James W. Coe, "Brief Summary of USS *S-39* War Patrol Report No. 1, December 11–21, 1941," U.S. Naval Academy Archives, Nimitz Library, U.S. Asiatic Fleet, Submarine Division 201, 1.

4. Gugliotta, *Pigboat 39,* 92.

5. Ibid., 93.

6. Casey, *Battle Below,* 74.

7. Gugliotta, *Pigboat 39,* 95.

8. Casey, *Battle Below,* 315.

9. Gugliotta, *Pigboat 39,* 98, 99.

10. George Grider, *Warfish* (Boston: Little, Brown, 1958), 254.

11. Casey, *Battle Below,* 316.

Chapter 12

1. Astor, *Greatest War,* 50, 56.

2. Ibid., 62.

3. Gugliotta, *Pigboat 39,* 109

4. Blair, *Silent Victory,* 132.

5. Gugliotta, *Pigboat 39,* 124.

6. Ibid., 141.

7. James W. Coe, "USS *S-39* Third War Patrol Report, Feb. 14–Mar. 18, 1942," U.S. Naval Academy Archives, Nimitz Library, U.S. Asiatic Fleet, Submarine Division 201, 5.

8. Ibid.

9. Ibid., 5–7.

10. Gugliotta, *Pigboat 39,* 150–51.

11. Coe, "USS *S-39* Third War Patrol Report," 10.

12. Casey, *Battle Below,* 318.

13. Gugliotta, *Pigboat 39,* 158.

14. Ibid., 165.

15. Ibid.

16. Holmes, *Undersea Victory,* 47.

17. Beach, *Submarine,* 111.

18. Casey, *Battle Below,* 315.

19. Blair, *Silent Victory,* 164.

Chapter 13

1. W. G. Winslow, *The Fleet the Gods Forgot* (Annapolis, Md.: Naval Institute Press, 1982), 161.

2. Ibid., 164.

3. Theodore Roscoe, *Submarine Operations in WWII* (Annapolis, Md.: U.S. Naval Institute, 1949), 96.

4. Morison, *History of United States Naval Operations,* 3:312.

5. Blair, *Silent Victory,* 159.

6. Winslow, *The Fleet the Gods Forgot,* 246.

7. Paul Fussell, *Wartime* (New York: Oxford University Press, 1989), 273.

8. Roscoe, *Submarine Operations,* 97.

9. Blair, *Silent Victory,* 165.

10. Samuel F. Simpson, "A Brief on the *USS Perch*" (unpublished manuscript in author's possession), 2.

11. Samuel F. Simpson, "USS *Perch* Experience," *Ex-Pow Bulletin* 10 (October 1984): 74.

12. Fussell, *Wartime,* 285.

Chapter 14

1. Robert Gannon, *Hellions of the Deep* (University Park: Pennsylvania State University Press, 1996), 81.

2. Roscoe, *Submarine Operations,* 34.

3. Blair, *Silent Victory,* 193.

4. Ibid., 161.

5. Douglas Murphy, "Hit or Miss," *Invention and Technology* (Spring 1998): 58.

6. Blair, *Silent Victory,* 167.

7. Ibid., 179–80.

Chapter 15

1. James W. Coe, "USS *Skipjack* Third War Patrol Report, April 14–June 3, 1942," NRS1968-51, Operational Archives, Naval Historical Center, Washington, D.C. (excerpts run throughout this chapter).

2. Roscoe, *Submarine Operations,* 113.

3. Blair, *Silent Victory,* 175.

4. Casey, *Battle Below,* 321.

5. Edward L. Beach, *Run Silent, Run Deep* (Annapolis, Md.: Naval Institute Press, 1986), 325–26.

6. Grider, *Warfish,* 64.

7. Fussell, *Wartime,* 272.

8. Dudley W. Morton, "USS *Wahoo* Third War Patrol Report, Jan. 16—Feb. 7, 1943," Operational Archives, Naval Historical Center, Washington, D.C. Material is also available online at http://www.warfish.com/warpatrolfrm3.html.

All attacks are given at least a paragraph. Here's a typical one: "This last one, fired at 1449, clipped him amidships in twenty-five seconds and broke his back. The explosion was terrific! . . . The topside was covered with Japs on turret tops and in the rigging. Over 100 members of the crew must have been acting as look-outs. . . . We took several pictures, and as her bow was settling fast we went to 150 feet and commenced the nine mile trip out of WEWAK. Heard her boilers go in between the noise of continuous shelling from somewhere" (2).

9. Fussell, *Wartime,* 272.

10. Casey, *Battle Below,* 319.

11. Tony Perry, "Ocean's Depths Demand Decisions Like No Others," *Los Angeles Times,* March 4, 2001, A24.

Chapter 16

1. Blair, *Silent Victory,* 249.

2. Coe, "USS *Skipjack* Third War Patrol Report" (excerpts run throughout chapter).

3. James DeRose, *Unrestricted Warfare* (New York: John Wiley and Sons, 2000), 33.

4. Blair, *Silent Victory,* 418.

5. W. F. Bennett, "USS *Skipjack* Day One," *Polaris,* October 2000, 10.

6. DeRose, *Unrestricted Warfare,* 4.

7. Edwin Hoyt, *Submarines at War* (New York: Stein and Day, 1983), 124–25.

8. Ibid., 199.

9. William R. McCants, *War Patrols of the USS* Flasher (Chapel Hill, N.C.: Professional Press, 1994), 234.

10. Blair, *Silent Victory,* 251.

11. Holmes, *Undersea Victory,* 126.

12. Blair, *Silent Victory*, 250.

13. Morison, *History of U.S. Naval Operations*, 4:221.

14. Blair, *Silent Victory*, 251.

15. Gannon, *Hellions of the Deep*, 84.

16. Ibid., 87.

17. Ibid., 89.

18. Blair, *Silent Victory*, 404.

19. Roscoe, *Submarine Operations*, 260.

20. Ibid., 261.

Chapter 17

1. Casey, *Battle Below*, 369.

2. James W. Coe, letter to Phoebe Coe, *Richmond (Indiana) Palladium Item*, August 11, 1942, 1.

3. James W. Coe, "Fourth War Patrol Report of USS *Skipjack*, July 18–Sept. 4, 1942," NRS1958-51, Operational Archives, Naval Historical Center, Washington, D.C. (excerpts throughout chapter taken from this report).

4. Gugliotta, *Pigboat 39*, 172.

5. A Q-ship was a merchant ship converted into a lethal fighting ship designed to decoy submarines into attack so they could be counterattacked.

6. David Jones, "Experiences of an Enlisted Man on U.S. Submarines during WWII," paper presented at Navy History Conference, King-Hall, Brisbane, Australia, July 2001.

7. Grider, *Warfish*, 207.

8. Ibid., 19.

9. Blair, *Silent Victory*, 258–59.

10. Ibid., 301.

11. Ibid., 268.

Chapter 18

1. C. Wayland Brooks to Randall Jacobs, letter of May 11, 1945, Textual Archives Services Division, Modern Military Records, National Archives and Record's Administration, College Park, Md.

2. H. Crommelin, letter of May 14, 1945, Textual Archives Services Division, Modern Military Records, National Archives and Records Administration.

3. Blair, *Silent Victory*, 418.

4. Ibid., 694.

5. Ibid., 714.

6. Grider, *Warfish,* 191.

7. Herman Wouk, *The Caine Mutiny* (Glasgow: Fontana Books, 1972), 499.

8. Blair, *Silent Victory,* 958–62.

9. *Richmond (Indiana) Palladium Item,* October 22, 1942, 1.

10. Blair, *Silent Victory,* 323.

11. Ibid., 327.

12. Ibid., 293.

13. James W. Coe, "Fifth War Patrol Report of USS *Skipjack,* Sept. 27–Nov. 26, 1942," NRS1968-51, Operational Archives, Naval Historical Center, Washington, D.C., 8.

14. Blair, *Silent Victory,* 327; Coe, "Fifth War Patrol Report," 19.

15. Beach, *Submarine,* 134.

16. Fussell, *Wartime,* 90.

17. Doug Smay, editorial, *Klaxon* (newsletter of U.S. Subvets WWII, San Diego Chapter), May 1999.

18. Fussell, *Wartime,* 268.

Chapter 19

1. Maynard Bertsch, "Coe Believes American People Must Realize Jap Fighting Power before Victory Can Be Won," *Richmond (Indiana) Palladium Item,* January 8, 1943, 12.

2. U.S. Navy Subs SoWesPac, Seventh Fleet, "Task Force/Group 71.1 Operation Plan 1-43, Sept. 1, '43," 5, in Records of Naval Operating Forces, COMSUBPAC CTF71.1, To/From Dispatches, Record Group 38, Box 303, National Archives and Records Administration, College Park, Md.

3. Lavo, *Back from the Deep,* 116.

4. "Silent Victory—WWII," *Submarine Centennial Log,* www.navy.mil.

5. McCants, *War Patrols,* 3.

6. Ibid., 7.

7. *Portsmouth (New Hampshire) Herald,* December 24, 1942, 1.

8. Ibid., December 26, 1942, 1.

9. Stefan Terzibaschitsch, *Submarines of the U.S. Navy* (London: Arms and Armour Press, 1991), 69.

10. Grider, *Warfish,* 26.

11. Ibid., 25.

12. USS *Cisco* SS-290 Administrative Log, May 10, 1943–August 31, 1943, Record Group 24, Stack 470, Row 32, National Archives and Records Administration.

13. Robert A. Knapp, testimony, "Board of Investigation of *Cisco* loss, Dec. 4, 1943," Record Group 38, Box 1346, Law and Justice Courts of Inquiry, National Archives and Records Administration.

14. James W. Coe, "Report of Trials of USS *Cisco*," July 13, 1943, Record Group 19, General Correspondence—Bureau of Ships, 1940–45, File SS290, Stack Area 470, Box 2127, National Archives and Records Administration, 4.

15. Beach, *Submarine,* 180.

Chapter 20

1. Dispatch No. 042030, Records of Naval Operating Forces, COMSUBPAC, CTF72 Dispatches May–August 1943, Record Group 313, Box 3, File 5-43, National Archives and Records Administration, College Park, Md.

2. DeRose, *Unrestricted Warfare,* 280–81.

3. U.S. Navy Subs SoWesPac, Seventh Fleet, "Task Force/Group 71.1 Operation Plan 1-43."

4. Blair, *Silent Victory,* 522.

5. "U.S. Navy Operation Order 30-43," September 10, 1943, Task Force 71, Records of Office of Chief of Naval Operations WWII—Plans, Orders, and Related Documents, Record Group 38, Box 303, National Archives and Records Administration.

6. "Board of Investigation of Cisco loss."

7. Ibid., 5.

8. Naval History Division, Office of the Chief of Naval Operations, *U.S. Submarine Losses, WWII* (Washington, D.C.: U.S. Department of the Navy, 1963), 57.

9. Jiro Kimata, *Japanese Attacks against Enemy Submarines,* trans. Y. Tamagawa (Tokyo: Military History Dept., National Institute for Defense Studies), 75, 76.

10. "Nautical Chart No. 678: Philippine Islands, Eastern Part of Sulu Sea," U.S. Charts to 1936, Military History Department, National Institute for Defense Studies, Tokyo, Japan.

11. National Geographic Society, *Atlas of the World,* 5th ed. (Washington, D.C.: National Geographic Society, 1981), 33.

Chapter 21

1. *Richmond (Indiana) Palladium Item,* "Coe Avenue at Pearl Harbor Sub Base Named in Honor of Local War Hero," February 26, 1950, 13.

2. Ralph Christie, papers, quoted by Bradley E. Gernand, senior archivist, Library of Congress, Washington, D.C., correspondence of December 2, 1999.

3. Blair, *Silent Victory,* 474.

4. William J. Ruhe, *War in the Boats* (Washington, D.C.: Brassey's, 1994), 151–54.

Personal Communications

The following is a list people who generously provided information in interviews and/or telephone conversations and e-mail and letter correspondence or were sources of family letters, memorabilia, and documents.

Captain Edward Arentzen, ret.

Commander John D. Alden, ret.

Robert C. Asin

Captain Edward L. Beach, ret.

Captain W. F. Bennett, ret.

Carolyn (Mrs. Lawrence) Bernard

Jim Coe

Phoebe Coe

Pat Niles Colyer

John Cowan

Ann King Cummings

Captain Slade Cutter, ret.

Tom Davis

Margaret Dikeman

Bob Fickett

Bradley E. Gernand

Captain Guy F. Gugliotta, ret.

Sara M. Gwynn

Charles W. Haislip

Captain William Hazard, ret.

Captain David Hurt, Jr., ret.

Agnes King

Captain Noritaka Kitazawa

Marcus Klein

Admiral John Lee, ret.

Captain Paul Loustaunau, ret.

Walter Lundgren

Bryan MacKinnon

Roberta (Mrs. John S. Jr.) McCain

Mary (Mrs. Rob Roy) McGregor

Captain Joseph McGrievy, ret.

Lil (Mrs. William) Nelson

Fred Niles

Robert Norton

Jean Noyes

Tom Parks

Howell Rice

Nancy Richards

Admiral Maurice "Mike" Rindskopf, ret.

John Rutkofske

Samuel F. Simpson

Captain Robert Slaven, ret.

Keiko Takada

Captain Y. "Tommy" Tamagawa

William Tebo

Myron "Turk" Turner

Admiral John A. Tyree, ret.

Jim Ward

George Watson

Sid Wellikson

Jane Weston

Edward Wilson

Charles Witt